# Female Genital Mutilation:
# Law and Practice

# Female Genital Mutilation: Law and Practice

**Zimran Samuel**
**Barrister**
Doughty Street Chambers, London
**Visiting Fellow**
The London School of Economics

*Foreword by*
The Honourable Mr Justice Keehan
Family Division Liaison Judge, Midland Circuit

LexisNexis©

Published by LexisNexis

LexisNexis
Regus
Terrace Floor
Castlemead
Lower Castle Street
Bristol BS1 3AG

**British Library Cataloguing-in-Publication Data**

A catalogue record for this book is available from the British Library.

ISBN 978 1 78473 333 9

Typeset by Letterpart Limited, Caterham on the Hill, Surrey CR3 5XL

Printed in Great Britain by Hobbs the Printers Limited, Totton, Hampshire SO40 3WX

For Amartya

# ABOUT THE AUTHOR

Zimran Samuel is a practising barrister at Doughty Street Chambers in London. He is an elected member of the Executive Committee of the Bar Human Rights Committee (BHRC) and holds a position as a Visiting Fellow at the London School of Economics.

'Words should not seek to please, to hide the wounds in our bodies, or the shameful moments in our lives. They may hurt, give us pain, but they can also provoke us to question what we have accepted for thousands of years.'[1]

Nawal El Saadawi

[1] Nawal El Saadawi, *Walking Through Fire: A Life of Nawal El Saadawi* (Zed Books Ltd, London & New York, 15 April 2009).

# FOREWORD

The practice of female genital mutilation (FGM) remains widespread across the globe – especially in parts of North Africa – but a substantial number of mutilations are reported to have been undertaken in this jurisdiction. Accordingly, the risk to girls and young women living in this jurisdiction is not limited to being taken abroad to be subjected to FGM but includes the risk of having the mutilation performed in this country. The adverse physical, emotional and psychological consequences of FGM are invariably severe and life-long.

Many health and social care professionals, politicians and lawyers have worked tirelessly to bring to wider public attention the extent of the practice of FGM and its brutal effects. They have sought effective protection to be provided to the potential victims of this cruel practice. The campaign culminated in the passing of legislation to introduce FGM Protection Orders (FGMPOs) with a statutory regime designed to prevent FGM and afford protection to vulnerable girls and young women.

One of the leading campaigners is Zimran Samuel, the author of this excellent tome. He is one of the country's foremost legal experts on the practice and prevention of FGM. This book is the culmination of his dedicated work in this field.

The Metropolitan Police have taken a proactive stance in commencing proceedings and seeking FGMPOs in appropriate cases. Their lead is being followed by many police forces and local authorities across the country. It is vital in order to prevent FGM that health and social care professionals, local authorities and law enforcement agencies have a clear understanding of the socio-cultural reasons for the practice of FGM, the factors which may indicate a girl or young woman is at a real risk of being forced to undergo FGM and of the effective legal steps which can and must be taken to prevent the same.

This book provides a comprehensive and readily accessible guide to all of these matters and, most especially, to the legal procedures to be followed to secure protective court orders. It contains a very helpful list of: (a) medical centres and practitioners who are experts in this field to give forensic clinical opinions, and (b) organisations who have the experience and expertise to undertake educative and preventative work with girls, young women and their families.

I am delighted and honoured to be asked to write the Foreword to this book. Those who are concerned with girls and young women who are feared to be at risk of being subjected to FGM will undoubtedly find this book to be an invaluable resource tool. I highly commend it to you.

The Honourable Mr Justice Keehan
*January 2017*

# PREFACE

This work was written in close consultation with survivors of female genital mutilation and frontline practitioners from across the spectrum of disciplines. It is intended to summarise the current legal provisions surrounding FGM in England, Wales and Northern Ireland.

Once clouded behind arguments of cultural relativism, FGM is now widely recognised both domestically and internationally as child abuse and a serious human rights abuse. However, it remains a practice shrouded in secrecy and one which all too often has escaped the reaches of our child protection system.

There has also been criticism that the law itself has been ineffective and inadequate in tackling FGM. Despite the existence over 30 years of a criminal law, there remains no successful prosecution of an offence of FGM. Whilst the Family Court and the High Court have creatively utilised other measures to address FGM, there has historically been no targeted provision to protect those at risk.

In what has been termed by campaigners and survivors as a quiet revolution, recent years have seen a proactive drive towards greater public awareness of the issue and a better frontline understanding of the complexities of FGM.[1]

This has now been accompanied by revised legislation and statutory guidance with the introduction of the Serious Crime Act 2015, offering strong reasons for optimism for both the criminal and civil jurisdictions.

Set within a human rights framework, this book aims to summarise the key legal developments and debates across international law, family law, immigration and criminal law.

It is hoped that it will be of use to judges, advocates, social workers, teachers, midwives, and other professionals as part of the on-going efforts to combat the scourge of FGM and violence against women and young girls.

The law is stated as at 6 March 2017.

Zimran Samuel

---

[1]    Karen McVeigh, 'FGM court orders: a quiet revolution in child protection', *The Guardian*, Thursday 31 December 2015.

# CONTENTS

# OPENING COMMENT: COUNTERING THE CATASTROPHE

I feel enormously privileged to have been invited by Zimran Samuel to contribute to the prefatory remarks of this crucial book. However, it would be a serious omission if I did not record at the very outset that Zimran has worked tirelessly over the last few years to protect young women and girls from the scourge that is FGM.

By his campaigning, policy work and expert advocacy in court, painstakingly fighting for the rights of young women and girls to enjoy what the rest of us take for granted – the right to bodily integrity – he has significantly reduced the sum of human suffering within affected communities in the United Kingdom. Therefore his work and his book, have to be situated within that broader struggle for the vindication of the rights of the vulnerable.

But why is there this fight? What is behind the controversy and contestation? To get at this, let us consider three questions: what, why, how.

- What is FGM?

- Why does it happen?

- How can we fight it?

## What

The question 'What is FGM?' is conceptually equivalent to asking what is crime, what is child abuse, what is gender violence, what is a human rights violation, what is the social control of women? The distinguishing feature of FGM is that it is all those things.

The World Health Organisation has identified four 'types' of FGM, different grades and degrees of genital mutilation. But typologies fail to capture the human cost. So what kind of human thing is it?

It is a commonplace to say that the scale of social harm inflicted by FGM is horrifying. Literally. It creates a cold sense of horror. The UN has 'upgraded' its estimate of the amount of women worldwide who are living with the legacy of

FGM. It is now estimated to be 200 million. What does that mean? Here is one attempt: imagine the entire population of Germany is female and has been genitally mutilated, then add the entire population of France, then add the entire United Kingdom. That many.

Every year 3 million more girls are mutilated. That is the population of Birmingham plus Leeds plus Liverpool plus Manchester plus Bristol. FGM has been around for a long time. An inconceivably long time. Its origins may indeed be Pharaonic. Therefore, it easily predates Islam. It predates Christianity. It is not restricted to any particular social or religious group. It is practised by Muslims, Christians, Jewish people and animists. It is not prescribed or officially ordained by any religion. It is not, contrary to certain myths and misinformation, authorised by the Koran. It has historically affected a broad swathe of countries from Iran and Kurdistan, through Egypt and the Horn of Africa, across the Sahara to the Atlantic Ocean, and then down towards the Equator in certain, but by no means all, Sub-Saharan African countries. There are other centres of concern such as Indonesia. It is a living thing. It is diffuse; it's spreading. It is complex, changing, adapting – mutating.

With the mass population movements of modern times, these historic practising communities have dispersed across the world, so that FGM is now found on every continent without exception. It is a global phenomenon. Yet as national and international initiatives seek to counter it, so it changes and mutates. It is becoming more 'medicalised' in certain countries such as Egypt. The age at which it is inflicted changes: lowering among some groups, so very young children or babies cannot speak about what has been done to them; being raised elsewhere, so girls in their teens are beyond the scope of routine childhood medical examinations.

There is a vivid sense in which there is no such thing as FGM. There are FGMs.

As French social theorist Pierre Bourdieu says of racial discrimination: there is no such thing as 'racism' but racisms. Bourdieu's idea is particularly apposite here, as what has come to be called FGM is in actuality a series of subtly different but seriously harmful social practices directed against young women and girls. The result is that wherever there are girls and young women and communities with links to the broad band of historically practising countries, there is the risk of a child or an adolescent, without any choice, with no control, against her will, possibly without anaesthetic, having her genitalia mutilated. And for what? That is the question. To what end? Why?

## Why

To ask the why question is even more problematic than asking what. After all: why do people do what they do?

Whole university departments and research institutes are devoted to this elusive quest; whole libraries are filled, conferences and compendia are prepared, and still the mystery remains. We remain shut out from the inner sanctum, the repository of the deeper truth. Let me propose some keys to unlocking the door. Three of them.

First, do not just ask who arranges or authorises or performs the 'cutting', but ask whom it is for. It is certainly the case that FGM is often arranged by the female members of the social group. In many communities, where it has not been medicalised, the cutting is performed by a female cutter. But there is a tripartite structure to FGM: it is arranged and performed by older women, on younger females, for – and this is at the heart of it – men. Unless we understand that third and final limb, we will not understand FGM. We will come in a moment to why it is of benefit to men.

Secondly, do not just look at surface effects but seek deeper causes. Many human behavioural sciences distinguish between proximate and distal causes. People will say that FGM is performed because of community, clan or kinship pressure. Yes. But why that pressure? From where does it come? We need to disentangle the visible contours of the practice from what underpins the social norm. There is a need to control the sexuality of females. But why?

Thirdly, then, scrutinise the reasons for the reasons. What does FGM target? What does it do? If it is sexual control, such control is achieved by a very distinctive method: the mutilation of female genitalia. Evolutionary biology and both social and evolutionary psychology tell us that one of the prime uncertainties in the relations between the sexes is what is called 'paternal uncertainty'. The father can rarely be sure that the offspring is his. In the modern world, equipped with sophisticated DNA testing, this habitual cloud of confusion can be alleviated. But in the geographical regions and historic epochs in which this harmful social practice developed, this was not an option. One obvious way to suppress the risk that the child you are bringing up contains the genes of another (possibly rival) male, is to reduce the risk that the mother of the child is having sex with other men.

In mediaeval Europe, a range of technologies developed including the chastity belt and the remorseless supervision and surveillance of young women. FGM can be conceived as another such technology: crude, punishing and painful. In one appalling sense, this brutalist logic works. Certainly, many of the survivors I have spoken to while working on this subject for a number of years will tell you that what they associate sex with is pain. In human behaviour, as Jeremy Bentham observed, nature has placed humankind under two sovereign masters: pleasure and pain. It is no coincidence that invariably targeted in FGM, even in the miscalled 'mildest' forms, is the clitoris, a seat of sexual pleasure for women. Thus following mutilation, sex is not pleasurable, but functional. Sex is removed from the sphere of pleasure and sequestrated within another zone: pregnancy and pain. This may be somewhere near the unsparing originating logic. It is unacceptable and anachronistic. It must be defeated. But how?

# How

There is a deep paradox in that the efficacy of the law tends to be overestimated by lawyers and underestimated by non-lawyers. Nevertheless, it is to be commended that the stance of this book, and the approach of many of the lawyers mentioned in it, is that the law is a tool for both social change and social justice, if we want it to be. In respect of FGM, do we?

What can we do about FGM with the law? That is the problem, the paradox, the puzzle. You will read within these pages that there has been a lamentable history of prosecuting FGM in the United Kingdom. I have no doubt that a greater awareness of the problem has developed in just the last two or three years than in the previous two or three decades. In part that is because of some of the courageous, in fact heroic, survivors of FGM, including those to whom the book is dedicated.

As part of the Bar Human Rights Committee's work on the Parliamentary Inquiry, Zimran Samuel worked with me to impress on parliamentarians that an overly punitive approach could be counterproductive. Prosecutions are important, to victims, as a public acknowledgement of the uncompromising stance of the nation towards this harmful social practice. They unquestionably have symbolic value. But prosecutions are not enough. You cannot prosecute FGM into extinction. Therefore, as with UN initiatives throughout Sub-Saharan Africa, the great emphasis should be on 'collective abandonment'. That is, collaborative work with all sections of civil society to assist affected communities to move away from the deep grooves of tradition. You cannot eradicate such deeply ingrained social practices instantly. But you can remove them. You can change social norms. Social norms are constantly changing around us. The challenge presented by FGM is to achieve this deliberately and swiftly.

The clock is ticking. Every year 3 million more young women and girls will be mutilated. There are already 200 million. How many million more before we achieve what must be achieved?

The law can help. Books like this can help. It aims its fire at the twin targets of justice in a courtroom and social justice for young women and girls beyond. It equips lawyers and judges with the legal tools to intervene to protect at-risk young women and girls; it arms affected communities, frontline professionals and (no less importantly) concerned citizens, with indispensable information to vindicate the right of all young women and girls to bodily integrity.

FGM remains one of the greatest human rights catastrophes in the world. But unlike hurricanes and earthquakes and tsunamis, we can do something about it. We can counter the catastrophic. We must.

Dexter Dias QC
Garden Court Chambers, London
Centre for Community, Gender and Social Justice, University of Cambridge
*November 2016*

# ACKNOWLEDGMENTS

This book is dedicated to *the survivors* Leyla Hussain, Hibo Wardere, Alimatu Dimonekene and all those who have campaigned tirelessly for greater action to eradicate the practice of female genital mutilation in the UK and globally.

This work would not have been possible without the dedicated assistance of all those who have given time into undertaking research and giving much invaluable advice.

In particular huge thanks is owed to Mr Justice Keehan, Kirsty Brimelow QC (Doughty Street Chambers), the Bar Human Rights Committee's Working Group on FGM, the Metropolitan Police Service, Seema Malhtra MP, Baroness Angela Smith, Dexter Dias QC (Garden Court Chambers), Alison Leivesley (Head of Family Law, TV Edwards solicitors), Sophie Lotte (FGM lead at the Forced Marriage Unit), Jean Mahon (FGM lead at the Home Office), Ria Palmer (trainee solicitor candidate at Freshfields Bruckhaus Deringer), Aisha Arden (Law & Anthropology, the LSE), Xenia June Stafford, Stephanie Cocker, Sabrina McKay (Burke Niazi Solicitors) and of course Jared Ficklin (University of Liverpool, Law Clinic) who is responsible for the insightful chapter summarising the relevant immigration law issues that practitioners should be aware of.

I am also very grateful to both Greg Woodgate and Kate Hather at LexisNexis for their guidance and encouragement over the last two years.

The image used for the cover of this book is the artwork of 14-year-old Feyrus Ali whose mother took a decision not to have her cut, notwithstanding pressure from within her community. Entitled *Girls all Rise* the artwork symbolises the cultural shift as many applicants who attend court are women who have been cut themselves but seek protection for their own daughters. I am indebted to Feyrus for her powerful contribution.

Finally, I wish to thank my loving and patient wife Ilham who gave birth to our son Amartya in the final days of this project's completion. Without her encouragement, none of this would have been close to being possible. *Merci pour ton soutien*. Our hope is that Amartya grows up in a world in which practices such as FGM are confined to the history books.

Zimran Samuel

# TABLE OF CASES

References are to paragraph numbers.

# TABLE OF STATUTES

References are to paragraph numbers.

# TABLE OF STATUTORY INSTRUMENTS

References are to paragraph numbers.

# TABLE OF INTERNATIONAL MATERIALS

References are to paragraph numbers.

# CHAPTER 1

# INTRODUCTION

**1.1**    Female Genital Mutilation (FGM) is a culturally deep-rooted practice involving procedures which include the partial or total removal of the external female genital organs for non-medical reasons. FGM is now recognised internationally and domestically as a form of child abuse and violence against women and girls. It serves as a complex form of social control of women's sexual and reproductive rights. The survivor and campaigner Hibo Wardere recounts her experience of being subjected to the FGM by a cutter when she was still a young child:

> 'She picked up a cloth and dabbed it between my legs; each time she took it away, I saw that more and more of it was soaked in red. I could smell my blood by now, the sickly metal tang of it filling the small hut that we were crammed into. The pain continued, each hack into my flesh seeming to hit a new place and every nerve ending screaming in agony.
>
> I knew in that moment that this wasn't humane, to make me suffer like this; we would never let one of our animals suffer in this way, we would put even a goat or a sheep out of its misery sooner than let it experience this pain. On and on it went, and then further, as she parted my vaginal lips and hacked away at more flesh inside. Everything was on fire, and all I could do was scream.'[1]

**1.2**    Hibo's experience has sadly been repeated on girls and women across the world, often with no pain relief and with serious resulting consequences. Men and women in practising communities are often unaware of the potential harmful health and welfare consequences of FGM. FGM has no known health benefits. The removal of or damage to healthy, normal genital tissue interferes with the natural functioning of the body and can have serious health consequences both at the time when the cutting is carried out and in later life. The immediate consequences can include:

- severe pain;
- shock;
- haemorrhage;
- wound infections;
- urinary retention;

---

[1]    Hibo Wardere, *Cut: One Woman's Fight Against FGM in Britain Today* (Simon & Schuster, 7 April 2016), p 33.

- injury to adjacent tissues;
- genital swelling; and/or
- death.

**1.3**    The long-term consequences can include:

- genital scarring;
- genital cysts and keloid scar formation;
- recurrent urinary tract infections and difficulties in passing urine;
- possible increased risk of blood infections such as hepatitis B and HIV;
- pain during sex, lack of pleasurable sensation and impaired sexual function;
- psychological concerns such as anxiety, flashbacks and post-traumatic stress disorder;
- difficulties with menstruation;
- complications in pregnancy or childbirth (including prolonged labour, bleeding or tears during childbirth, increased risk of caesarean section); and increased risk of stillbirth and death of child during or just after birth.

**1.4**    FGM is predominantly carried out amongst specific ethnic populations in Africa and parts of the Middle East and Asia.[2] The cultural underpinnings and motives underlying FGM are often grounded in culture or perceptions that it makes a girl more sexually pure or clean. Infibulation (Type III) is strongly linked to virginity and chastity, and used to 'protect' girls from sex outside marriage and from having sexual feelings. In some cultures, it is considered necessary at marriage for the husband and his family to see her 'closed' and, in some instances, both mothers will take the girl to be cut open enough to be able to have sex.

**1.5**    FGM is most often claimed to be carried out in accordance with religious beliefs. However, FGM predates Christianity, Islam and Judaism. The Bible, Quran and Torah do not advocate for or justify FGM. Mona Eltahawy writes:

> 'The cultural origins of FGM are obscure. In Sudan, infibulation (the most extreme form of FGM) is described as the "Pharaonic" method, and in Egypt the same procedure is known as the "Sudanese" method. This history matters little to the girls brutalised and butchered as their own mothers watch, and sometimes even help to hold them down. Can there be a greater betrayal? And in the name of love! Yes, love. These mothers do not hate their daughters. They have not forgotten the brutalisation they themselves endured as their own mothers held them down. How could they? Surely they have not forgotten the pain. Yet they understand – as they hear their daughters' screams, echoes of their own screams of decades earlier – that

---

[2]    Multi-agency statutory guidance on female genital mutilation, HM Government, (April 2016), pp 8–9.

without such butchery, their girls will be considered sexually out of control and unmarriageable. So they cut away to make them complete – the irony of cutting, of mutilating, to make whole!'[3]

**1.6** Although the exact number of girls and women alive today who have undergone FGM is unknown, UNICEF estimates the current figure at 200 million across 30 countries.[4] The age at which girls undergo FGM varies enormously according to the community. The procedure may be carried out when the girl is newborn, during childhood or adolescence, just before marriage or during the first pregnancy. However, the majority of cases of FGM are thought to take place between the ages of 5 and 8. Countries with the highest prevalence among girls and women aged 15 to 49 are Somalia 98%, Guinea 97% and Djibouti 93%.[5]

**1.7** How the practice is undertaken and whom it is physically done by also depends on the country and sub-community. The 'cutter' may be a professional cutter as in Sierra Leone, an elder woman in the family as in parts of East Africa, or it may even be a medical doctor or medical professional as sometimes tends to be the case in Egypt.

**1.8** The medicalisation of FGM raises its own unique problems. The fact that the cutting may be undertaken in a professional or medical environment is often presented as a positive development in that girls are cut in hygienic conditions and with provision for pain relief. However, survivors and campaigners have continued to argue powerfully that although the 'medicalisation' of FGM, reduces immediate medical risks, it serves only to legitimise and prolong the practice in some communities.

**1.9** FGM has been a specific criminal offence in the UK since 1985 when the (UK-wide) Prohibition of Female Circumcision Act (the 1985 Act) was passed. The Female Genital Mutilation Act 2003 (the 2003 Act) replaced the 1985 Act in England, Wales and Northern Ireland.[6] It modernised the offence of FGM and the offence of assisting a girl in carrying out FGM on herself while also creating extra-territorial offences to deter people from taking girls abroad for mutilation. To reflect the serious harm caused, the 2003 Act increased the maximum penalty for any of the FGM offences from 5 to 14 years' imprisonment. To date, no-one has been convicted of FGM in England and Wales.

**1.10** FGM continues to take place within the UK and girls are also taken out of the jurisdiction for the practice to be performed. In July 2014, the UK Government hosted the first international summit aimed at mobilising domestic

3    M Eltahawy, *Headscarves and Hymens: Why the Middle East Needs a Sexual Revolution* (Weidenfeld & Nicholson, 21 April 2015), pp 118–119.
4    UNICEF, *Female Genital Mutilation/Cutting: A Global Concern* (2016).
5    UNICEF, *Female Genital Mutilation/Cutting: A Global Concern* (2016).
6    The Prohibition of Female Genital Mutilation (Scotland) Act 2005 replaced the 1985 Act in Scotland.

and international efforts to end FGM. The Government subsequently made a number of commitments for further resources and new legislation to tackle the practice.[7] The new provisions in the form of the Serious Crime Act 2015 (the 2015 Act) make provision for mandatory reporting of FGM and the introduction of civil protection orders.

**1.11** Fundamental to the recent campaign against FGM and the new legal provisions, is the unequivocal message that FGM is not only a serious crime and child abuse, but a fundamental breach of human rights and gender based violence against women and girls.

## DEFINITION

**1.12** FGM, also known as Female Genital Cutting (FGC) and female circumcision is a collective term for a range of procedures that involve partial or total removal of the external female genitalia for non-medical reasons. It is sometimes referred to as female circumcision, or female genital cutting.

## International classification of FGM (2007)

**1.13** In 1997, the World Health Organization (WHO), the United Nations Children's Fund (UNICEF) and the United Nations Population Fund (UNFPA) issued a Joint Statement on FGM which described the implications of the practice for public health and human rights and declared support for its abandonment. The Joint Statement classified FGM into four types.[8] This classification has subsequently been sub-divided into categories to capture more closely the variety of procedures.[9]

**1.14** The extent of genital tissue cutting generally increases from Type I to Type III. Severity and risk are closely related to the anatomical extent of the cutting, including both the type of FGM performed and the amount of tissue that is cut, which may vary between the types. Type IV comprises a variety of practices that do not involve removal of tissue from the genitals. The complete typology with sub-divisions is as follows:

- Type I – Partial or total removal of the clitoris and/or the prepuce (clitoridectomy). When it is important to distinguish between the major variations of Type I mutilation, the following subdivisions are proposed:
    - Type Ia, removal of the clitoral hood or prepuce only;
    - Type Ib, removal of the clitoris with the prepuce.

---

[7]   The Girl Summit, HM Government, July 2014: https://www.gov.uk/government/topical-events/girl-summit-2014.

[8]   WHO/UNICEF/UNFPA Joint Statement on Female Genital Mutilation (Geneva, 1997).

[9]   Eliminating female genital mutilation: An interagency statement – OHCHR, UNAIDS, UNDP, UNECA, UNESCO, UNFPA, UNHCR, UNICEF, UNIFEM, WHO (2008).

- Type II – Partial or total removal of the clitoris and the labia minora, with or without excision of the labia majora (excision). When it is important to distinguish between the major variations that have been documented, the following subdivisions are proposed:
  - Type IIa, removal of the labia minora only;
  - Type IIb, partial or total removal of the clitoris and the labia minora;
  - Type IIc, partial or total removal of the clitoris, the labia minora and the labia majora.
- Type III – Narrowing of the vaginal orifice with creation of a covering seal by cutting and appositioning the labia minora and/or the labia majora, with or without excision of the clitoris (infibulation). When it is important to distinguish between variations in infibulations, the following subdivisions are proposed:
  - Type IIIa, removal and apposition of the labia minora;
  - Type IIIb, removal and apposition of the labia majora.
- Type IV – All other harmful procedures to the female genitalia for non-medical purposes, for example: pricking, piercing, incising, scraping and cauterisation.

## Statutory definition: Female Genital Mutilation Act 2003

**1.15** Section 1(1) of the 2003 Act definition stipulates that a person is guilty of an offence if he excises, infibulates or otherwise mutilates the whole or any part of a girl's labia majora, labia minora or clitoris.[10] However, no offence is committed by an approved person who performs:

(a) a surgical operation on a girl which is necessary for her physical or mental health, or

(b) a surgical operation on a girl who is in any stage of labour, or has just given birth, for purposes connected with the labour or birth.[11]

**1.16** The question of whether the WHO classifications of FGM, which are widely used internationally, should be formally adopted into domestic legislation was carefully considered by Parliament during the Parliamentary debates for the Serious Crime Bill.[12] It was argued strongly by Baroness Smith of Basildon (as Shadow leader of the House of Lords) that the WHO definition should be adopted as the definition to be used in the 2003 Act, particularly as there had been confusion historically, for example from the Royal College of Midwives (RCM) and the Royal College of Obstetricians and Gynaecologists (RCOG), in relation to whether re-infibulation was covered within the definition.[13]

---

[10] 2003 Act, s 1(1).
[11] 2003 Act, s 1(2).
[12] Hansard, Parliamentary debate, Serious Crime Bill [House of Lords], Col 1621, Third Reading, Clause 61: Appeal against decision under s 60, Amendment 1, 5 November 2014.
[13] Hansard, Parliamentary debate, Serious Crime Bill [House of Lords], Col 1621, Third Reading, Clause 61: Appeal against decision under s 60, Amendment 1, 5 November 2014.

**1.17**   Baroness Smith contended that adopting the WHO definition:

> 'would ensure that our law is consistent with recognised international standards and understandings and clarifies any existing confusion around offending conduct such as re-infibulation'.[14]

**1.18**   Ultimately, Parliament resolved not to adopt or incorporate the WHO definition into the legislation, amid concerns that such clarification could affect any existing or current cases.[15]

**1.19**   Whilst the WHO definition was not formally incorporated into the definition of FGM within s 1(1) of the 2003 Act, it was adopted by the President of the Family Division, Sir James Munby, in the matter of *Re B and G (Children) (No 2)*.[16] The President observed that knowledge and understanding of the classification and categorisation of the various types of FGM is vital and that the WHO classification is the one widely used for forensic purposes.[17] The WHO definition was also adopted by Mr Justice McDonald in *Re E (Female Genital Mutilation and Permission to Remove)*.[18]

The WHO Fact Sheet N241 summarises the four major types of FGM as follows:[19]

- Type I: Often referred to as clitoridectomy, this is the partial or total removal of the clitoris (a small, sensitive and erectile part of the female genitals), and in very rare cases, only the prepuce (the fold of skin surrounding the clitoris).

- Type II: Often referred to as excision, this is the partial or total removal of the clitoris and the labia minora (the inner folds of the vulva), with or without excision of the labia majora (the outer folds of skin of the vulva).

- Type III: Often referred to as infibulation, this is the narrowing of the vaginal opening through the creation of a covering seal. The seal is formed by cutting and repositioning the labia minora, or labia majora, sometimes through stitching, with or without removal of the clitoris (clitoridectomy).

- Type IV: This includes all other harmful procedures to the female genitalia for non-medical purposes, eg pricking, piercing, incising, scraping and the cauterisation of the genital area.

---

[14]   Hansard, Parliamentary debate, Serious Crime Bill [House of Lords], Col 1621, Third Reading, Clause 61: Appeal against decision under s 60, Amendment 1, 5 November 2014.

[15]   Hansard, Parliamentary debate, Serious Crime Bill [House of Lords], Col 1621, Third Reading, Clause 61: Appeal against decision under s 60, Amendment 1, 5 November 2014.

[16]   [2015] EWFC 3 at para 7.

[17]   [2015] EWFC 3 at para 79.2.

[18]   [2016] EWHC 1052 (Fam) at para 58.

[19]   WHO Fact Sheet N241, published in February 2014 and updated in February 2016.

**1.20** Furthermore, UNICEF's statistical overview sets out the following typology:[20]

(1)  cut, no flesh removed;

(2)  cut, some flesh removed;

(3)  sewn closed; and

(4)  type not determined/not sure/doesn't know.

**1.21**  As noted in *B and G (Children) (No 2)*,[21] these categories do not fully match the WHO typology. 'Cut, no flesh removed' describes a practice known as nicking or pricking, which currently is categorised as Type IV. 'Cut, some flesh removed' corresponds to Type I (clitoridectomy) and Type II (excision) combined'. 'Sewn closed' corresponds to Type III, infibulation. Excision and infibulation are examples of what constitutes mutilation in accordance with the 2003 Act. However, the term 'mutilate' is not defined in the Act.[22]

## Re-infibulation

**1.22**  Re-infibulation is the term used to describe when the raw edges of the wound are sutured again following childbirth, recreating a small vaginal opening similar to the original FGM Type III appearance. Whilst s 1 of the 2003 Act does not refer explicitly to re-infibulation the statutory guidance states that if it is an offence to infibulate it must equally be an offence to re-infibulate.[23]

## De-infibulation

**1.23**  Fact Sheet N241 describes de-infibulation as the practice of cutting open the sealed vaginal opening in a woman who has been infibulated, which is often necessary for improving health and well-being as well as to allow intercourse or to facilitate childbirth.

**1.24**  De-infibulation involves a minor surgical procedure to divide the scar tissue sealing the vaginal entrance in Type III FGM. De-infibulation is sometimes termed a 'reversal' of FGM. The current statutory guidance states that this description is incorrect as the procedure does not replace genital tissue or restore normal genital anatomy and function.[24]

---

[20]  UNICEF, *Female Genital Mutilation/Cutting: A statistical overview and exploration of the dynamics of change* (2013), p 48.

[21]  [2015] EWFC 3.

[22]  Multi-agency statutory guidance on female genital mutilation, HM Government (April 2016), para 3.1.4.

[23]  Multi-agency statutory guidance on female genital mutilation, HM Government (April 2016).

[24]  Multi-agency statutory guidance on female genital mutilation, HM Government (April 2016).

## Other terms

**1.25**  Terms used for FGM in other languages include the following:[25]

| Country | Term used for FGM | Language |
|---|---|---|
| CHAD – the Ngama Sara subgroup | Bagne | French |
| | Gadja | Arabic |
| EGYPT | Thara | Arabic |
| | Khitan | Arabic |
| | Khifad | Arabic |
| ETHIOPIA | Megrez | Amharic |
| | Absum | Harrari |
| ERITREA | Mekhnishab | Tigregna |
| GAMBIA | Niaka | Mandinka |
| | Kuyango | Mandinka |
| | Musolula Karoola | Mandinka |
| GUINEA-BISSAU | Fanadu di Mindjer | Kriolu |
| IRAN | Xatna | Farsi |
| KENYA | Kutairi | Swahili |
| | Kutairi was ichana | Swahili |
| NIGERIA | Ibi/Ugwu | Igbo |
| | didabe fun omobirin/ila kiko fun omobirin | Yoruba |
| SIERRA LEONE | Sunna | Soussou |
| | Bondo | Temenee |
| | Bondo/Sonde | Mendee |
| | Bonde | Mandinka |
| | Bonde | Limba |

---

[25]   Multi-agency statutory guidance on female genital mutilation, HM Government (April 2016).

| Country | Term used for FGM | Language |
|---------|-------------------|----------|
| SOMALIA | Gudiniin | Somali |
|         | Halalays | Somali |
|         | Qodiin | Somali |
| SUDAN | Khifad | Arabic |
|       | Tahoor | Arabic |
| TURKEY | Kadin Sunneti | Turkish |

# CHAPTER 2

## STATISTICAL OVERVIEW[1]

**2.1** Treated with the right caution, statistics can provide a useful way of analysing and assessing risk in FGM cases. This chapter aims to provide a brief summary of the global context of FGM, alongside a more detailed study of domestic variables. The use of multi-agency reports, national reports by governmental agencies, and studies by international organisations such as UNICEF and the WHO have contributed to building our understanding of FGM in the UK.

**2.2** The international context becomes essential in understanding and responding to risk at a domestic level, especially with respect to assessing the probability of risk within particular diaspora.

**2.3** Equally important to formulating a holistic UK-wide picture of FGM are contributing variables such as age at which the procedure is performed, the method by which it is identified, the classification or type of FGM performed, and other regional factors such as urban-rural prevalence and place of residence within the UK.[2] Each of these, among others, is covered within this chapter, alongside correlative data.

**2.4** FGM is strongly anchored in the customs and traditions of 30 African and Middle Eastern countries, including some in Asia.[3] The WHO's estimates indicate that 200 million women and girls have experienced some form of FGM or excision, and approximately 3 million face the risk of undergoing the procedure annually.[4]

## MULTI-FRAMEWORK APPROACH

**2.5** To meaningfully address the incidence of FGM and its risk requires a multi-disciplinary and multi-framework approach. As put forward by

---

[1]   This chapter was written with the research assistance of Ms Ria Palmer.

[2]   Health & Social Care Information Centre (HSCIC), Female Genital Mutilation (FGM) Enhanced Dataset (April 2015 to March 2016, experimental statistics), Table 6, 13.

[3]   Multi-agency statutory guidance on female genital mutilation, HM Government (April 2016), p 2.

[4]   United Nations Children's Fund, 'At least 200 million girls and women alive today living in 30 countries have undergone FGM/C' (UNICEF, Current Status and progress, updated September 2016), http://data.unicef.org/topic/child-protection/female-genital-mutilation-and-cutting/# accessed 17 September 2016.

UNICEF's Deputy Director, Deepa Rao Gupta, this includes accelerated efforts from a range of actors, notably governments, health professionals, community leaders, parents, and families.[5] A comprehensive and accessible database is crucial to enable this approach. To this effect, a number of important reports and a support portal are cited, as go-to points of reference.

## UNICEF'S STATISTICAL OVERVIEW

**2.6**    The UNICEF report entitled *Female Genital Mutilation/Cutting: A statistical overview and exploration of the dynamics of change* analyses prevalence and trends in 29 countries.[6] Drawing on data from more than 70 nationally representative surveys over a 20-year period, the report finds that the practice has declined in a number of countries.

**2.7**    UNICEF published its first statistical exploration of FGM in 2005, helping to increase awareness of the magnitude and persistence of the practice. The more recent 2013 report casts additional light on how the practice is changing and on the progress being made. The report also makes clear that in some countries little or no change is apparent yet and further programmatic investments are needed.

## THE OHCHR

**2.8**    Other UN bodies such as the Office of the High Commissioner for Human Rights (OHCHR) also publish statistics and wider analysis in relation to several countries in which prevalence of the practice is high.[7]

## *Case study*

**2.9**    According to the April 2016 OHCHR report, Guinea has the second highest prevalence of FGM worldwide, after Somalia. Although FGM is forbidden by law, it is practised in every region, by all ethnic or religious groups and social classes, and 97% of Guinean women and girls aged 15–49 have

---

[5]    UNICEF, *New statistical report on female genital mutilation shows harmful practice is a global concern* (5 February 2016), http://www.unicef.org.hk/en/new-statistical-report-on-female-genital-mutilation-shows-harmful-practice-is-a-global-concern-unicef/ accessed 12 September 2016.

[6]    UNICEF, *Female Genital Mutilation/Cutting: A statistical overview and exploration of the dynamics of change* (2013).

[7]    OHCHR, *Summary of the OHCHR Report on human rights and the practice of female genital mutilation and excision in Guinea* (April 2016).

suffered excision.[8] FGM is decreasing worldwide, although a national Demographic and Health Study (EDS) found in 2012 that FGM had slightly increased since 2002.[9]

**2.10** Guinea's estimated 11 million inhabitants stem from various ethnic groups. In terms of religious belief, Islam dominates in Upper and Middle Guinea and to a lesser extent in Lower Guinea (85% of the population). Most Guinean women have suffered Type II FGM. According to the 2012 EDS study, 84% of women aged 15 to 49 have suffered ablation; 8%, infibulation; and 6%, cutting with no removal of flesh. The most extreme forms of FGM are practised among the Peuhle ethnic group and by the Tomas.[10] Age appears to have no impact on the type of FGM practised. The EDS found a 96% prevalence of FGM among women aged 15–49 in 2005, and a 97% prevalence in 2012. FGM was practised by all ethnic groups without significant disparities, excepting the Guerzé, a mostly Christian and animist group of Guinée forestière. While the prevalence of the practice did not shift significantly from 1999–2012 among most ethnic groups, among the Guerzé, the EDS noted a significant decline, from 89% in 1999 to 66% in 2012.[11] Studies are underway to determine the reasons for this decrease; relevant stakeholders feel it may be the result of awareness campaigns in Guinée forestière.

**2.11** In Guinea there is no significant difference in prevalence in urban areas (96.8% of women aged 15–49) and rural zones (97%).[12] The prevalence of excision decreases among girls whose mother is more highly educated, and support for FGM is greatest among women and girls from poor households (92%) compared to more well-off households (68%).[13] The study also indicates that the practice is being inflicted on girls at a younger age than previously: according to the 2012 EDS study, 69% of women aged 20–24 were excised before the age of 10, compared to 61% of women aged 45–49.

**2.12** In Guinea, FGM is an initiation rite, not only in the transition from childhood to adolescence and adulthood but also to prepare the young girl for active life within specific communities.[14] Groups of girls from multiple families[15] are usually excised together, either at home or in camps established for the purpose, with or without ceremonies and festivities. FGM usually takes place during school holidays or at harvest time.[16] There is an increasing trend

---

[8]   See mapping in UNICEF, Female Genital Mutilation/Cutting: A statistical overview of exploration of the dynamics of change (July 2013, New York).

[9]   Institut national de la staistique (INS), Guinea's 4th Demographic and Health Study, October 2012.

[10]  EDS-MICS 2012, pp 328–329.

[11]  EDS-MICS 2012, pp 327–328.

[12]  EDS-MICS 2012, table 17.2, p 327.

[13]  EDS-MICS 2012, p 331; UNICEF, *Female Genital Mutilation/Cutting: A statistical overview of exploration of the dynamics of change* (July 2013, New York), graph 6.6, p 60.

[14]  Plan International, *Tradition and rights – Excision in West Africa, Regional Office for West Africa, Dakar* (July 2006), p 9.

[15]  CRC/C/GIN/2, para 361.

[16]  CRC/C/GIN/2, para 361; General Commissariat for Refugees and Stateless Persons

to fewer celebrations and an increase in individual excisions, because of limited financial resources and a desire for greater discretion, due to the potential for legal sanctions. The excision of infants or very young girls is easier to hide from the authorities than the ceremonious excision of large groups.[17]

## NATIONAL FGM CENTRE – THE KNOWLEDGE HUB

**2.13**   The online database known as the *Knowledge Hub* has been set up by the Barnardos National FGM Centre.[18] It provides users with statistics and resources pertaining to specific regions within the UK and correlates this with the user's selection of information regarding a preferred industry or profession. For instance, it attempts to filter a geographically accurate resource base relevant to a range of practitioners such as social care professionals and health care professionals.[19] It is highly user-friendly, and contains more specific sub-categories that cover particular services, information on events, guidance and policy. More detail and a link to the portal can be found below at the following website: https://barnardosfgm.custhelp.com/app/home.

**2.14**   This hub is in the initial stages of developing into a comprehensive resource bank, with links to essential government reports on FGM, independent assessments by international organisations such as the WHO and UNICEF, policy, guidance and legislation, as well as crucial data on prevalence rates.

## HEALTH AND SOCIAL CARE INFORMATION CENTRE (HSCIC), ENHANCED DATASET

**2.15**   The Enhanced Dataset (April 2015–March 2016, Experimental Statistics), published by the Health and Social Care Information Centre (HSCIC), acts as a 'repository of individual data collected by healthcare providers in England'.[20] These include 'acute hospital providers, mental health providers and GP practices'.[21] The data represent statistics collected from April 2015 until March 2016, prior to which monthly data was collected. As stated in their annual report as part of the FGM Prevention Programme led by the Department of Health the datasets are key to improving the NHS response to

---

(CGRA/Belgium), French Office for the Protection of Refugees and Stateless Persons (OFPRA/France) and Federal Office for Migration (ODM/Switzerland), *Report on the Mission to the Republic of Guinea*, 29 October–19 November 2011, (Belgium-France-Switzerland Cooperation, March 2012), p 18.

[17]   Plan International, *Tradition and rights – Excision in West Africa, Regional Office for West Africa, Dakar* (July 2006), p 11.

[18]   National FGM Centre Knowledge Hub https://barnardosfgm.custhelp.com/app/home accessed 14 September 2016.

[19]   National FGM Centre Knowledge Hub https://barnardosfgm.custhelp.com/app/home accessed 14 September 2016.

[20]   Health & Social Care Information Centre (HSCIC), *Female Genital Mutilation (FGM) Enhanced Dataset* (April 2015–March 2016, experimental statistics), 4.

[21]   Health & Social Care Information Centre (HSCIC), *Female Genital Mutilation (FGM) Enhanced Dataset* (April 2015–March 2016, experimental statistics), 4.

safeguarding women and girls from the risk of FGM by increasing awareness and improving access to services and management of the issue.[22]

**2.16** The Enhanced Dataset improves upon its predecessor, the FGM Prevalence Dataset, in that it extends its overall radius for data collection. For instance, the Prevalence Dataset collection was confined to acute NHS trusts between September 2014 and March 2015, focusing primarily on 'non-identifiable aggregate data about the prevalence of FGM within the female population as treated by NHS trusts'.[23] The Enhanced Dataset extends to all mental health trusts[24] and GP practices.[25]

**2.17** The FGM Enhanced Dataset Information Standard (SCCI2026) brings with it is a higher degree of alignment with the multi-agency statutory guidelines.[26] Both require that clinicians across the NHS make a note of when patients are identified with FGM, as well as classify the type of FGM performed. The Enhanced Dataset avoids double counting patients who have visited more than one NHS trust, as was the case with the Prevalence Dataset.[27] This is because data is collected at 'patient-level' and avoids confusion.[28]

**2.18** Nonetheless, the Enhanced Dataset collection process is relatively recent (initiated in 2015) and should be interpreted with caution. This is usually due to the high proportion of unknown figures. This will be elaborated upon when considering each variable separately. Further, the recent annual report concerning the Enhanced Dataset has been criticised by practitioners.[29] For instance, it has been cited by Professor Alison Macfarlane as data that does not adequately address the stated goal of helping to eradicate FGM, and to provide services and support for women. In summary, the data collected quarterly by these sets covers an estimated 1% of the 134,600 women who have been subject to the procedure.

**2.19** Dr Brenda Kelly, who is a consultant obstetrician and Director of Oxford Rose (specialist FGM) Clinic in Oxford, makes a useful point in questioning whether data collection through the Enhanced Dataset, usually done when a

[22] Health & Social Care Information Centre (HSCIC), *Female Genital Mutilation (FGM) Enhanced Dataset* (April 2015–March 2016, experimental statistics), 4.
[23] Health & Social Care Information Centre (HSCIC), *Female Genital Mutilation (FGM) Enhanced Dataset* (April 2015–March 2016, experimental statistics), 6.
[24] Health & Social Care Information Centre (HSCIC), *Female Genital Mutilation (FGM) Enhanced Dataset* (April 2015–March 2016, experimental statistics), 6; from 1 July 2015.
[25] Health & Social Care Information Centre (HSCIC), *Female Genital Mutilation (FGM) Enhanced Dataset* (April 2015–March 2016, experimental statistics), 6; from 1 October 2015.
[26] Health & Social Care Information Centre (HSCIC), *Female Genital Mutilation (FGM) Enhanced Dataset* (April 2015–March 2016, experimental statistics), 6.
[27] Health & Social Care Information Centre (HSCIC), *Female Genital Mutilation (FGM) Enhanced Dataset* (April 2015–March 2016, experimental statistics), 7.
[28] Health & Social Care Information Centre (HSCIC), *Female Genital Mutilation (FGM) Enhanced Dataset* (April 2015–March 2016, experimental statistics), 7.
[29] Letters, 'We need better data on FGM, not propaganda' (*The Guardian*, 31 July 2016; Dr Brenda Kelly and Yana Richens) https://www.theguardian.com/society/2016/jul/31/we-need-better-data-on-fgm-not-propaganda, accessed 18 September 2016.

woman or girl visits a medical practitioner, is the best way to gauge prevalence rates amongst the female population.[30] The HSCIC's first annual Enhanced Dataset reported 5,702 newly recorded cases of FGM. Whilst the meaning of newly recorded is defined and made clear, it is important to note that within some media coverage of the same report,[31] it may have come across as 5,702 new cases of FGM were reported, rather than the number of women and girls with FGM who have been recorded for the first time under this particular dataset. Admittedly, the 'call for better data on FGM' is entirely valid, but as stated by Yana Richens, co-founder of FGM National Clinical Group stated in response to the 5,700 figure mentioned previously, 'that is still 5,700 newly recorded cases too many'.[32]

**2.20**    Despite some inaccuracies, collecting this essential information enables better planning of services, support, and protection to FGM survivors. In agreement with Professor Macfarlane, the data will need extensive development before substantially enabling it to contribute towards the elimination and prevention of FGM more directly. However, the Dataset provides a starting point for creating a more comprehensive statistical picture of FGM prevalence within the UK. In the long term, the Enhanced Dataset gathers essential information regarding women and girls who have already faced FGM and currently live in the UK. For instance, identifying a particular demographic that has undergone FGM or whose family history indicates a customary adherence to the practice, arguably allows for earlier planning and support for the next generation of females within these households.

## STATISTICS FROM THE ENHANCED DATASET ANNUAL REPORT (EXPERIMENTAL STATISTICS REPORT)

**2.21**    The data presented covers the reporting period between April 2015 and March 2016, and is collected at a 'national and NHS commissioning region level'.[33] Additional reports are available by region, clinical commissioning group (CCG), and local authority level.[34]

---

[30]   Letters, 'We need better data on FGM, not propaganda' (*The Guardian*, 31 July 2016; Dr Brenda Kelly and Yana Richens) https://www.theguardian.com/society/2016/jul/31/we-need-better-data-on-fgm-not-propaganda, accessed 18 September 2016.

[31]   Letters, 'We need better data on FGM, not propaganda' (*The Guardian*, 31 July 2016; Dr Brenda Kelly and Yana Richens) https://www.theguardian.com/society/2016/jul/31/we-need-better-data-on-fgm-not-propaganda, accessed 18 September 2016.

[32]   Letters, 'We need better data on FGM, not propaganda' (*The Guardian*, 31 July 2016; Dr Brenda Kelly and Yana Richens) https://www.theguardian.com/society/2016/jul/31/we-need-better-data-on-fgm-not-propaganda, accessed 18 September 2016.

[33]   Health & Social Care Information Centre (HSCIC), *Female Genital Mutilation (FGM) Enhanced Dataset* (April 2015–March 2016, experimental statistics), 8.

[34]   Health & Social Care Information Centre (HSCIC), *Female Genital Mutilation (FGM) Enhanced Dataset* (April 2015–March 2016, experimental statistics), 8.

## Number and type of submitting organisations

**2.22** The report states that within the reporting period 150 organisations, namely 112 NHS Trusts and 38 GP practices recorded one or more attendances.[35] It is also notable that out of the 112 NHS trusts, 15 provide mental health services.[36] The general trend showed that trust coverage remained similar across the Enhanced Dataset and the earlier Prevalence Dataset.

## Referring organisation type

**2.23** The Enhanced Dataset warns of interpreting data in relation to referring organisation with caution due to what it cites as a 'high proportion of unknowns' (52.1%). From the known data, 92% of women were referred 'either by an NHS organisation (50.5% or a GP practice (42.1%)'.[37] Amongst these, most known referrals in London are reported as coming from a GP practice (53%), whilst the North of England presents a referral trend from NHS organisations (75.9%). In addition to this, the HSISC report notes that self-referrals are more common in the South of England NHSCR (16%), relative to the rest of the country.[38]

## Number of total attendance

**2.24** Under the Enhanced Dataset, it is clearly stated that newly recorded women and girls[39] does not preclude the possibility that these women had data collected from them prior to 1 April 2015. The report acknowledges that it is fully possible that these women were recorded in the Prevalence Dataset (prior to 2015) if the information of identified FGM survivors was passed on by health providers.[40] In the four quarters between April 2015 and March 2015, a total number of 8,656 attendances were reported. This refers to every attendance 'where FGM was identified or a procedure/treatment for the same was undertaken'.[41] This factors in that some women may have more than one attendance during this reporting period.

---

[35] Health & Social Care Information Centre (HSCIC), *Female Genital Mutilation (FGM) Enhanced Dataset* (April 2015–March 2016, experimental statistics), 10.

[36] Care Quality Commission (CQC) – Trusts that provide mental health services – (Intelligent monitoring, February 2016) http://www.cqc.org.uk/download/a-to-z/mh- imonitoring-feb-2016, accessed 14 September 2016.

[37] Health & Social Care Information Centre (HSCIC), *Female Genital Mutilation (FGM) Enhanced Dataset* (April 2015–March 2016, experimental statistics), 15.

[38] Health & Social Care Information Centre (HSCIC), *Female Genital Mutilation (FGM) Enhanced Dataset* (April 2015–March 2016, experimental statistics) 15; self-referrals refer to those situations where a women or girl refers herself (directly) to the health service that oversees the care contact.

[39] Health & Social Care Information Centre (HSCIC), *Female Genital Mutilation (FGM) Enhanced Dataset* (April 2015–March 2016, experimental statistics), 11.

[40] Health & Social Care Information Centre (HSCIC), *Female Genital Mutilation (FGM) Enhanced Dataset* (April 2015–March 2016, experimental statistics), 11.

[41] Health & Social Care Information Centre (HSCIC), *Female Genital Mutilation (FGM) Enhanced Dataset* (April 2015–March 2016, experimental statistics), 11.

## Newly recorded attendances

**2.25**   Newly Recorded cases were recorded at 5,702.[42] Here, it is essential to clarify that this indicates that 5,702 women and girls who had been identified as having had FGM or had sought some treatment for the same, had their data collected under the Enhanced Dataset for the first time. In summary, 5,702 of 8,656 women and girls had their data collected under the Enhanced Dataset for the first time. This does not necessarily signify that it was the girl or woman's first attendance with a health provider concerning FGM. Since the Enhanced Dataset operates on a patient level, it would follow that this figure probably avoids a double count for the same patient, in the event that they have visited more than one health provider on more than one occasion. It has also been noted within this report and in the media,[43] that Birmingham reported the highest rate of newly recorded cases (435 cases), followed by Bristol (385) and the London Borough of Brent (325).[44]

## AGE: GLOBAL PERSPECTIVE

**2.26**   The UNICEF statistical overview provides a country-wise break-up by age, for example, age bracket: 15–49.[45]

**2.27**   A global overview of regions with the highest FGM prevalence rates provides a useful base for assessing the probability of a girl or young woman undergoing FGM or its imminent risk. It also helps to create a context for which countries of origin consider it a custom or a rite of passage to adulthood. Within Africa, UNICEF estimates that approximately 3 million girls are at the risk of FGM annually.[46] Within the Middle East, the practice is prevalent across Iraq, Yemen, Oman, Saudi Arabia, and the UAE, albeit to a relatively lesser degree vis-à-vis most African countries. Within Asia, Indonesia, Malaysia, and to a lesser extent, Pakistan and India have also been reported as countries where the practice takes place.[47]

---

[42]   Health & Social Care Information Centre (HSCIC), *Female Genital Mutilation (FGM) Enhanced Dataset* (April 2015–March 2016, experimental statistics), 12.

[43]   Alexandra Topping, 'FGM affects females in every local authority in England and Wales – study' Birmingham highest rate of new cases of FGM (*The Guardian*, 17 August 2015) https://www.theguardian.com/society/2015/jul/21/fgm-affects-females-in-every-local-authority-in-england-and-wales-study, accessed 19 August 2016.

[44]   Health & Social Care Information Centre (HSCIC), *Female Genital Mutilation (FGM) Enhanced Dataset* (April 2015–March 2016, experimental statistics), 14.

[45]   UNICEF, *Female Genital Mutilation/Cutting: A statistical overview and exploration of the dynamics of change* (2013).

[46]   United Nations Children's Fund, *Female Genital Mutilation/Cutting: A statistical overview and exploration of the dynamics of change* (UNICEF, 22 July 2013) http://data.unicef.org/resources/female-genital-mutilationcutting-statistical-overview-exploration-dynamics-change/, accessed 18 August 2016, 2.

[47]   United Nations Children's Fund, *Female Genital Mutilation/Cutting: A statistical overview and exploration of the dynamics of change* (UNICEF, 22 July 2013) http://data.unicef.org/resources/female-genital-mutilationcutting-statistical-overview-exploration-dynamics-change/, accessed 18 August 2016, 6.

**2.28**  In relation to the women cut between the ages of 15–49 the following counties are currently the most widely cited as the highest prevalence: Guinea (96%), Somalia (96%), Djibouti (93%), Eritrea (89%), Mali (89%) and Sudan (88%). Overall, there has been a move to reduce prevalence rates of FGM, which has resulted in a decline within the 15–19 age group, falling to over 41% in Liberia, 31% in Burkina Faso, 30% in Kenya and 27% in Egypt.[48]

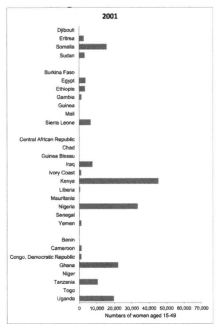 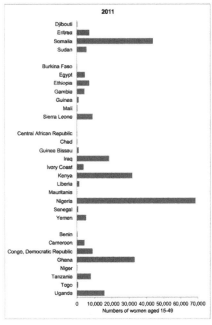

Comparison of numbers of women between ages 15–49 born in FGM practising countries in England and Wales census, 2001 and 2011.[49]

Source: *Prevalence of Female Genital Mutilation in England and Wales: National and local estimates* (City University London, July 2015).

**2.29**  As can be seen from the census comparisons above, from the number of women aged 15–49 who were born in FGM practising countries, the figures have considerably increased since 2001 in many countries including Nigeria and Ghana.[50] In contrast, women within this age group in countries such as

48  UNICEF, 'FGM/Cutting: A global concern' (5 February 2016) http://www.unicef.org/media/files/FGMC_2016_brochure_final_UNICEF_SPREAD(2).pdf, accessed 18 August 2016, 1.
49  Alison Macfarlane and Efua Dorkenoo, *Prevalence of Female Genital Mutilation in England and Wales: National and local estimates* (City University London, July 2015), 15; the statistical data within the report is the property of ONS (Crown copyright).
50  Alison Macfarlane and Efua Dorkenoo, *Prevalence of Female Genital Mutilation in England and Wales: National and local estimates* (City University London, July 2015), 15, Figure 3 (ONS Crown copyright).

Kenya, Tanzania, and Uganda have seen a drop.[51] According to the City University Report, this is because the 2001 census represented women and girls who had previously migrated from South Asia but have now crossed the age of 50, and so are outside the purview of this census.

**2.30**   The UNICEF report also notes that girls who are below 14 or younger make up 44 million of the total number of those cut, with the highest prevalence within this age bracket existing in Gambia (56%), Mauritania (54%) and Indonesia. In contrast to these statistics, on 28 December 2015 Gambia passed a law criminalising and banning FGM after President Yahya Jammeh promised to end the practice. It was acknowledged that the practice can cause lifelong health complications, and that offenders would have to pay a fine of 50,000 delasi and could face up to three years in prison. Until now, as of 2010, over 80% of Gambia's women had been cut.[52]

## AGE: UK PERSPECTIVE

**2.31**   The City University study *Prevalence of Female Genital Mutilation in England and Wales: National and local estimates* (City University London, July 2015) by Professor Macfarlane and Efua Dorkenoo, provides useful data in respect of the ages at which FGM is undertaken within the domestic context.

**2.32**   Connecting the data in the two graphs above, it can be helpful to draw a linkage between global statistics and the domestic estimates within the UK:

---

[51]   Alison Macfarlane and Efua Dorkenoo, *Prevalence of Female Genital Mutilation in England and Wales: National and local estimates* (City University London, July 2015), 15, Figure 3 (ONS Crown copyright).

[52]   Lily Kuo, 'Gambia bans female circumcision and then orders women to cover their hair at work' (*Quartz Africa*, 5 January 2016), http://qz.com/586480/gambia-bans-female-circumcision-and-then-orders-women-to-cover-their-hair-at-work/, accessed 26 September 2016.

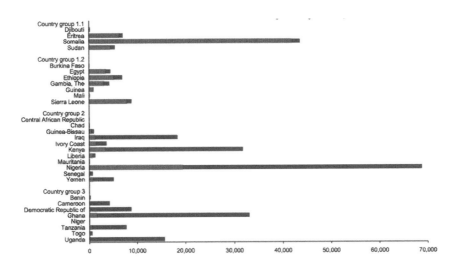

Estimated numbers of women between 15–49 who are permanently resident in England and Wales with (light grey) and without FGM (dark grey) by country of birth, 2011.[53]

Source: *Prevalence of Female Genital Mutilation in England and Wales: National and local estimates* (City University London, July 2015).

## Age at attendance

**2.33**  Within the reporting period, 56.3% of the women were aged between 25–34. This age represents the time at which they met with a medical practitioner at an NHS trust or GP practice, and not the age at which they were cut.[54] It is also reported that 106 girls (1.9%) were below 18 at their attendance. Moreover, 87% of the women at attendances were identified with a known pregnancy status and were pregnant at the time of attendance.[55] In relation to the age at the time when the FGM procedure was carried out 96.4% of women were below 18 and 43% of these were young girls aged between 5–9 years old.[56]

---

[53]  Alison Macfarlane and Efua Dorkenoo, *Prevalence of Female Genital Mutilation in England and Wales: National and local estimates* (City University London, July 2015), 21, Figure 4 (ONS Crown copyright).

[54]  Alison Macfarlane and Efua Dorkenoo, *Prevalence of Female Genital Mutilation in England and Wales: National and local estimates* (City University London, July 2015), 21.

[55]  Health & Social Care Information Centre (HSCIC), *Female Genital Mutilation (FGM) Enhanced Dataset* (April 2015–March 2016, experimental statistics), 19.

[56]  http://content.digital.nhs.uk/catalogue/PUB21206/fgm-apr-2015-mar-2016-exp-rep.pdf.

## FGM Type identified and the age at which it was done

**2.34**  Data from HSCIC on the FGM type identified and the age at which it was done should be treated as highly relevant when connecting regions in which the FGM procedure was conducted, with the number of newly recorded women whose data was collected within the reporting period. This data must be correlated with the type of FGM, as classified by the WHO.[57] These percentages represent prevalence rates amongst types of FGM that are known.

**2.35**  The countries where the procedure was undertaken and the FGM Type are as follows:

- Eastern Africa: FGM Type II (32%) and Type III (33.7%) prevalence rates are similar, whereby Type II is more common in Eritrea, Ethiopia and Kenya, and Type III in Somalia.[58] Most FGM procedures in this region, according to the HSISC report, were carried out between the ages from 5–9 years (48.3%), with Eritrea recording a majority of cases under the age of one year (50.5%).[59]

- Northern and Western Africa: Type I (36%) and Type II (48%) are most common. The former is found mostly in Egypt whereas Type II is more often found in Sudan, the Gambia, and Sierra Leone.[60] In Northern Africa, 62.4% of the newly recorded cases were cut between the ages of 5–9. In Western Africa, of the newly recorded women and girls, 32.4% underwent FGM under the age of one year. This trend is in alignment with the data taken from Nigeria, the country with the highest FGM prevalence in the region.

- Asia: Type I is predominant amongst the known types (66.7%).[61] 40 newly recorded women were classified with Type I, five cases with Type II and 10 cases with Type IV. The age at which the procedure was undertaken ranged between 1–9 years in the majority of the cases.[62]

- FGM undertaken within the UK: Amongst the 18 known cases, 70% were reported as Type IV (piercings).

**2.36**  The figure below shows a steep rise in the number of girls born to women who were born in countries that practice FGM. A direct correlation is shown, with a steady increase, escalating between 2001–2004, and again more sharply between 2004–2011, after which a slight drop is noted (indicated by a slightly

---

[57]  WHO/UNICEF/UNFPA, *Joint Statement on Female Genital Mutilation* (Geneva, 1997).
[58]  Health & Social Care Information Centre (HSCIC), *Female Genital Mutilation (FGM) Enhanced Dataset* (April 2015–March 2016, experimental statistics), 29.
[59]  Health & Social Care Information Centre (HSCIC), *Female Genital Mutilation (FGM) Enhanced Dataset* (April 2015–March 2016, experimental statistics). 31.
[60]  Health & Social Care Information Centre (HSCIC), *Female Genital Mutilation (FGM) Enhanced Dataset* (April 2015–March 2016, experimental statistics), 29.
[61]  Health & Social Care Information Centre (HSCIC), *Female Genital Mutilation (FGM) Enhanced Dataset* (April 2015–March 2016, experimental statistics), 29.
[62]  Health & Social Care Information Centre (HSCIC), *Female Genital Mutilation (FGM) Enhanced Dataset* (April 2015–March 2016, experimental statistics), Table 19.

gentler downward curve). The type of FGM is indicated by the coloured index in the left corner of the graph. The report suggests that the number of girls who were born to women from countries that practice FGM saw an increase. This increase is related in particular to women from countries where FGM is 'near universal and Type 3 is commonly practised.'[63]

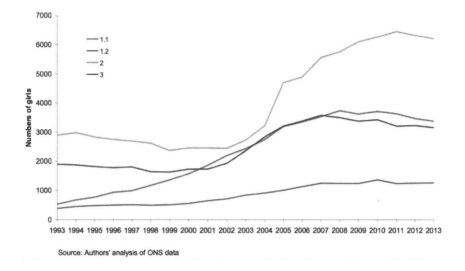

Source: Authors' analysis of ONS data

Numbers of girls born to women born in countries known to practice FGM, England and Wales, 1993–2013

Source: *Prevalence of Female Genital Mutilation in England and Wales: National and local estimates* (City University London, July 2015).

According to data collected between 2011–2013, 17,300 girls were born in England and Wales to mothers with FGM.

## REGIONAL PREVALENCE

**2.37** According to Professor Macfarlane and Efua Dorkenoo on the 'Prevalence of Female Genital Mutilation in England and Wales',[64] the estimated number of women who have undergone FGM between 15–49 in England and Wales amounts to approximately 103,000.[65] These prevalence rates vary by region, with London having the highest prevalence rate per 1000 women (28.2%).

---

[63]  Alison Macfarlane and Efua Dorkenoo, *Prevalence of Female Genital Mutilation in England and Wales: National and local estimates* (City University London, July 2015), 27.

[64]  Alison Macfarlane and Efua Dorkenoo, *Prevalence of Female Genital Mutilation in England and Wales: National and local estimates* (City University London, July 2015) 21, Figure 4 (ONS Crown copyright).

[65]  Alison Macfarlane and Efua Dorkenoo, *Prevalence of Female Genital Mutilation in England and Wales: National and local estimates* (City University London, July 2015), 20.

Overall, London continues to maintain the highest prevalence rates across all ages.

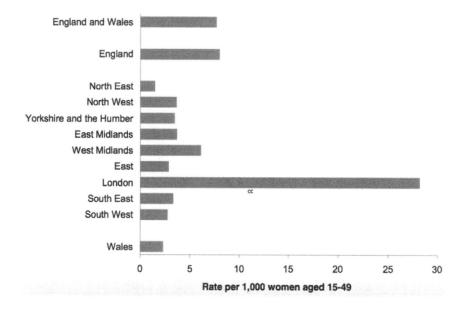

Estimated prevalence of FGM among women aged 15–49 by region.[66]

Source: *Prevalence of Female Genital Mutilation in England and Wales: National and local estimates* (City University London, July 2015).

## PLACE OF RESIDENCE AND THE INFLUENCE OF AN URBAN-RURAL DIVIDE

**2.38**   According to the Enhanced Dataset, 99.6% of newly recorded women and girls live in urban areas, and a definite majority of women and girls lived in 'major urban conurbations'.[67] This is reflected at 42.1% higher than the equivalent figure for the entire English population.[68] In contrast to a sharp urban prevalence rate, only 0.4% of newly recorded women and girls belong to rural areas.[69] Analysing this at a local authority level, there appears to be considerable variation, with the three local authorities with the highest newly recorded cases being in the London Borough of Brent, the London Borough of Southwark and in Bristol. According to the HSISC report, Brent alone accounts

---

[66]   Alison Macfarlane and Efua Dorkenoo, *Prevalence of Female Genital Mutilation in England and Wales: National and local estimates* (City University London, July 2015), 21.

[67]   Health & Social Care Information Centre (HSCIC), *Female Genital Mutilation (FGM) Enhanced Dataset* (April 2015–March 2016, experimental statistics).

[68]   Health & Social Care Information Centre (HSCIC), *Female Genital Mutilation (FGM) Enhanced Dataset* (April 2015–March 2016, experimental statistics), 13.

[69]   Health & Social Care Information Centre (HSCIC), *Female Genital Mutilation (FGM) Enhanced Dataset* (April 2015–March 2016, experimental statistics), 13.

for one in seven of total attendances for FGM within the reporting period (14.6%). This comes in stark contrast to other local authorities where fewer than 12 newly recorded cases are reported across the entire reporting period.[70] This amounts to one case per month, on average.

## FGM Identification method and commissioning region (NHSCR)

**2.39**  The HSISC warns that a degree of caution is exercised when interpreting this data due to the high proportion of 'unknowns' within this collection, for the relevant reporting period (33.4%).[71]

**2.40**  73% of the known submissions were identified via self-reporting, which is when the woman or girl records having had FGM at the attendance. The regional variation was as follows: 58.1% in the North of England NHSCR reported through this method, and self-reporting was the predominant method in the South of England (92.9%). The number of newly recorded women identified by commissioning region was reportedly the highest in London (1,340) via self-reporting, and the total number across England amounted to 2,771 cases recorded through this route.

## UPDATED NHS STATISTICS

**2.41**  From July to September 2015 healthcare providers in England reported 1,385 newly recorded cases of FGM.[72] FGM Types I, II and III covered over 90% of women and girls with a known FGM Type in the cohort, with a relatively low incidence of the remaining categories (Type IV, history of Type III and Type III – re-infibulation identified).[73]

**2.42**  The most recent figures from NHS digital, which began collating data in April 2015, reveal that more than 8,000 women across England have recently been identified as being victims of FGM.[74] Between July and September 2016 there were 1,971 attendances reported at NHS trusts and GP practices where FGM was identified or a procedure for FGM was undertaken.[75] There were 1,204 women and girls who had their FGM information collected in the Enhanced Dataset for the first time. This does not indicate how recently the FGM was undertaken, nor does it necessarily mean that this is the woman or

---

[70]  Health & Social Care Information Centre (HSCIC), *Female Genital Mutilation (FGM) Enhanced Dataset* (April 2015–March 2016, experimental statistics), 13.

[71]  Health & Social Care Information Centre (HSCIC), *Female Genital Mutilation (FGM) Enhanced Dataset* (April 2015–March 2016, experimental statistics), 19.

[72]  Female Genital Mutilation (FGM) – July 2015–September 2015, *Experimental Statistics, Health and Social Care Information Centre* (HSCIC), 2 December 2015.

[73]  Female Genital Mutilation (FGM) – July 2015–September 2015, *Experimental Statistics, Health and Social Care Information Centre* (HSCIC), 2 December 2015.

[74]  http://www.content.digital.nhs.uk/catalogue/PUB22619.

[75]  http://www.content.digital.nhs.uk/catalogue/PUB22619.

girl's first attendance for FGM. It is the first time their information has been collected in the FGM Enhanced Dataset.[76]

## CURRENT TRAJECTORY OF FGM

**2.43**  Statistical data in relation to FGM should be treated with appropriate caution. However, the use of multi-agency reports, national reports by governmental agencies and studies by international organisation such as UNICEF and the WHO have significantly contributed to the building of a comprehensive understanding of FGM.

**2.44**  There are approximately 70 million more women and girls subjected to the practice since 2014.[77] This is partly due to population growth and increased data submissions by governments such as Indonesia. Overall, there has been a decline of FGM over the past three decades but the decline has been uneven. The current extent of FGM is nevertheless considerable.[78]

---

[76]   http://www.content.digital.nhs.uk/catalogue/PUB22619.

[77]   UNICEF, *FGM/Cutting: A global concern* (5 February 2016) http://www.unicef.org/media/files/ FGMC_2016_brochure_final_UNICEF_SPREAD(2).pdf, accessed 18 August 2016.

[78]   UNICEF, *FGM/Cutting: A global concern* (5 February 2016), http://www.unicef.org/media/ files/FGMC_2016_brochure_final_UNICEF_SPREAD(2).pdf, accessed 18 August 2016.

# CHAPTER 3

# INTERNATIONAL LEGAL FRAMEWORK

**3.1** The United Kingdom has long-standing and wide-ranging international legal obligations in relation to FGM. International law requires that the UK creates an effective mechanism to tackle FGM that operates in a multi-level and multi-agency manner (including legal, administrative, educational and health) and that it maintains a proactive commitment to protecting girls in the UK from FGM.

**3.2** By ratifying the Convention on the Elimination of All Forms of Discrimination against Women 1979 (CEDAW)[1] the UK committed itself to eliminate discrimination against women. FGM unambiguously constitutes a form of discrimination against young women and girls.

**3.3** Under the UN Convention on the Rights of the Child 1989 (CRC) the UK has positive obligations in international law to ensure that children are not subjected to cruel, inhuman or degrading treatment.[2] FGM constitutes an irreparable violation of the child's bodily integrity and physical and psychological health.

**3.4** The Committee on the Convention of the Rights of the Child has described FGM as a 'harmful traditional practice'.[3]

**3.5** The Convention against Torture and Other Cruel, Inhuman or Degrading Treatment or Punishment (CAT) was adopted and opened for signature by General Assembly resolution 39/46 and was ratified by the UK in 1988, entering into force in 1990.[4]

**3.6** The UK has a positive obligation to take legislative, administrative, judicial or other measures to prevent acts of torture within its jurisdiction.[5] The Committee against Torture clearly stated in General Comment No 2 in 2008 that FGM falls within its mandate. The UN Special Rapporteur on violence

---

[1] Convention on the Elimination of All Forms of Discrimination against Women (CEDAW), adopted in 1979 by the UN General Assembly, signed by the UK in 1981 and ratified 1986.

[2] United Nations Convention on the Rights of the Child 1989. Signed by the UK in 1990, and came into force in the UK in 1992, Art 37.

[3] CRC Committee, *Consideration of reports submitted by states parties under article 44 of the Convention*, 3 May 2007, CRC/C/MLI/CO/2, para 53(d).

[4] Convention on the Elimination of All Forms of Discrimination against Women (CEDAW), adopted in 1979 by the UN General Assembly, signed by the UK in 1981 and ratified 1986.

[5] United Nations Convention against Torture 1984. Ratified by the UK in 1988, Art 2.

against women and the UN Special Rapporteur on torture have both recognised that FGM can amount to torture under this Convention.

**3.7**   In the CAT Committee's General Comment No 2, it identified gender-based violence as within the ambit of the prohibition of torture and cruel, inhuman or degrading treatment. The Committee on the Convention on the Elimination of Discrimination against Women has identified FGM as a form of gender-based violence, thus bringing it within the scope of the prohibition.[6]

**3.8**   The UN Human Rights Committee has identified the practice of FGM is in breach of Article 7 of the Covenant, in its General Comment No 28.[7]

**3.9**   In 2010, the Commission on the Status of Women (CSW) resolved that States should ensure the effective implementation of national legislative frameworks and institute adequate accountability mechanisms to monitor the impact of anti-FGM measures.[8]

**3.10**  The European Parliament resolved in 2012 that the Member States should not only enact legislation, but also develop 'a full range of prevention and protection measures, including mechanisms to coordinate, monitor, and evaluate law enforcemen'.[9] The European Parliament's Resolution called for the allocation of appropriate financial resources to actively support targeted programmes and to 'disseminate best practice guidelines that address the needs and priorities of girls in vulnerable situations, including those subjected to female genital mutilation.'[10]

**3.11**  The call for adequate resources to combat FGM echoed the Istanbul Convention which observed that States should allocate adequate resources to prevent forms of violence against women, of which FGM is undoubtedly one of the most serious.[11] The UK has a legal duty to ensure that such preventative and protective mechanisms are adequately resourced to the maximum extent of available resources.[12]

---

[6]   CEDAW Committee, General Recommendation Number 14 (1992). Available at: http://www.un.org/womenwatch/daw/cedaw/recommendations/recomm.htm#recom14 [last accessed 20 October 2016].

[7]   See Human Rights Committee, General Comment No 28 on Art 3: The equality of rights between men and women (2000), para 11; see also concluding observations on Uganda, CCPR/CO/80/UGA, para 10; Mali, CCPR/CO/77/MLI, para 11; Sweden, CCPR/CO/74/SWE, para 8; Yemen, CCPR/CO/84/YEM, para 11.

[8]   Ending female genital mutilation, Resolution 54/7 of 2010, United Nations Commission on the Status of Women.

[9]   European Parliament Resolution 2012/2684 (RSP) on ending female genital mutilation of 14 June 2012, para 4.

[10]  European Parliament Resolution 2012 /2684 (RSP) on ending female genital mutilation of 14 June 2012, para 4.

[11]  Council of Europe Convention on preventing and combating violence against women and domestic violence, 12 April 2011 (Treaty No 210).

[12]  United Nations Convention on the Rights of the Child 1989, signed by the UK in 1990 and came into force in the UK in 1992, Art 4.

**3.12** Lord Justice Auld observed in *Fornah v Secretary of State for the Home Department*[13] that FGM is '... an evil practice internationally condemned and in clear violation of Article 3 of the European Convention on Human Rights (ECHR)'.

**3.13** The United Nations General Assembly passed a significant resolution on FGM in 2007 with overwhelming international support. The UN General Assembly emphasised that custom, tradition or religious consideration cannot be used as justifications for avoiding the obligation to eliminate violence against women and girls.[14]

**3.14** The UN Human Rights Council adopted on 1 July 2016 a resolution on the elimination of FGM.[15] The Resolution recognises FGM as an act of violence against women and girls and urges Member States to place special emphasis on education of youth, parents and religious, traditional and community leaders and especially to encourage men and boys to become more involved in information and awareness-raising campaigns and to become agents of change.

**3.15** The Human Rights Council also urges States to adopt national legislation prohibiting FGM and to take steps to ensure its strict application, as well as develop, support and promote education programmes including on sexual and reproductive health that challenge the negative stereotypes and harmful attitudes and practices that sustain FGM and gender-based violence and discrimination.

**3.16** States are called to increase technical and financial assistance for the effective implementation of policies, programmes and action plans and the international community is encouraged to devote special attention to the issue of FGM in the implementation of the Sustainable Development Goals by 2030. The need for systematic collection of data and financial support for research on FGM is also highlighted.

---

[13] [2005] EWCA Civ 680 (9 June 2005).
[14] United Nations General Assembly, Resolution A/RES/61/143, adopted by the General Assembly on 19 December 2006.
[15] Human Rights Council, 32nd session, 29 June 2016, A/HRC/32/L.31/Rev.1.

# CHAPTER 4

# CRIMINAL OFFENCES AND GUIDANCE FOR POLICE AUTHORITIES

**4.1**   FGM has been a specific criminal offence in the United Kingdom since 1985 when the UK-wide Prohibition of Female Circumcision Act 1985 (the 1985 Act) was passed.[1] The Female Genital Mutilation Act 2003 (the 2003 Act) replaced the 1985 Act in England, Wales and Northern Ireland.[2] One of the changes the 2003 Act instituted was an increase in the sentence for the offence. At present, the maximum penalty for any of the FGM offence is 14 years' imprisonment.[3]

**4.2**   The 2003 Act made it an offence for any person in England, Wales or Northern Ireland (regardless of their nationality or residence status) to perform FGM (s 1); or to assist a girl to carry out FGM on herself (s 2). The term 'girl' is defined to include woman.[4] It is also an offence to assist (from England, Wales or Northern Ireland) a non-UK national or non-UK resident to carry out FGM outside the UK on a UK national or a UK resident (s 3). These provisions were further amended and supplemented by the Serious Crime Act 2015 (the 2015 Act).

## OFFENCE OF EXCISING, INFIBULATING OR MUTILATING

**4.3**   The substantive FGM offence of FGM, as set out in s 1 of the 2003 Act, stipulates that:[5]

'(1)   A person is guilty of an offence if he excises, infibulates or otherwise mutilates the whole or any part of a girl's labia majora, labia minora or clitoris.[6]

---

[1]   It has been argued that FGM has been illegal since the Offences Against the Person Act 1861.
[2]   The Prohibition of Female Genital Mutilation (Scotland) Act 2005 replaced the 1985 Act in Scotland.
[3]   2003 Act, s 5(1)(a). A person guilty of offences under ss 1, 2 and 3 of the legislation is liable on conviction on indictment, to imprisonment for a term not exceeding 14 years or a fine (or both); on summary conviction, to imprisonment for a term not exceeding six months or a fine not exceeding the statutory maximum (or both).
[4]   2003 Act, s 6(1).
[5]   2003 Act, s 1.
[6]   2003 Act, s 1(1).

(2)    But no offence is committed by an approved person who performs:[7]
   (a)    a surgical operation on a girl which is necessary for her physical or mental health,[8] or
   (b)    a surgical operation on a girl who is in any stage of labour, or has just given birth, for purposes connected with the labour or birth.'[9]

**4.4**    The legislation makes clear that no offence is committed by an approved person who performs a surgical operation.[10] An approved person is defined as a medical practitioner. In relation to an operation on a girl who is in any stage of labour, or for any purpose connected with the labour or birth, an approved person would be a medical practitioner, a registered midwife or a person undergoing a course of training with a view to becoming such a practitioner or midwife.[11]

**4.5**    Section 1 also details lines of defence where the procedure is performed by an approved person. First, where FGM is performed because it is necessary for the mental or physical health of a girl. Secondly, when it is performed on a girl who is in any stage of labour, or who has just given birth, for purposes connected to the labour or birth.[12]

**4.6**    Importantly, in determining whether an operation is necessary for the mental health of a girl it is immaterial whether the girl or any other person believes that the operation is required as a matter of custom or ritual.[13]

## Aiding and abetting

**4.7**    Section 2 deals with secondary participation. It provides that a person is guilty of an offence if he aids, abets, counsels or procures a girl to excise, infibulate or otherwise mutilate the whole or any part of her own labia majora, labia minora or clitoris.[14]

## ASSISTING A NON-UK PERSON TO MUTILATE OVERSEAS A GIRL'S GENITALIA

**4.8**    Section 3 of the 2003 Act provides for the offence of assisting a non-UK person to mutilate overseas a girl's genitalia. A person is guilty of an offence if he aids, abets, counsels or procures a person who is not a United Kingdom national or United Kingdom resident to do a relevant act of FGM outside the

---

7    2003 Act, s 1(2).
8    2003 Act, s 1(2)(a).
9    2003 Act, s 1(2)(b).
10   2003 Act, s 1(2).
11   2003 Act, s 1(3)(a) and (b).
12   2003 Act, s 1(2)(a) and (b).
13   2003 Act, s 5.
14   2003 Act, s 2.

United Kingdom.[15] An act is deemed as a relevant act which would constitute FGM if it were performed on a UK national or UK resident and it would fall under s 1.[16]

**4.9** No offence is committed if the relevant act is a surgical operation falling within s 1(2)(a) or (b), and it is performed by a person who, in relation to such an operation, is an approved person or exercises functions corresponding to those of an approved person.[17]

## OFFENCE OF ASSISTING A GIRL TO MUTILATE HER OWN GENITALIA

**4.10** The 2003 Act makes provision for an offence of assisting a girl to mutilate her own genitalia.[18] A person is guilty of an offence if 'he aids, abets, counsels or procures a girl to excise, infibulate or otherwise mutilate the whole or any part of her own labia majora, labia minora or clitoris'.[19]

**4.11** Consequently, a person can be charged with this offence even though they were not present when the offence itself was committed. Where a person has knowledge of the crime and assists in its commission through advice, financial support or action, they may also fall foul of this offence. It is a defence if the relevant act of FGM is a surgical operation performed by a person who is an approved person.[20]

## THE SERIOUS CRIME ACT 2015

**4.12** The Serious Crime Act 2015 (the 2015 Act) introduced several new provisions on FGM which have a direct effect on the criminal legal framework. These changes include the provision for the extra-territorial reach of the substantive offence of FGM, reflecting the transnational nature of this crime. It is intended to cover UK residents who assist in the commission of FGM outside of the jurisdiction. Further changes brought in by the 2015 Act include provision for the anonymity of victims and an offence of failing to protect a girl from risk of FGM.

### Extension of extra-territorial jurisdiction

**4.13** The 2003 Act was originally concerned solely with acts done by UK nationals, or permanent UK residents, to girls or women who are UK nationals or permanent UK residents. Perpetrators and victims of FGM who fell outside

---

[15]   2003 Act, s 3(1).
[16]   2003 Act, s 3(1).
[17]   2003 Act, s 3(3)(a) and (b).
[18]   2003 Act, s 2.
[19]   2003 Act, s 2.
[20]   2003 Act, s 1(2)(a) and (b).

this category were not covered by this legislation. Submissions were made during the Parliamentary Inquiry on FGM identifying the limits of this in relation to safeguarding.[21] The Government adopted these concerns and consequently s 70(1) of the 2015 Act amended s 4 of the 2003 Act so as to extend the scope of the offences contained within ss 1–3 to habitual residents rather than only permanent UK residents.[22]

**4.14**  These changes mean that the 2003 Act can extend its reach to offences of FGM committed abroad by or against those who at the time are habitually resident in the UK irrespective of whether they are subject to immigration restrictions. This includes the offence of assisting a non-UK person to mutilate overseas a girl's genitalia.

**4.15**  'UK resident' is defined as an individual who is habitually resident in the UK. The term 'habitually resident' covers a person's ordinary residence, as opposed to a short, temporary stay in a country. It will be for the courts to determine on the facts of individual cases whether or not those affected are habitually resident in the UK and thus covered by the 2003 Act, as amended.

**4.16**  If the offence is committed outside the UK, proceedings may be taken and the offence may be treated as having been committed anywhere in England, Wales or Northern Ireland.[23] Section 70(2) of the 2015 Act makes equivalent amendments to the Prohibition of Female Genital Mutilation (Scotland) Act 2005.

## Anonymity of victims of FGM

**4.17**  It is believed that the reluctance to be identified as a victim of FGM is one of the reasons for the low incidence of reporting of FGM.[24] It is hoped that providing for the anonymity of complainants of alleged offences of FGM will encourage more victims to come forward.

**4.18**  Section 71 of the 2015 Act amends the 2003 Act to prohibit the publication of any information that would be likely to lead to the identification of a person against whom an FGM offence is alleged to have been committed. Publication is given a broad meaning and includes traditional print media, broadcasting and social media such as Twitter or Facebook.[25] Anonymity will commence once an allegation has been made and will last for the duration of

---

[21]  See particularly: Bar Human Rights Committee submissions to Parliamentary Inquiry 2014.
[22]  2003 Act, s 4, as amended by s 70(1) of the 2015 Act.
[23]  2003 Act, s 4.
[24]  See Dias QC, Gerry and Burrage, *The Guardian*, 7 February 2014: https://www.theguardian.com/commentisfree/2014/feb/07/fgm-female-genital-mutilation-prosecutions-law-failed.
[25]  CPS, *Female Genital Mutilation Legal Guidance*, http://www.cps.gov.uk/legal/d_to_g/female_genital_mutilation/, accessed 27 September 2016.

the victim's lifetime.[26] This is similar, although not identical, to the anonymity given to alleged victims of sexual offences by the Sexual Offences (Amendment) Act 1992.[27]

**4.19** There are two circumstances in which the court may dis-apply the restrictions on publication.[28] The first is where a person being tried for FGM could have their defence substantially prejudiced if the restriction to prevent identification of the person against whom the allegation of FGM was committed is not lifted.[29] The second is where anonymity of the FGM victim could be seen as a substantial and an unreasonable restriction on the reporting of the proceedings and it is considered in the public interest to remove the restriction.[30]

**4.20** Contravention of the prohibition on publication is an offence.[31] It will not be necessary for the prosecution to show that the defendant intended to identify the victim.[32] In relation to newspapers or other periodicals (whether in print form or online editions) and radio and television programmes, the offence is directed at proprietors, editors, publishers or broadcasters rather than individual journalists.[33] Any prosecution for the offence requires the consent of the Attorney General. This is a summary only offence.

**4.21** There are two defences to publishing information that is prohibited:[34]

(1) where the defendant had no knowledge (and no reason to suspect) that the publication included content that would be likely to identify a victim or that a relevant allegation had been made; or[35]

(2) where the victim (when aged 16 or over) had freely given written consent to the publication.[36]

---

[26] 2003 Act, Sch 1, s 1(2).

[27] Section 1 provides that 'where an allegation has been made that an offence to which this Act applies has been committed against a person, neither the name nor address, and no still or moving picture, of that person shall during that person's lifetime be published in England and Wales in a written publication available to the public; or be included in a relevant programme for reception in England and Wales, if it is likely to lead members of the public to identify that person as the person against whom the offence is alleged to have been committed'.

[28] CPS, *Female Genital Mutilation Legal Guidance*, http://www.cps.gov.uk/legal/d_to_g/female_genital_mutilation/, accessed 27 September 2016.

[29] CPS, *Female Genital Mutilation Legal Guidance*, http://www.cps.gov.uk/legal/d_to_g/female_genital_mutilation/, accessed 27 September 2016.

[30] CPS, *Female Genital Mutilation Legal Guidance*, http://www.cps.gov.uk/legal/d_to_g/female_genital_mutilation/, accessed 27 September 2016.

[31] CPS, *Female Genital Mutilation Legal Guidance*, http://www.cps.gov.uk/legal/d_to_g/female_genital_mutilation/, accessed 27 September 2016.

[32] CPS, *Female Genital Mutilation Legal Guidance*, http://www.cps.gov.uk/legal/d_to_g/female_genital_mutilation/, accessed 27 September 2016.

[33] 2003 Act, Sch 1, s 2(3).

[34] 2003 Act, Sch 1, s 3.

[35] 2003 Act, Sch 1, s 3(2).

[36] 2003 Act, Sch 1, s 3(3).

**4.22**  These defences impose a reverse burden on the defendant. It is for the defendant to prove on the balance of probabilities that the defence is made out, rather than requiring the prosecution to show beyond reasonable doubt that the defence does not apply.[37] In relation to newspapers or other periodicals (whether in print form or online editions) and radio and television programmes, the offence is directed at proprietors, editors, publishers or broadcasters rather than individual journalists. Any prosecution for the offence requires the consent of the Attorney General or the Director of Public Prosecutions for Northern Ireland as the case may be.[38]

## Offence of failing to protect

**4.23**  Section 72 of the 2015 Act inserts new s 3A into the 2003 Act, creating the offence of failing to protect a girl from FGM. The provision, which was initially tabled and discussed in broader terms of public encouragement of FGM being unlawful, was introduced to tackle the deep-rooted cultural aspects of FGM and the secrecy with which it is often shrouded. During the Parliamentary debates that preceded the 2015 Act, Baroness Smith stated:

> 'Many activists tell us that pressures from others in the community on parents can become too difficult to resist, even when they have no wish to cut their daughters. Affected communities often retain a strong hierarchical structure, and encouragement or admonishment from elders can carry enormous weight. Not only are parents told that their daughters will never get married, but whole families can be ostracised and isolated as unclean.

> We need to support those who are seeking to change the culture in affected communities and send the message that the practice is breaking the law. We know from research by the Bar human rights committee and others that there is still significant support among affected communities in Britain for sunna: that is, type 1 and type 2 FGM. The process by which FGM occurs is complex, and sometimes encouragement takes place in small gatherings and in informal settings behind the scenes, where it is difficult to intervene. Many campaigners and activists unanimously support a distinct offence of making the public encouragement of female genital mutilation unlawful.'[39]

**4.24**  The offence of failing to protect as it was eventually termed in s 3A of the 2003 Act states that 'if FGM is committed against a girl under the age of 16, each person who is responsible for her will be guilty of the offence'.[40]

---

[37]  CPS, *Female Genital Mutilation Legal Guidance*, http://www.cps.gov.uk/legal/d_to_g/female_genital_mutilation/, accessed 27 September 2016.

[38]  Multi Agency Statutory Guidance on FGM, section 3.1.4 April 2016, section, 3.2.2.

[39]  http://www.publications.parliament.uk/pa/cm201415/cmpublic/seriouscrime/150120/am/150120s01.htm.

[40]  2003 Act, s 3A(1).

**4.25**  In order to be deemed 'responsible' for a girl, a person will have parental responsibility for the girl (such as mothers, fathers married to the mothers at the time of birth and guardians) and have frequent contact with her.[41]

**4.26**  The term 'parental responsibility':

(a)  in England Wales, has the same meaning as in the Children Act 1989;[42]

(b)  in Northern Ireland, has the same meaning as in the Children (Northern Ireland) Order 1995, SI 1995/755 (NI 2);[43]

Where the person is aged 18 or over they may have assumed responsibility for caring for the girl 'in the manner of a parent'.

**4.27**  This in loco parentis provision caters for extended family members to whom the girl may be sent by parents during vacations, for instance, family members parents might send their child to stay with during the summer holidays.[44] The requirement for frequent contact is intended to ensure that a person who in law has parental responsibility for a girl, but who in practice has little or no contact with her, would not be liable. A carer with irregular, haphazard or very short-term responsibility would not be liable.

**4.28**  Similarly, the requirement that the person should be caring for the girl 'in the manner of a parent' is intended to ensure that a person who is looking after a girl for a very short period, such as a babysitter, would not be liable.[45] However, where frequent contact between a person and a girl is interrupted temporarily, for example, by her going somewhere on holiday, that contact is deemed to have continued during her stay there.[46]

**4.29**  In order to establish the commission of an offence under s 3A, the following evidence may be considered:[47]

- Evidence of the relationships between the girl and her parents/their parental responsibility.

- Evidence showing the girl has suffered FGM which includes medical evidence as well as expert evidence confirming the type of FGM and that the procedure has been done.

---

[41]  2003 Act, s 3A(2) and (3).

[42]  2003 Act, s 3A(8).

[43]  2003 Act, s 3A(8).

[44]  Alexandra Topping, 'Schools warned over FGM risk to girls during summer holidays', *The Guardian*, 25 May 2014, https://www.theguardian.com/society/2014/may/25/schools-warned-fgm-risks-summer-holidays, accessed 26 September 2016.

[45]  CPS, *Female Genital Mutilation Legal Guidance*, http://www.cps.gov.uk/legal/d_to_g/female_genital_mutilation/, accessed 27 September 2016.

[46]  2003 Act, s 3A(7). Under subsection (8), 'an offence of FGM means an offence under section 1, 2 or 3 and for the purposes of subsection (1) the prosecution does not have to prove which section it is'.

[47]  CPS, *Female Genital Mutilation Legal Guidance*, http://www.cps.gov.uk/legal/d_to_g/female_genital_mutilation/, accessed 27 September 2016.

- Evidence that the FGM procedure is illegal in the country in which it was performed.
- Where possible, evidence that the girl was born with normal genitalia.

**4.30**  The offence of failing to protect a girl from risk of genital mutilation as provided for by s 3A, covers the offences provided for under ss 1, 2 or 3 of the 2003 Act. The prosecution does not have to prove which section it is.[48]

**4.31**  The legislation makes provision for a statutory defence to this offence. It is a defence for a defendant to show that at the relevant time, he or she did not think there was a significant risk of FGM being committed against the girl and they could not reasonably have been expected to be aware of this risk.[49] Alternatively, it will be a defence if the defendant can show they took such steps as were reasonably expected to protect the girl from being the victim of FGM.[50] A person will be deemed to have raised the above defences 'if sufficient evidence of the fact is adduced to raise with respect to it and the contrary is not proved beyond reasonable doubt'.[51] Therefore there is an evidential burden on the defendant. Once raised by the defence evidentially, the prosecution retains the overall burden of disproving this line of defence to the criminal standard.

**4.32**  Where a defence is raised based on having left the child with another for some time, consideration might be given to obtaining evidence of the immediate effects of the operation.[52] In many cases the child is bound by the legs for days or weeks – the recovery period is not short. They will be in pain and bed-bound for a significant time. An FGM expert may be able to assist here.[53]

## PENALTIES FOR FGM OFFENCES

**4.33**  All offences (with the exception of s 4A which is summary only) are triable either way; in essence, they can be tried either in the Magistrates' or in the Crown Court.[54] A person guilty of an offence under ss 1, 2 or 3 of the 2003 Act is liable on conviction on indictment to imprisonment for a term not exceeding 14 years or a fine (or both).[55] However, where tried summarily, a person is liable to imprisonment for a term not exceeding six months or a fine not exceeding the statutory maximum (or both).[56]

---

[48]  2003 Act, s 3A(8).
[49]  2003 Act, s 3A(5).
[50]  2003 Act, s 3A(5)(a) and (b).
[51]  2003 Act, s 3A(6)(b).
[52]  CPS, *Female Genital Mutilation Legal Guidance*, http://www.cps.gov.uk/legal/d_to_g/female_genital_mutilation/, accessed 27 September 2016.
[53]  CPS, *Female Genital Mutilation Legal Guidance*, http://www.cps.gov.uk/legal/d_to_g/female_genital_mutilation/, accessed 27 September 2016.
[54]  CPS, *Female Genital Mutilation Legal Guidance*, http://www.cps.gov.uk/legal/d_to_g/female_genital_mutilation/, accessed 27 September 2016.
[55]  2003 Act, s 5(1)(a).
[56]  2003 Act, s 5(1)(b).

**4.34**  A person guilty of an offence of failing to protect a girl from the risk of FGM is liable on conviction on indictment to imprisonment for a term not exceeding seven years and/or an unlimited fine; and on summary conviction, to imprisonment for a term not exceeding six months and/or an unlimited fine.[57] A person guilty of an offence under s 4A of this Act is liable on summary conviction to an unlimited fine.[58]

## Other offences

**4.35**  Under provisions of the law which apply generally to criminal offences it is also an offence to:

- aid, abet, counsel or procure a person to commit an FGM offence;[59]
- encourage or assist a person to commit an FGM offence;[60]
- attempt to commit an FGM offence:[61] and
- conspire to commit an FGM offence.[62]

Any person found guilty of such an offence faces the same maximum penalty as for the offences under the 2003 Act.

## Additional considerations for police authorities

**4.36**  Police authorities should refer to the College of Policing's Authorised Professional Practice on FGM which includes guidance on prevention, protection and evidence-gathering in FGM cases.[63] In addition, the police should also consider section D.2 of the statutory guidance which provides details of additional considerations for police authorities.[64]

### *Initial investigations*

**4.37**  If an officer or a member of police staff believes that a girl may be at risk of undergoing FGM, the duty inspector must be made aware and an immediate referral should be made to their local child abuse specialist team or similar. If this is outside their core hours, the duty inspector must ensure that effective protection measures are put in place to ensure the safety of the victim in addition to undertaking an effective primary investigation. The safety and welfare of the girl is of paramount importance. The specialist team will in turn make an immediate referral to the relevant local authority's children's social

---

[57]  2003 Act, s 5(2).
[58]  2003 Act, Sch 1, s 2(2).
[59]  Common law.
[60]  Serious Crime Act 2007, ss 44–46.
[61]  Criminal Attempts Act 1981, s 1.
[62]  Criminal Law Act 1977, s 1.
[63]  www.app.college.police.uk/app-content/major-investigation-and-public-protection/female-genital- mutilation/?s=female+genital+mutilation#prevention.
[64]  Multi Agency Statutory Guidance on FGM, section 3.1.4 April 2016, section D.2.

care team if this has not already been done by the first responders/primary investigators.[65] Officers should consider the use of police protection powers under s 46 of the Children Act 1989.

**4.38**   If it is believed or known that a girl has undergone FGM, a multi-agency strategy meeting should be held as soon as practicable (and in any case within two working days) to discuss the implications for the child and the coordination of the criminal investigation.

**4.39**   There is a risk that the fear of prosecution will prevent those concerned from seeking help, resulting in possible health complications for the girl; thus police action will need to be in partnership with other agencies, affected communities and specialist non-government organisations. This should also be used as an opportunity to assess the need for specialist support services such as counselling and medical help as appropriate.[66]

**4.40**   Police officers should refer to the CPS's guidance *Provision of Therapy for Child Witnesses Prior to a Criminal Trial.*[67] Investigating officers must refer to the Police/CPS Protocol for the investigation and prosecution of FGM cases, which has been signed by the 43 police forces in England and Wales.

## *Conducting interviews about FGM*

**4.41**   As with all criminal investigations, children and young people should be interviewed under the Achieving Best Evidence procedure to obtain the best possible evidence for use in any prosecution. Consent should be obtained to record the interview and for allowing the use of the interview in family and/or criminal courts. In addition, information gained from the interview process will enable a risk assessment to be conducted as to the risk to any other children or siblings.

## Female Genital Mutilation Prosecution Policy and Guidance, Crown Prosecution Service, 2015

**4.42**   The Crown Prosecution Service (CPS) has published Legal Guidance on FGM for Crown Prosecutors and Associate Prosecutors to assist in the exercise of their discretion in making charging decisions. Reference to the Legal Guidance does not override the need for Crown Prosecutors to consider each case on its individual merits, and to take into account special circumstances when applying the principles set out in the Code of Crown Prosecutors.

---

[65]   Multi Agency Statutory Guidance on FGM, section 3.1.4 April 2016, section D.2.
[66]   Multi Agency Statutory Guidance on FGM, section 3.1.4 April 2016, section D.2.
[67]   www.cps.gov.uk/publications/prosecution/therapychild.html.

## Charging decisions

**4.43** Cases involving FGM should be referred to the CPS Area FGM lead prosecutor, given their experience and knowledge in dealing with these cases.[68] In circumstances where the nationality or residence of the suspect(s) or victim is relevant and it may be difficult to support an offence under the 2003 Act, prosecutors should consider the full range of relevant offences, which are outlined in Annex C: aide memoire: offence/behaviours experienced by victims of FGM.[69]

**4.44** It is important for prosecutors to be aware that when dealing with a case of FGM, the victim may not just be a victim of FGM. The aide memoire sets out similar offences or behaviours that are often experienced by victims of FGM. For example, victims of FGM may be a victim of forced marriage and may also suffer humiliation, intimidation, emotional blackmail or verbal abuse (telling a child that she must conform) or being persistently asked to accept that FGM should be performed with the verbal threat of violence at the hands of their parents or guardian. In such instance, prosecutors should be aware of and consider possible offences such as distress or harassment.[70] Likewise, parents/guardians may subject the girl to violence such as punishing, kicking, broken bones or other child cruelty offences.[71]

**4.45** In cases of FGM, where there is sufficient evidence to support a prosecution, it is likely to be in the public interest to prosecute; however each case must be considered on its own facts and merits.[72] When considering the public interest stage of the Full Code Test, prosecutors should always take into account the circumstances and consequences for the victim of the decision to prosecute, and any views expressed by the victim.[73] Prosecutors should ask the police to provide information about family circumstances and the likely effect of a prosecution on the victim. Social services and specialist FGM support agencies may be able to help by providing the police with this information.

## Evidential considerations

**4.46** FGM cases may be challenging to prosecute for a number of reasons, but primarily because of difficulties in obtaining evidence from the victim and

[68] Police and the Crown Prosecution Service in the investigation and prosecution of allegations of FGM (2013), http://www.cps.gov.uk/london/assets/uploads/files/fgm_protocol_cps_mps_2013.pdf, accessed 26 September 2016.

[69] CPS, *Female Genital Mutilation Legal Guidance*, http://www.cps.gov.uk/legal/d_to_g/female_genital_mutilation/, accessed 27 September 2016.

[70] Public Order Act 1986, s 4. Where this has occurred on more than one occasion the action can be construed as harassment; lawyers should consider the Protection from Harassment Act 1997, s 2.

[71] Criminal Justice Act 1988, s 39 for Common Assault. Offences Against the Person Act 1861, s 20 or s 18 for Actual Bodily Harm (ABH) or Grievous Bodily Harm (GBH) respectively.

[72] CPS, *Female Genital Mutilation Legal Guidance*, http://www.cps.gov.uk/legal/d_to_g/female_genital_mutilation/, accessed 27 September 2016.

[73] CPS, *Female Genital Mutilation Legal Guidance*, http://www.cps.gov.uk/legal/d_to_g/female_genital_mutilation/, accessed 27 September 2016.

ensuring their continued engagement with criminal proceedings.[74] When reviewing a case of FGM, prosecutors should establish a number of key things. The first is early consultation with the police. This is vital in establishing the willingness of a victim to testify at the trial, as well as discussing other evidential issues such as if the victim is likely to give evidence.[75] Victims are often reluctant to make a statement or, if they do, retract because of family and cultural pressures. Secondly, whether there has been a risk assessment for the victim and for any other (female) siblings.[76] This will prove necessary if it is suspected that others may be at risk of FGM. Thirdly, prosecutors should consider if other evidence is available.[77] It is always worth considering if other family members, close friends or medical practitioners can provide evidence. Finally, prosecutors should consider instructing a medical expert to confirm FGM and ensure special measures applications are made on time.[78]

## Protection for victims of FGM

**4.47** When prosecuting FGM, a victim may indicate before trial that she no longer wishes to give evidence.[79] In such an instance, prosecutors should consider whether the prosecutor may proceed without the victim. The police should be advised to take a statement setting out why the victim no longer wishes to give evidence. A key issue is whether the decision to withdraw support for the prosecution is voluntary or as a result of pressure on the victim by family members or others.[80]

**4.48** Prosecutors should assess as soon as possible whether there is other sufficient evidence to proceed without the need for the victim to give live evidence (for example by weight of direct, indirect and circumstantial evidence such as admissions in interview, evidence of a medical expert, travel or planned travel out of the UK, passports, flight tickets and bookings, flight manifests, diary entries, dates and notes of where and when the procedure is to take place, or payment for procedure).[81] Where a victim is reluctant to attend court and the case can only continue with her evidence to prove the case, a witness summons may be considered. The victim should be made aware of the range of special measures that can be applied for at court to support and assist them in

---

[74]   CPS, *Female Genital Mutilation Legal Guidance*, http://www.cps.gov.uk/legal/d_to_g/female_genital_mutilation/, accessed 27 September 2016.

[75]   CPS, *Female Genital Mutilation Legal Guidance*, http://www.cps.gov.uk/legal/d_to_g/female_genital_mutilation/, accessed 27 September 2016.

[76]   CPS, *Female Genital Mutilation Legal Guidance*, http://www.cps.gov.uk/legal/d_to_g/female_genital_mutilation/, accessed 27 September 2016.

[77]   CPS, *Female Genital Mutilation Legal Guidance*, http://www.cps.gov.uk/legal/d_to_g/female_genital_mutilation/, accessed 27 September 2016.

[78]   CPS, *Female Genital Mutilation Legal Guidance*, http://www.cps.gov.uk/legal/d_to_g/female_genital_mutilation/, accessed 27 September 2016.

[79]   CPS, *Female Genital Mutilation Legal Guidance*, http://www.cps.gov.uk/legal/d_to_g/female_genital_mutilation/, accessed 27 September 2016.

[80]   CPS, *Female Genital Mutilation Legal Guidance*, http://www.cps.gov.uk/legal/d_to_g/female_genital_mutilation/, accessed 27 September 2016.

[81]   CPS, *Female Genital Mutilation Legal Guidance*, http://www.cps.gov.uk/legal/d_to_g/female_genital_mutilation/, accessed 27 September 2016.

giving their evidence.[82] These include methods to adjust the conventional court procedure by making testifying less daunting. Available means include the use of screens and live links.

## Local authority evidence

**4.49** In cases involving a young victim of FGM, the local authority or social services are likely to have material or information which might be relevant to the prosecution case. If the material or information might be capable of undermining the prosecution case or of assisting the defence, prosecutors should take steps to obtain it.[83] Equally, should the material undermine the prosecution or elements of it, then there is a high duty on the prosecution to disclose it also. Third party disclosure such as this can be complex and take time and thus consideration should be given to this in a timely fashion.

## Expert evidence

**4.50** Prosecutors should consider instructing an expert witness to confirm that FGM has been carried out and the type of FGM.[84] The Royal College of Obstetricians and Gynecologists has recommended the kinds of expert evidence that may assist for women and child victims respectively. For women who have undergone FGM, a list of obstetricians and gynecologists who can assist as experts in criminal proceedings should be considered; and two key clinicians for child victims.[85]

**4.51** In cases where the FGM procedure has been carried out overseas, prosecutors should request the police to investigate and obtain evidence from that country.[86] Evidence may be obtained from travel or flight records, or the Home Office Border Force. Assistance in making enquiries may also be provided by the CPS International Division.

---

[82] Prosecutors are reminded of the guidance of *Provision of Therapy to Child Witnesses prior to a Criminal Trial*.

[83] For further guidance see 2013 Protocol and Good Practice Model: *Disclosure of information in cases of alleged child abuse and linked criminal and care directions hearings*, http://www.cps.gov.uk/publications/docs/third_party_protocol_2013.pdf, accessed 25 September 2016.

[84] For further guidance see 2013 Protocol and Good Practice Model: *Disclosure of information in cases of alleged child abuse and linked criminal and care directions hearings*, http://www.cps.gov.uk/publications/docs/third_party_protocol_2013.pdf, accessed 25 September 2016.

[85] For further guidance see 2013 Protocol and Good Practice Model: *Disclosure of information in cases of alleged child abuse and linked criminal and care directions hearings*, http://www.cps.gov.uk/publications/docs/third_party_protocol_2013.pdf, accessed 25 September 2016.

[86] CPS, *Female Genital Mutilation Legal Guidance*, http://www.cps.gov.uk/legal/d_to_g/female_genital_mutilation/, accessed 27 September 2016.

## *Guidance for schools*

**4.52**   With the help of the Metropolitan Police Service, guidance is available for schools helpfully listing FGM indicators to enable school staff to identify those at risk.[87] Some of the indicators of a child being at risk of FGM are: the girl confiding that she is having a 'special procedure' which will make her a woman, or talk of a ceremony taking place for her or other siblings, or the girl or her family may talk about a long holiday.[88] Similarly, staff should be alert to the possible signs that FGM may have occurred. For instance, prolonged absence from school with a noticeable change in behaviour on return; asking to be excused from PE or swimming; finding it difficult to sit still and appearing to experience discomfort or pain.[89]

**4.53**   School staff members are advised to prevent FGM by reporting signs that a child may be at risk.[90] If a teacher believes a child is at risk they must inform their designated teacher for child protection; a referral must be completed to the social services and in urgent cases they should contact children's social care or the police by phoning 999.[91]

## Why has there been a lack of prosecutions?

**4.54**   To date there have been no prosecutions of FGM in England and Wales leading to a conviction. This has been a cause of increasing concern in light of the statistics detailing the prevalence of FGM.[92]

**4.55**   The Home Affairs Committee concluded in its 2016 report:

> 'It is beyond belief that there still has not been a successful prosecution for an FGM offence since it was made illegal over 30 years ago. That is a lamentable

---

[87]   Met Police guidance for schools Project Azure and The Metropolitan Police Service, *Female Genital Mutilation (FGM) Guidance for schools* (2015), https://www.gov.uk/government/uploads/system/uploads/attachment_data/file/276657/Project_Azure_FGM_school_guidance.pdf, accessed 27 September 2016.

[88]   Met Police guidance for schools Project Azure and The Metropolitan Police Service, *Female Genital Mutilation (FGM) Guidance for schools* (2015), https://www.gov.uk/government/uploads/system/uploads/attachment_data/file/276657/Project_Azure_FGM_school_guidance.pdf, accessed 26 September 2016, accessed 27 September 2016.

[89]   Met Police guidance for schools Project Azure and The Metropolitan Police Service, *Female Genital Mutilation (FGM) Guidance for schools* (2015), https://www.gov.uk/government/uploads/system/uploads/attachment_data/file/276657/Project_Azure_FGM_school_guidance.pdf, accessed 27 September 2016.

[90]   Met Police guidance for schools Project Azure and The Metropolitan Police Service, *Female Genital Mutilation (FGM) Guidance for schools* (2015), https://www.gov.uk/government/uploads/system/uploads/attachment_data/file/276657/Project_Azure_FGM_school_guidance.pdf, accessed 27 September 2016.

[91]   Met Police guidance for schools Project Azure and The Metropolitan Police Service, *Female Genital Mutilation (FGM) Guidance for schools* (2015), https://www.gov.uk/government/uploads/system/uploads/attachment_data/file/276657/Project_Azure_FGM_school_guidance.pdf, accessed 27 September 2016.

[92]   FGM: Lack of convictions 'a national scandal', BBC News, 15 September 2016, http://www.bbc.co.uk/news/uk-37364079, accessed 18 September 2016.

record and the failure to identify cases, to prosecute and to achieve convictions can only have negative consequences for those who are brave enough to come forward to highlight this crime. In the absence of successful prosecutions, FGM remains a national scandal that is continuing to result in the preventable mutilation of thousands of girls. We welcome the measures that the Government has introduced in recent years to deter parents and others from attempting to inflict FGM on girls and to bring those to justice who succeed in this.'[93]

**4.56**  There are numerous and varying reasons often cited for the lack of successful prosecutions. Traditionally the issue was seen to be very much one of insufficient public and professional awareness and accompanied by a general perception that reporting FGM was interfering with an important and deep-rooted cultural tradition. With the increasing awareness of the health implications of FGM over recent years and wider recognition of it both domestically and internationally as child abuse, the problem in obtaining convictions is now more as a result of the challenges of gathering necessary evidence and testing the evidence.

**4.57**  FGM is a practice which remains shrouded in secrecy and there are many cases in which children are taken out of the jurisdiction for the practice to be undertaken, where it is also carried out amidst secrecy and ritual. In Sierra Leone, which is a country that has a high FGM rate, cutting is carried out in secret at night in the Bondo bush.[94] Within this culture, FGM is a practice carried out as a ceremony, with the face of the cutters hidden behind masks.[95] In this instance, it can be seen why there is low reporting because the cutters are never seen and the girls are sworn to secrecy.[96] There are therefore often significant challenges for the police in collecting the necessary evidence needed to propose a prosecution to the CPS. The difficulties were demonstrated following paediatric research at the specialist FGM clinic at UCL, which found that out of 47 girls, 10 cases were potentially illegal cases of FGM, yet despite police involvement there were no prosecutions.[97]

**4.58**  FGM is often carried out or organised by family members or other people that are known to the victims or by influential leaders in their community.[98] As seen in cases of forced marriage, victims often do not want the full force of the criminal law to come down their family or community members. A

---

[93]  Female genital mutilation: abuse unchecked, House of Commons Home Affairs Committee, Ninth Report of Session 2016–17. Published on 15 September 2016 by authority of the House of Commons.

[94]  *28 Too Many, FGM in Sierra Leone: Country Profile* (2014), http://www.28toomany.org/media/uploads/sierra_leone_(june_2014).pdf, accessed 15 September 2016.

[95]  *28 Too Many, FGM in Sierra Leone: Country Profile* (2014), http://www.28toomany.org/media/uploads/sierra_leone_(june_2014).pdf, accessed 15 September 2016.

[96]  *28 Too Many, FGM in Sierra Leone: Country Profile* (2014), http://www.28toomany.org/media/uploads/sierra_leone_(june_2014).pdf, accessed 15 September 2016.

[97]  D Hodes, A Armitage, K Robinson, S Creighton, 'Female genital mutilation in children presenting to a London safeguarding clinic: a case series', *Arch Dis Child* doi:10.1136/archdischild-2015-308243, 27 July 2015.

[98]  FGM: Lack of convictions 'a national scandal', BBC News, 15 September 2016, http://www.bbc.co.uk/news/uk-37364079, accessed 18 September 2016.

longstanding difficulty therefore has been in persuading victims, in most cases children, to give oral evidence against the perpetrators (usually including their parents) due to their conflicting loyalties and emotions.

**4.59** FGM is commonly perceived as a practice that initiates a girl to womanhood or prepares them for marriage. In addition, responsible adults in these cases often have no history of offending. They are often otherwise caring and exhibit little external indication that they are about to commit a serious criminal offence against their child.

**4.60** Furthermore, there is often difficulty detecting cases of FGM and gathering evidence due to the low reporting by victims and others.[99] It is often contended that the burden of gathering evidence and the necessary information should rest with professionals such as the police and social services. The fact that those subjected to FGM are often children means that they are not able to readily self-refer. This places the onus on professionals to pass on information to the police and take the necessary ancillary actions.

**4.61** Local authorities, medical professionals and schools are now reporting FGM to the police with increasing frequency. It is hoped that with the new provisions on mandatory reporting for professionals combined with greater public awareness of the issue, more cases will be referred to the police and when appropriate the CPS will prosecute.

## THE FIRST PROSECUTION: *R V DHARMASENA* [2014]

**4.62** On 21 March 2014, the CPS announced its first prosecution for FGM under the 2003 Act. The defendants were not 'professional cutters' or family members, but were medical doctors working in an NHS hospital.[100]

**4.63** The main defendant was Dr Dharmasena, a junior registrar in obstetrics and gynaecology at the Whittington Hospital in North London. Dr Dharmasena had successfully delivered a baby from an adult woman who had already been a victim of FGM when she was a child of six years old. He had needed to undo the earlier stitches in order to allow the birth and then reinstated a stitch (re-infibulation) of 1.5 cm, in order to stop the substantial bleeding which had followed the birth (and which had been caused by the cutting of the original stitches). Later, when Dr Dharmasena had the opportunity to speak to a consultant, he was advised of another way of stopping the bleeding. Mr Mohamed, who had assisted Dr Dharmasena with the re-infibulation, was also indicted as his accomplice.

---

[99]  Bindel, *An Unpunished Crime: The lack of prosecutions for female genital mutilation in the UK*, (2014) The New Culture Forum, http://www.justiceforfgmvictims.co.uk/the-report/, accessed 28 July 2016.

[100]  Unreported, 4 February 2015 (Crown Court (Southwark)). Being a Crown Court (and thus first instance) case it is unreported in the law reports; nevertheless, it was widely reported in the media eg, *The Daily Telegraph*, 5 February 2015 at 13.

**4.64**  The trial started on 19 January 2015. The jury took just 30 minutes to retire and find both defendants not guilty on 4 February 2015. It has been subsequently argued that it was not in the public interest for the Crown Prosecution Service to ever have brought such a prosecution.[101]

**4.65**  Conceivably, the prosecution was motivated to test the definition of 'necessary' in s 1(2) of the 2003 Act. It might also have been thought that this prosecution could have an effective educative aim; to inform doctors that their duties under the Act are strict.[102]

**4.66**  On the face of it the decision to prosecute was misconceived. First, s 1(3) of the 2003 Act makes it clear that Dr Dharmasena was an 'approved person' for the purposes of s 1(2). Dr Dharmasena had undertaken the procedure in good faith. Secondly, the victim was unwilling to give evidence as she was said to be grateful to Dr Dharmasena for successfully delivering her baby.[103]

## Case study: the French experience

**4.67**  In France, FGM was criminalised in 1983. It is punishable by 10 years in prison or up to 20 years for cutting a girl under the age of 15.[104] In comparison to the UK, there is no specific legislation in France banning FGM; rather prosecutions are brought under its existing laws against grievous bodily harm and violence to children.[105] There have been approximately 40 trials in France, which have resulted in approximately 100 convictions.[106]

**4.68**  It is frequently contended that the UK could reflect on France's experience of prosecuting FGM and adopt similar practices. In France, children up to the age 16 may undergo regular medical check-ups, which can include examination of the genitals. Although the check-ups are not mandatory, they are routinely considered good practice for communities thought to be at risk. Girls that are identified to be at risk of FGM may generally be examined every year and when they return from abroad. This practice is deemed useful to detect FGM, especially during school holidays when girls are taken abroad to be cut.

---

[101] J Rogers, 'The First Prosecution for FGM' (2015) 179(9) *Criminal Law and Justice Weekly* JPN 177.

[102] J Rogers, 'The First Prosecution for FGM' (2015) 179(9) *Criminal Law and Justice Weekly* JPN 177.

[103] J Rogers, 'The First Prosecution for FGM' (2015) 179(9) *Criminal Law and Justice Weekly* JPN 177.

[104] Willsher, 'France's tough stance on female genital mutilation is working, says campaigners', *The Guardian*, 10 February 2014, https://www.theguardian.com/society/2014/feb/10/france-tough-stance-female-genital-mutilation-fgm, accessed 25 September 2016.

[105] In France, FGM can be treated as a crime according to the provisions of the Penal Code. Particularly, Articles 221-2, 22-3 and 22-5 which refer to acts of torture and barbarity can be used. Articles 222-9 and 220-10 refer to intended bodily harm causing permanent mutilation, which could be applied to FGM.

[106] Willsher, 'France's tough stance on female genital mutilation is working, says campaigners', *The Guardian*, 10 February 2014, https://www.theguardian.com/society/2014/feb/10/france-tough-stance-female-genital-mutilation-fgm, accessed 25 September 2016.

The first conviction was secured in 1988 against a father and his two wives, who all received three year suspended prison sentences.

**4.69** The French approach to reporting is a principal reason for their successful prosecutions. There are many who advocate that the UK adopt similar practices to France in relation to prosecuting FGM.[107] In France, following a medical examination, should the healthcare staff find a girl has undergone FGM, they are required to report this.[108] At this point, prosecutions are initiated. In contrast to the UK, the bringing of a prosecution is not dependent upon the girl. In France, the parents being guardians of the child would be prosecuted because the mutilation would not have been carried out without their knowledge or funding.

---

[107] Home Affairs Committee – Second Report, *Female Genital Mutilation: The case for a national action plan*, 3 July 2014, http://www.publications.parliament.uk/pa/cm201415/cmselect/cmhaff/201/20105.htm, accessed 3 September 2016.

[108] House of Lords Hansard, *Female Genital Mutilation*, (2016) 773, https://hansard.parliament.uk/lords/2016-06 09/debates/16060935000289/FemaleGenitalMutilation, accessed 3 September 2016.

# CHAPTER 5

# MEDICALISATION OF FGM

**5.1**   The medicalisation of FGM refers to when FGM is practiced not by a family member or elder, but rather by a professional 'cutter' or a medical professional and/or in a professional or medical setting. This is the case in countries such as Sierra Leone and Egypt, where 'cutters' as opposed to family members perform FGM.

**5.2**   In Egypt it is has been reported that 77% of FGM is conducted in a medical environment or by a medical professional. The growing rate of FGM medicalisation in Egypt is something that concerns anti-FGM campaigners, particularly because the rate of medicalisation has risen from 55% to 77% in just over 20 years.[1]

## MEDICALISATION OF FGM IN THE UK

**5.3**   There are increasing examples of FGM being performed by professionals in the UK. Charities and survivor's groups have long warned about professional cutters advertising their services in the UK. FGM 'parties' in cities across England which girls are taken to have long been reported on. The Black Health Initiative in Leeds has reported that midwives from practicing communities are being flown into the UK to carry out the practice.[2]

**5.4**   Consultant paediatrician, Deborah Hodes, who is based at the FGM clinic at University College London Hospital published a paediatric study with the aim of describing the presentation and management of children referred with suspected FGM to a UK safeguarding clinic. The study is a useful snapshot of FGM within the UK and a worrying demonstration of the significant medicalisation of FGM domestically which matches recent trends in international data.[3]

**5.5**   The research study was based on cases of children under 18 years of age who were referred to the UCL clinic with suspected FGM between June 2006

---

[1]   M Eltahawy, *Headscarves and Hymens: Why the Middle East Needs a Sexual Revolution* (Weidenfeld & Nicolson, 21 April 2015), pp 118–119.

[2]   www.bbc.co.uk/news/uk-england-38290888.

[3]   D Hodes, A Armitage, K Robinson, S Creighton, 'Female genital mutilation in children presenting to a London safeguarding clinic: a case series', *Arch Dis Child* doi:10.1136/archdischild-2015-308243, 27 July 2015.

and May 2014. The study found that of the 47 girls referred, 27 (57%) had confirmed FGM. According to the WHO classification of genital findings, FGM Type I was found in two girls, Type II in eight girls and Type IV in 11 girls. No Type III FGM was seen. The circumstances of FGM were known in 17 cases, of which 12 (71%) were performed by a health professional or in a medical setting (medicalisation).[4]

**5.6**    The increase in the medicalisation of FGM might appear at first to be a positive development. Compared to it being inflicted without the use of any anaesthetic and in unhygienic conditions, the thought of a girl being cut under anaesthetic, in a sterile environment and being cared for afterwards has a superficial appeal.

**5.7**    Anthropologists such as Bettina Shell-Duncan have contended with force that the international campaign to eliminate female genital cutting (FGC) has, since the early 1990s, actively attempted to divorce itself from a health framework, adopting instead a human rights framework to justify intervention.[5] Shell-Duncan has questioned whether the medicalisation of FGM could be seen as 'harm reduction' or as promotion of a dangerous practice. She writes:

> 'Indeed harm reduction through medicalization may represent an important avenue for reducing risk and promoting health among those who currently view abandonment as an unacceptable option. If improvement in women's health is truly targeted as a priority, the harm reducing potential of medicalization of FGC warrants careful investigation'.[6]

**5.8**    Shell-Duncan wrote in 2001 and it is arguable that the understanding of FGM has moved on since then. Indeed, survivors and campaigners have long contended that although the medicalisation of FGM may reduce immediate medical risks, it serves only to legitimise and prolong the harmful practice in affected communities.[7]

**5.9**    The multi-agency statutory guidance on FGM makes clear that some who support the practice have sought to mitigate risks of infection (by, for example, carrying it out in a medical environment) in order to legitimise FGM. However, in addition to the immediate risks associated with FGM being carried out, it

---

[4]    D Hodes, A Armitage, K Robinson, S Creighton, 'Female genital mutilation in children presenting to a London safeguarding clinic: a case series', *Arch Dis Child* doi:10.1136/archdischild-2015-308243, 27 July 2015.

[5]    B Shell-Duncan, 'From Health to Human Rights: Female Genital Cutting and the Politics of Intervention' (2008) 110(2) *American Anthropologist*.

[6]    B Shell-Duncan, 'The medicalization of female "circumcision": harm reduction or promotion of a dangerous practice?' (2001) 52 *Social Science & Medicine* 1013–1028.

[7]    M Eltahawy, *Headscarves and Hymens: Why the Middle East Needs a Sexual Revolution* (Weidenfeld & Nicolson, 2015), pp 125–126.

can have serious and harmful long-term psychological and physical effects, regardless of how the procedure is done.[8]

## COSMETIC PROCEDURES AND PIERCING
### Female genital cosmetic surgery

**5.10**  An equally longstanding concern of campaigners and survivors is that piercing parlours or clinics offering female genital cosmetic surgery (FGCS) can provide a legitimate environment for practicing communities to take their young daughters for FGM. The Home Affairs Select Committee has observed that, 'We cannot tell communities in Sierra Leone and Somalia to stop a practice which is freely permitted on Harley Street'.[9]

**5.11**  Others have argued that piercings or cosmetic procedures should be treated differently as they represent the right of women to choose.[10] Many campaigners and survivors of FGM however remain concerned that such arguments ignore the substantial pressure on women and girls within several communities.

**5.12**  In Alice Edward's research paper on this issue, she concludes:

'Examining the "cosmetic versus cultural surgery" discourse has compelled me to re-examine my perspective towards FGM within the wider field of women's rights, where the cultural imperative of FGM cannot easily be separated from a woman's "choice" to modify the appearance of her genitals to conform to a "social norm". The cultural norms that encourage, or coerce women into having FGM procedures may be less explicit but I would argue that FGM can be associated in terms of cementing societal expectations of a woman's body, and the "Convention on the Elimination of all forms of Discrimination Against Women" calls for all appropriate measures to be taken to modify social and cultural patterns which are based on stereotyped roles for men and women. Therefore, whether or not they are recognised as one and the same, FGM both demand to receive attention if the UK is committed to achieving women's rights and equality.'[11]

**5.13**  The Female Genital Mutilation Act 2003 (the 2003 Act) does not require consent to the procedure and nor does it set an age requirement.[12] The issue of

---

[8]  Multi-agency statutory guidance on female genital mutilation, HM Government (April 2016), ss 3.1.4, A.2.

[9]  Female genital mutilation: follow-up, 14 March 2015, Home Affairs Select Committee.

[10]  Butterly, 'Counting genital piercings as FGM "undermines" abuse says union', BBC Newsbeat 19 March 2015, http://www.bbc.co.uk/newsbeat/article/31938409/counting-genital-piercings-as-fgm-undermines-abuse-says-union, accessed 25 September 2016.

[11]  Alice Edwards 'Between these poles of beauty and butchery: What is the dynamic between the 'cosmetic' versus cultural surgery discourse and efforts to end FGM in the UK?' 27 September 2013, http://www.halsburyslawexchange.co.uk/wp-content/uploads/sites/25/2015/03/Alice_ Edwards_Dissertation_Dec_13_FGM.pdf, accessed 25 September 2016.

[12]  There are some campaigners, eg in Sierra Leone, who advocate for FGM to be done on those over 18 only. They are sometimes referred to as 'anti-child' FGM campaigners. See the end of the chapter for further information on this topic.

consent and self-election for a clitoris piercing may no doubt pose a challenge when determining whether it is in the public interest to prosecute such a case in accordance with the Code of Conduct for Prosecutors.

**5.14**   The 2003 Act contains no specific exemption for 'cosmetic' surgery or Female Genital Cosmetic surgery (FGCS). If a procedure involving any of the acts prohibited by s 1 of the 2003 Act is not necessary for physical or mental health, or is not carried out for purposes connected with childbirth, then it is an offence (even if the girl or woman on whom the procedure is carried out consented).[13]

**5.15**   The Royal College of Obstetricians and Gynecologists is clear in its guideline that 'all surgeons who undertake FGCS must take appropriate measures to ensure compliance with the FGM Act'.[14] It is for the police to investigate any alleged offence and for the CPS to decide whether a prosecution under the 2003 Act is appropriate. Ultimately, it would be for a criminal court to determine, as and when the point arises for decision in a particular case, if non-medically indicated genital surgery constitutes mutilation and is therefore an offence under the 2003 Act.[15]

## Piercings

**5.16**   Piercings for cosmetic purposes or to enhance sexual pleasure may comprise Type IV FGM.[16] Again, the 2003 Act does not provide for consent as a defence. It is currently unclear whether a vaginal piercing could lead to a prosecution due to the public interest test. Piercing parlours remain unregulated. Historically, the lack of regulation for piercing parlours and clinics and the absence of clear guidance for health professionals has served to deepen concerns about the manner in which such places may be used. There are challenges in this area. Adult women may have genital piercings and it is doubtful whether it would ever be in the public interest to prosecute, but in some communities girls and adult women are forced to have them, which is why the WHO has defined this as a form of FGM. Accordingly, hospitals are now required to record women and girls with genital piercings.[17]

---

[13]   Multi-agency statutory guidance on female genital mutilation, HM Government (April 2016), ss 3.1.4, 3.1.8.

[14]   The Royal College of Obstetricians and Gynaecologists, 'Female Genital Mutilation and its Management (Green-top Guideline No. 53)', published on 10 July 2015, https://www.rcog.org.uk/globalassets/documents/guidelines/gtg-53-fgm.pdf, accessed 25 September 2016.

[15]   Multi-agency statutory guidance on female genital mutilation, HM Government (April 2016), ss 3.1.4, 3.1.8.

[16]   Sanghani, 'Got a vaginal piercing? According to the NHS you're a victim of FGM', *The Telegraph*, 18 March 2015, http://www.telegraph.co.uk/women/womens-health/11480359/FGM-Vaginal-piercing-to-be-recorded-as-female-genital-mutilation.html, accessed 25 September 2016.

[17]   Department of Health, *Guidance and resources about FGM for healthcare professionals*, last updated 27 May 2016.

**5.17** The multi-agency statutory guidance states that excision and infibulation are examples of what constitutes mutilation for the purpose of the 2003 Act, but the term 'mutilate' is not defined in the Act.[18] The interpretation of the legislation, including whether a particular procedure amounts to mutilation, is a matter for the criminal courts to determine in cases brought before them. In the absence of any conviction for FGM, there is currently no criminal case-law casting light on what does or does not amount to mutilation for the purpose of the 2003 Act.[19]

**5.18** The statutory guidance also refers to the judgment in *B and G (Children) (No 2)* in which Sir James Munby observes, 'it will be seen that for the purposes of the criminal law what is prohibited is to "excise, infibulate or otherwise mutilate" the "whole or any part" of the "labia majora, labia minora or clitoris"'.[20] This brings within the ambit of the criminal law all forms of FGM of WHO Types I, II and III (including, it may be noted, Type Ia). But WHO Type IV comes within the ambit of the criminal law only if it involves 'mutilation'.[21]

**5.19** Sir James Munby further stated:

> 'whether a particular case of FGM Type IV ... involves mutilation is in my determination not a matter for determination by the family court and certainly not a matter I need to determine in the present case. It is a matter properly for determination by a criminal court as and when the point arises for decision in a particular case.'[22]

**5.20** The statutory guidance concludes that unless and until a criminal court decides the point in a particular case, there can be no certainty that any of the procedures classified by WHO as Type IV FGM, including piercing, amounts to mutilation. The most that can be said is that Type IV FGM may be an offence under s 1 of the 2003 Act.[23] Whether it does in fact constitute such an offence would depend on the particular circumstances. It is for the police, upon receipt of a report, to investigate the circumstances and to conduct enquiries into any alleged offence. The Crown Prosecution Service (CPS) will decide whether a person should be charged with a criminal offence and, if so, what that offence should be and whether a prosecution will take place. As with every criminal offence, the CPS will apply the two-stage test in the Code for Crown Prosecutors in deciding whether to proceed with a prosecution: (1) whether

---

[18] Multi-agency statutory guidance on female genital mutilation, HM Government (April 2016), s 3.1.4.

[19] Multi-agency statutory guidance on female genital mutilation, HM Government (April 2016), s 3.1.4.

[20] *B and G (Children) (No 2)* [2015] EWFC 3, at para 11.

[21] Multi-agency statutory guidance on female genital mutilation, HM Government (April 2016), s 3.1.4.

[22] At para 70.

[23] Multi-agency statutory guidance on female genital mutilation, HM Government (April 2016), s 3.1.4.

there is sufficient evidence to provide a realistic prospect of conviction; and, if so, (2) whether a prosecution is in the public interest.

## PROFESSIONAL CUTTERS AND EXCLUSION ORDERS

**5.21**  The law in the UK is generally designed to protect named individuals from FGM. However, there remains a loophole which fails to protect the rights of unnamed individuals who are believed to be at risk generally from FGM professional cutters, who are still seemingly able to travel to the UK to undertake their work.

**5.22**  This threat was recently illustrated in an unreported case of *Metropolitan Police; Request to Home Secretary*.[24] The police applied for an order under the High Court's inherent jurisdiction to stop a professional cutter advertising her services in the UK amid evidence that she would be travelling to London.[25]

**5.23**  The individual, later named in the media as Kharday Zorokong, was part of a Sierra Leonean delegation that included the minister for gender, Dr Sylvia Blyden, to the 73rd session of the UN committee on the rights of the child in Geneva. Zorokong performs FGM, but is now opposed to operations on children under 18. Campaigners feared that she would come to the UK as part of Blyden's delegation after the meeting in Geneva.[26]

**5.24**  Anti-FGM campaigners from Sierra Leone condemned Zorokong's appearance before the UN. At the meeting, Blyden spoke about protecting under-18s from FGM, but insisted that an adult woman should be allowed to 'do what she wants to her body', arguably ignoring the pressure on women to undergo mutilation in countries such as Sierra Leone.

**5.25**  Hearing the application, Mr Justice Holman stated that he found FGM 'abhorrent and a terrible scourge on women', but 'the right thing is to try to get the Secretary of State not to let this woman in'. After the judge declined to make any orders, the police applied to the Home Secretary for an exclusion order.[27] As a result of the case, the Solicitor General is set to consider ways to extend the current law to protect girls generally from professional cutters who come to the UK.

---

[24]  As reported in *The Guardian*, Police urge Home Secretary to ban FGM practitioner from entering UK, Monday 19 September 2016, Karen McVeigh.

[25]  Karen McVeigh, 'Police urge Home Secretary to ban FGM practitioner from entering the UK', *The Guardian*, 19 September 2016, https://www.theguardian.com/society/2016/sep/19/police-urge-home-secretary-to-ban-fgm-practitioner-from-entering-uk, accessed 19 September 2016.

[26]  Karen McVeigh, 'Police urge Home Secretary to ban FGM practitioner from entering the UK', *The Guardian*, 19 September 2016, https://www.theguardian.com/society/2016/sep/19/police-urge-home-secretary-to-ban-fgm-practitioner-from-entering-uk, accessed 19 September 2016.

[27]  Karen McVeigh, 'Police urge Home Secretary to ban FGM practitioner from entering the UK', *The Guardian*, 19 September 2016, https://www.theguardian.com/society/2016/sep/19/police-urge-home-secretary-to-ban-fgm-practitioner-from-entering-uk, accessed 19 September 2016.

**5.26** An exclusion order is an official order excluding a person from a particular place, especially to prevent a crime being committed. The Home Secretary and immigration officials have the power to exclude persons from entering the UK by refusing or revoking permission already granted, for reasons related to an individual's character, conduct or associations.[28] This power to exclude can be exercised by the Home Secretary over a person even if they have not indicated an intention to defraud the UK. There is no statutory right to appeal against exclusion by the Home Secretary, although the decision can be challenged by judicial review.

**5.27** An exclusion order can only be made against a person who is outside the UK. The effect of the order prohibits the person's admission to the UK. The exclusion remains in place until the Home Secretary revokes it. Section 3(5)(a) of the Immigration Act 1971 provides that 'a person who is not a British citizen is liable to deportation if the Secretary of State deems his deportation to be conducive to the public good'. Whilst the above provision does not specifically refer to a power to exclude, the Immigration Rules state that entry to the UK is to be refused 'where the Secretary of State has personally directed that the exclusion of a person from the United Kingdom is conducive to the public good'.[29]

**5.28** Paragraph 320(19) sets out guidance for staff handling visa applications indicating the type of behaviour, which might warrant refusal:

> '(...) While a person does not necessarily need to have been convicted of a criminal offence, the key to establishing refusal in this category will be the existence of reliable evidence necessary to support the decision that the person's behaviour calls into question their character and/or conduct and/or associations such that it makes it undesirable to grant them entry clearance.'

**5.29** This can certainly include a professional cutter. It can also include, for example, those associated with terrorism, known criminals and individuals who pose a public order risk.

---

[28] Non-EEA nationals seeking permission to enter or remain in the UK are subject to the various general grounds for refusal within Part 9 of the Immigration Rules. Immigration Rules (HC 395 of 1993–4, as amended), Part 9 (paras A320–324) https://www.gov.uk/guidance/immigration-rules/immigration-rules-part-9-grounds-for-refusal, accessed 15 September 2016.
[29] Paragraph 320(6).

# CHAPTER 6

## FEMALE GENITAL MUTILATION PROTECTION ORDER

### THE EVOLUTION OF THE FGM PROTECTION ORDER

#### Home Affairs inquiry on FGM

**6.1**    The criminal law on FGM has been in place since 1985 but there has yet to be a single successful prosecution. To address the historical failure to tackle this issue, in February 2014 the Home Affairs Select Committee opened an inquiry into the practice of FGM within the UK.[1] The Bar Human Rights Committee of England & Wales (BHRC) gave evidence to the Select Committee based on its experience of working with UNICEF in Nigeria and the expertise of members of its Working Group on FGM.[2]

**6.2**    The BHRC's evidence noted the historical challenges in tackling FGM and submitted that the UK lacked sufficiently tailored or targeted legal powers to assist in intervening in cases where FGM is suspected. It was submitted that better reporting would alert authorities to cases where serious risk of mutilation is suspected. In these cases, the state's response would be strengthened by having a series of powers whereby the court could intervene without necessarily resorting to the criminal law or care proceedings.

**6.3**    The BHRC report highlighted that there are many situations in which victims are reluctant to come forward for fear that the only possible result may be that the full force of the criminal law is brought down against their family members.[3]

**6.4**    The report called for a number of legal changes, including the introduction of civil injunctive orders loosely modelled on forced marriage protection orders as provided for in Part 4A of the Family Law Act 1996 (inserted by the Forced Marriage Civil Protection Act 2007). This was proposed to be a civil measure available through the family courts, which could be accompanied by ancillary restrictions against potential perpetrators. It was

---

[1]    Home Affairs Select Committee Inquiry on Female Genital Mutilation, report published 3 July 2014. Female Genital Mutilation Protection Order.

[2]    *Female Genital Mutilation*, BHRC submissions to the Parliamentary Inquiry on FGM (Home Affairs Select Committee) 12 February 2014.

[3]    *Female Genital Mutilation*, BHRC submissions to the Parliamentary Inquiry on FGM (Home Affairs Select Committee) 12 February 2014.

hoped that such orders could act as a strong deterrent against the practice of FGM and offer a means of protecting potential victims from FGM.

**6.5**    The BHRC report submitted that the framework of civil injunctive orders offers much more flexibility in terms of how a court proceeds.[4] The court can hear full evidence and make findings of fact. However, it does not always need to do so in order to offer protection.

**6.6**    Importantly, whereas the criminal law is generally geared towards punishing perpetrators after FGM has happened, civil orders allow for targeted intervention to prevent potential victims from being subjected to FGM in the first place.

## Ministry of Justice consultation

**6.7**    Following the evidence given to the Home Affairs Select Committee, at the Girl Summit on 22 July 2014 a consultation on the proposals was launched. The BHRC and the Family Law Bar Association (FLBA) submitted detailed responses to the Ministry of Justice consultation that followed. The consultation was also widely circulated and responded to by academics, legal professionals, non-government organisations, healthcare professionals, local authorities, victims and members of the public, police, social workers and others.[5]

**6.8**    85% of the respondents to the consultation supported the BHRC's recommendation for the introduction of protection orders.[6] The respondents felt that current criminal legislation was not enough and considered a civil protection order would deter the practice of FGM and provide additional protection to victims. 64% were of the view that the introduction of a civil protection order for FGM could protect girls (including babies) or women who had already been subjected to FGM.[7] Most argued for the category of persons who could apply for an FGM protection order to be wide, for the duration of the order to be flexible and for the breach of the order to be a criminal offence.[8]

**6.9**    A significant majority of the respondents stated that a civil protection order for FGM could also protect girls or women who had already been subjected to FGM, pointing to the benefits of an order that required relatives or associates to disclose the location of victims who had been taken abroad and

---

[4]    *Female Genital Mutilation*, BHRC submissions to the Parliamentary Inquiry on FGM (Home Affairs Select Committee) 12 February 2014.

[5]    *Female Genital Mutilation: Proposal to Introduce a Civil Protection Order*, Response to consultation, Ministry of Justice, 20 October 2014.

[6]    *Female Genital Mutilation: Proposal to Introduce a Civil Protection Order*, Response to consultation, Ministry of Justice, 20 October 2014, p 1.

[7]    *Female Genital Mutilation: Proposal to Introduce a Civil Protection Order*, Response to consultation, Ministry of Justice, 20 October 2014, p 1.

[8]    *Female Genital Mutilation: Proposal to Introduce a Civil Protection Order*, Response to consultation, Ministry of Justice, 20 October 2014, p 1.

forbidden from returning. In addition, it was felt that civil protection orders would work well alongside formal liaison with embassy staff overseas to facilitate the repatriation of victims.[9]

**6.10**  Only 8% of respondents stated that civil orders in relation to FGM would not enable vulnerable young victims, including babies, to be protected.[10] 58% of the respondents stated that victims of FGM should be able to use the civil enforcement route if they prefer, even if the breach of an order was a criminal offence. 17% of respondents thought that victims should not be able to use a civil route to deal with breaches and 25% of respondents were unsure.[11]

**6.11**  However, many of the respondents who felt that a civil and criminal enforcement route should both exist also noted that there had to be an absence of coercion for victims to be fully empowered to use a civil route. Their responses recognised that victims might come under pressure not to criminalise their families and take the civil route instead.

**6.12**  A number of respondents who disagreed that victims should be able to use the civil enforcement route for breaches, felt that the creation of a civil route for dealing with breaches could undermine the criminal legislation and alter perceptions of FGM being a serious criminal offence. They also submitted that children should not be forced to decide whether to support a prosecution against their parents.[12] Some of those unsure of whether victims should be able to use the civil route thought that minors – unlike adults – were not capable of making a decision about whether to take the civil or criminal route. The consultation response from the Office of the Police and Crime Commissioner stated that, 'It is absolutely vital that there must be a civil enforcement route that does not deter enforcement through the concern of criminalising the victim's own family.'[13]

**6.13**  The underground nature of FGM and the surrounding issues of 'honour' based violence draw significant similarities with cases of forced marriage. Figures for forced marriage protection order applications were examined as part of the consultation. The figures indicated that of the 173 applications made in 2013, 72 were made by the person to be protected (or their legal representative); 51 by the relevant third party; and 50 by other third parties (ie, a family member, friend or someone in the community). The figures for this period also show that the majority of applications for forced marriage

---

[9]   *Female Genital Mutilation: Proposal to Introduce a Civil Protection Order*, Response to consultation, Ministry of Justice, 20 October 2014, p 9.

[10]  *Female Genital Mutilation: Proposal to Introduce a Civil Protection Order*, Response to consultation, Ministry of Justice, 20 October 2014, p 11.

[11]  *Female Genital Mutilation: Proposal to Introduce a Civil Protection Order*, Response to consultation, Ministry of Justice, 20 October 2014, p 13.

[12]  *Female Genital Mutilation: Proposal to Introduce a Civil Protection Order*, Response to consultation, Ministry of Justice, 20 October 2014, p 13.

[13]  *Female Genital Mutilation: Proposal to Introduce a Civil Protection Order*, Response to consultation, Ministry of Justice, 20 October 2014, p 13.

protection orders were made to protect minors (persons aged 17 or under). Of the 173 applications made, 112 were to protect persons aged 17 or under; 57 to protect persons over 17; and in four cases, the age of the person to be protected was unknown.

## Serious Crime Bill 2015

**6.14** Following the extensive consultation the government resolved to legislate for the proposed changes through the Serious Crime Bill 2015.

**6.15** The BHRC advised Parliament in the drafting of several of the key provisions within the Bill and was acknowledged in both the House of Lords and the House of Commons for its assistance.[14] In the House of Commons, Seema Malhotra MP also noted the motivation behind moving FGM matters into the civil sphere and, in doing so, emphasised the critical role individuals, communities and public bodies will play alongside the new law.[15]

**6.16** Parliament had considered whether the amendments proposed to the Serious Crime Bill 2015, particularly the provision for FGM protection orders, should be implemented by inserting new schedules into the Family Law Act 1996.[16] This indeed had been the approach that had been adopted when the Forced Marriage (Civil Protection) Act 2007 inserted the provisions for forced marriage protection orders into the Family Law Act 1996.

**6.17** The reasoning behind this approach, as advocated for by Baroness Smith, was that such civil protection orders would ultimately be used in the family courts and so should be placed within legislation and injunctive language which family lawyers were already familiar with.[17] There was also concern that introducing the new provision into the existing criminal statute (the Female Genital Mutilation Act 2003 (the 2003 Act)) would send the wrong message to survivors of FGM, who had long campaigned that the criminal law had completely failed to address FGM in England and Wales. However, ultimately Parliament resolved to insert the new provisions into the 2003 Act on the basis that it made more sense from a policy point of view to have all the legislation relating to FGM in one place.[18]

---

[14] For example, see Hansard, Parliamentary debate, Serious Crime Bill [House of Lords], Col 1621, Third Reading, Clause 61: Appeal against decision under s 60, Amendment 1, 5 November 2014 and see Hansard, Parliamentary debate, Serious Crime Bill [House of Lords], Clause 67, Public Bill Committee, Session 2014–15, Tuesday 20 January 2015.

[15] *FGM protection orders – impact for girls at risk*, BHRC seminar on Doughty Street Chambers, Thursday 16 July.

[16] Hansard, Parliamentary debate, Serious Crime Bill [House of Lords], Col 1621, Third Reading, Clause 61: Appeal against decision under s 60, Amendment 1, 5 November 2014.

[17] Hansard, Parliamentary debate, Serious Crime Bill [House of Lords], Col 1621, Third Reading, Clause 61: Appeal against decision under s 60, Amendment 1, 5 November 2014.

[18] Hansard, Parliamentary debate, Serious Crime Bill [House of Lords], Col 1621, Third Reading, Clause 61: Appeal against decision under s 60, Amendment 1, 5 November 2014.

**6.18** Notwithstanding those differences of approach in the Commons and in the Lords, the relevant provisions of the Serious Crime Bill 2015 were debated and approved with a large degree of consensus across the political spectrum. It was met with considerable optimism from campaigners and frontline practitioners such as midwives.

**6.19** The introduction of the civil injunctive orders was brought forward to 17 July 2015.[19]

## THE INTRODUCTION OF THE FGM PROTECTION ORDER

**6.20** Section 73 of the Serious Crime Act 2015 (the 2015 Act) inserts a new s 5A and Schedule 2 into the 2003 Act, making provision for FGM protection orders in England, Wales and Northern Ireland and offers the means of protection to girls and women who are victims, or may be at risk of FGM.

**6.21** FGM protection orders can be made by the High Court or the Family Court pursuant to Schedule 2, paragraph 1 of the 2003 Act (as amended). Applications for an FGM protection order can be made by: (1) the girl or women to be protected, (2) a Relevant Third Party, or (3) any other person with the permission of the court.[20] The purpose of such orders is to offer civil injunctive protection for girls at risk from the practice of FGM as defined in s 1(1) of the 2003 Act or to protect girls against whom such an offence has already been committed.[21] The breach of an FGM protection order is a criminal offence.[22]

### Commencement and progress

**6.22** The commencement of the FGM protection order provisions was brought forward to coincide with school summer holidays on 17 July 2015, when the risk of girls being taken abroad for FGM is particularly high.[23] On Thursday 16 July 2015, the eve of the commencement of the orders, the BHRC and Seema Malhotra MP (then Shadow Home Office Minister for Preventing Violence Against Women and Girls) launched the legislation with the support of

---

[19] *FGM protection orders – impact for girls at risk*, BHRC seminar on Doughty Street Chambers, Thursday 16 July.
[20] 2003 Act, Sch 2, para 2 (as inserted by s 73 of the 2015 Act).
[21] 2003 Act, s 1(1).
[22] 2003 Act, para 4(1) of Sch 2 (as inserted by s 73 of the 2015 Act).
[23] The Family Procedure (Amendment No 2) Rules 2015, SI 2015/1420, r 1(2). Also, see Commencement Schedule, Serious Crime Act, available at https://www.gov.uk/government/uploads/system/uploads/attachment_data/file/501179/Commencement_schedule.pdf.

campaign groups and survivors organisations.[24] The first order was obtained on the same day by Luton County Council in collaboration with Bedfordshire police.[25]

**6.23**   On 23 June 2016 a woman from the West Midlands reportedly became the first person in the UK to be given civil orders to protect her from both forced marriage and FGM.[26]

**6.24**   From 17 July 2015 to March 2016 there were 60 applications for FGM protection orders resulting in 46 orders made. [27] From July to September 2016, there were 20 applications and 11 orders made for FGM protection orders. In total, there have been 97 applications and 79 orders made since their introduction up to the end of September 2016.[28] Several applications have been made by (or on behalf of) mothers who were cut themselves and have made applications in order to protect their daughters.

**6.25**   The early use of these civil orders, particularly by applicant mothers, has been termed by many as a cultural shift and a quiet revolution, particularly in the context of the historical difficulties experienced in tackling FGM.[29] Despite the progress of these applications, the extent of the prevalence of FGM in the UK suggests that these figures reflect superficial evidence of a much larger problem. The latest figures from NHS digital, which began collating data in April 2015, reveal that more than 8,000 women across England have recently been identified as being victims of FGM.[30]

## Procedural rules

**6.26**   Rules 3–17 of the Family Procedure (Amendment No 2) Rules 2015 amend Part 11 of the Family Procedure Rules 2010[31] to make provision for the practice and procedure to be followed on an application for an FGM protection order under Part 1 of Schedule 2 to the 2003 Act.

**6.27**   Part 1 of Schedule 2 to the 2003 Act sets out:

(a)   the power of the court to make an FGM protection order, including prohibitions, restrictions, requirements or any other terms it considers necessary to protect the girl, including in relation to the conduct of the

---

[24]   *FGM protection orders – impact for girls at risk*, BHRC seminar on Doughty Street Chambers, Thursday 16 July.

[25]   K Rawlinson, 'Police obtain first FGM protection order', *The Guardian*, Friday 17 July 2015.

[26]   http://www.bbc.co.uk/news/uk-36587667.

[27]   Ministry of Justice (MoJ) family court statistics quarterly: https://www.gov.uk/government/collections/family-court-statistics-quarterly.

[28]   *Family Court Statistics Quarterly*, England and Wales, July to September 2016, Statistics bulletin, Ministry of Justice.

[29]   K McVeigh, 'FGM court orders: a quiet revolution in child protection', *The Guardian*, Thursday 31 December 2015.

[30]   http://www.content.digital.nhs.uk/catalogue/PUB22619.

[31]   SI 2010/2955.

respondents. The court can also specify that the order can be made for a period of time or until varied or discharged;

(b) the circumstances in which an order can be applied for, made, varied or discharged, including the occasions on which a court can make an order without an application being made to it, including in criminal proceedings for genital mutilation offences;

(c) the consequences if the order is breached, including proceedings for a criminal offence or for contempt of court;

(d) provisions for applying for a warrant of arrest for breach and remanding respondents in custody; and

(e) the court's power to make an FGM protection order without notice being given to the respondent.

**6.28** Paragraph 16 of Schedule 2 to the 2003 Act makes it clear that nothing in the provisions in relation to FGM protections order affects any other protection or assistance available to a girl who is, or may become, the victim of a genital mutilation offence.[32] In particular, it does not affect:

(a) the inherent jurisdiction of the High Court;

(b) any criminal liability;

(c) any civil remedies under the Protection from Harassment Act 1997;

(d) any right to an occupation order or a non-molestation order under Part 4 of the Family Law Act 1996;

(e) any right to a forced marriage protection order under Part 4A of that Act;

(f) any protection or assistance under the Children Act 1989;

(g) any claim in tort.[33]

## LEGAL AID AND COURT FEES

**6.29** Civil legal aid is available for legal representation in an FGM protection matter subject to meeting the relevant means and merits criteria.[34] This applies to victims, potential victims and third parties seeking to make, vary, discharge or appeal an FGM protection order.

**6.30** Where breach of an FGM protection order is dealt with as contempt of court in the Family Court, the applicant/person to be protected may also obtain legal aid to commence proceedings. Legal representation for the individual alleged to have breached the FGM Protection Order is provided under the criminal legal aid scheme.

---

[32] 2003 Act, Sch 2, para 16.
[33] 2003 Act, Sch 2, para 16.
[34] https://www.gov.uk/check-legal-aid.

**6.31**   Alternatively, where breach of an FGM protection order is dealt with in a criminal court, as prosecution would be taken forward by the Crown/CPS, there would be no requirement for the victim to receive legal aid. Criminal legal aid, would, however, be available to defendants in criminal proceedings, subject to meeting the criteria to qualify for criminal legal aid.

**6.32**   There is no fee for issuing an application for an FGM protection order. Article 2(2) of The Family Proceedings Fees (Amendment No 2) Order 2015[35] disapplies fees in proceedings relating to FGM orders under Schedule 2 to the 2003 Act. Article 2(3) disapplies fees for requests for service by a bailiff of FGM protection orders, or applications for, or to vary or discharge, FGM protection orders. There is therefore also no court fee for any additional court procedures associated with the case, such as applications to vary or discharge an order or applications to the Family Court to consider how the person who has breached the order should be dealt with.

## FORMS

**6.33**   An application for an FGM protection order can be made on form FGM001 (set out at Appendix 1) which is also available at http://formfinder. hmctsformfinder.justice.gov.uk/fgm001-eng.pdf.

**6.34**   If the applicant is applying for someone else to be protected and the leave of the court is therefore needed then form FGM006 should be completed and filed with the court: http://formfinder.hmctsformfinder.justice.gov.uk/fgm006-eng.pdf.

**6.35**   In the event that the person to be protected, or the person applying on her behalf does not want his or her address to be shared with the respondent, then Form C8 should be completed and filed.

**6.36**   Guidance on completing the court forms and the procedure around applications for FGM protection orders is provided for in FGM700 which is available at https://formfinder.hmctsformfinder.justice.gov.uk/fgm700-eng.pdf. This guidance is available in Amharic, Arabic, English, Farsi, French, Somali, Swahili, Tigrinya, Turkish, Urdu and Welsh.

**6.37**   All forms are available from any of the designated court centres that deal with applications for FGM protection orders or can be downloaded from the Her Majesty's Court Service website.[36]

---

[35]   SI 2015/1419.
[36]   hmctsformfinder.justice.gov.uk.

# WHO CAN MAKE AN APPLICATION?

**6.38** Section 2 of Schedule 2 makes provision as to the categories of people who may apply for an FGM protection order.[37] An application for an FGM protection order can be made by (1) the girl or women to be protected, (2) a Relevant Third Party or (3) any other person with the permission of the court.

## The girl or women to be protected

**6.39** A girl seeking protection can make an application for an FGM protection order without the leave of the court.[38] A girl is defined in the legislation to include a woman.[39] An application may be in person or with legal representation.

**6.40** Children do not need leave of the court to apply. Where the person who is the subject of proceedings is not the applicant and is a child, the court must consider, at every stage in the proceedings, whether to make that child a party to proceedings.[40] For when a child should be made a party to proceedings generally see paragraph 7 of Practice Direction 16A.

## Relevant third party

**6.41** Under paragraph 2(2)(b) of Schedule 2, an application for an FGM protection order may also be made by a relevant third party without the leave of the court.[41]

**6.42** Paragraph 2(7) defines that a relevant third party means a person specified, or falling within a description of persons specified, by regulations made by the Lord Chancellor (and such regulations may, in particular, specify the Secretary of State).[42]

**6.43** Regulations under paragraph 2(7) are made and updated by statutory instrument. The Lord Chancellor has currently issued the Female Genital Mutilation Protection Order (Relevant Third Party) Regulations 2015.[43] Currently, only local authorities have been classified as relevant third parties for the purposes of seeking FGM protection orders.[44]

---

[37] 2003 Act, para 2(2)(a) of Sch 2 inserted by s 73 of the 2015 Act.

[38] 2003 Act, Sch 2, para 2, as inserted by s 73 of the 2015 Act.

[39] 2003 Act, s 6(1).

[40] The Family Procedure (Amendment No 2) Rules 2015, SI 2015/1420, r 9.

[41] 2003 Act, para 2(2)(b) of Sch 2 as inserted by s 73 of the 2015 Act.

[42] 2003 Act, para 2(7) of Sch 2 as inserted by s 73 of the 2015 Act.

[43] SI 2015/1422.

[44] A local authority is defined in para 2 of the Female Genital Mutilation Protection Order (Relevant Third Party) Regulations 2015, SI 2015/1422 as: (a) a county council in England; (b) a metropolitan district council; (c) a non-metropolitan district council for an area for which there is no county council; (d) the council of a county or county borough in Wales; (e) a London borough council; (f) the Common Council of the City of London; (g) the Council of the Isles of Scilly.

## Any other person

**6.44**  Paragraph 2(3) goes on to provide that an application may be made by any other person with the leave of the court.[45] This is a wide-ranging provision. In practice, the person making the application is often a police authority, a voluntary sector support service, a healthcare body or a friend or family member of the person for whom that protection is sought.

**6.45**  In deciding whether to grant leave, the court must have regard to all the circumstances including:

(a)   the applicant's connection with the girl to be protected;

(b)   the applicant's knowledge of the circumstances of the girl.[46]

## OTHER OCCASIONS FOR MAKING ORDERS

### Existing family proceedings

**6.46**  An application for an FGM protection order may be made in other family proceedings. 'Family proceedings' has the same meaning as in Part 4 of the Family Law Act 1996.[47]

'Family proceedings' also include:[48]

(a)   proceedings under the inherent jurisdiction of the High Court in relation to adults;

(b)   proceedings in which the court has made an emergency protection order under s 44 of the Children Act 1989 which includes an exclusion requirement (as defined in s 44A(3) of that Act); and

(c)   proceedings in which the court has made an order under s 50 of the Children Act 1989 (recovery of abducted children, etc).

### *No application*

**6.47**  An FGM protection order can also be made without any other family proceedings being instituted.[49] Paragraph 2(6) of Schedule 2 of the 2003 Act provides that the circumstances in which the court may make an FGM protection order without an application being made are where:

(a)   any other family proceedings are before the court ('the current proceedings');

---

[45]  2003 Act, para 2(3) of Sch 2 as inserted by s 73 of the 2015 Act.
[46]  2003 Act, para 2(4)(b) of Sch 2 as inserted by s 73 of the 2015 Act.
[47]  Family Law Act 1996, s 3(1) and (2) of Part 4.
[48]  2003 Act, para 2(7) of Sch 2, as inserted by s 73 of the 2015 Act.
[49]  2003 Act, para 2(5) of Sch 2, as inserted by s 73 of the 2015 Act.

(b)   the court considers that an FGM protection order should be made to protect a girl (whether or not a party to the proceedings), and

(c)   a person who would be a respondent to any proceedings for an FGM protection order is a party to the current proceedings.

## *Protection orders within criminal proceedings*

**6.48**   The court before which there are criminal proceedings in England and Wales for a genital mutilation offence may make an FGM protection order (without an application being made to it) if: (a) the court considers that an FGM protection order should be made to protect a girl (whether or not the victim of the offence in relation to the criminal proceedings), and (b) a person who would be a respondent to any proceedings for an FGM protection order is a defendant in the criminal proceedings.[50]

## EX PARTE HEARINGS

**6.49**   The court is able to make an FGM protection order even though the respondent has not been given such notice of the proceedings as would otherwise be required by rules of court. The court has the power to do this in any case where it is just and convenient to do so.[51]

**6.50**   In considering whether to make an order on an ex parte basis, the court must have regard to all the circumstances including:

(a)   the risk to the girl, or to another person, of becoming a victim of a genital mutilation offence if the order is not made immediately;

(b)   whether it is likely that an applicant will be deterred or prevented from pursuing an application if an order is not made immediately; and

(c)   whether there is reason to believe that:
    (i)   the respondent is aware of the proceedings but is deliberately evading service; and
    (ii)  the delay involved in effecting substituted service will cause serious prejudice to the girl to be protected or (if different) an applicant.[52]

**6.51**   Where an FGM protection order is made at an ex parte hearing, the court must give the respondent an opportunity to make representations about the order made.[53] The opportunity for the respondent to make representations must be afforded at a return hearing of which notice has been given to all the parties in accordance with rules of court.[54]

---

[50]   2003 Act, para 3 of Sch 2, as inserted by s 73 of the 2015 Act.
[51]   2003 Act, Sch 2, para 5(1).
[52]   2003 Act, Sch 2, para 5(2).
[53]   2003 Act, Sch 2, para 5(3).
[54]   2003 Act, Sch 2, para 5(4).

**6.52**  It is incumbent on an applicant for without notice relief to provide a full attendance note of the hearing (to include a note of the submissions that were made and the documents placed before court) to those affected by any order as soon as reasonably practicable.

**6.53**  In *Local Authority 1 & Others v AF (Mother) & Others*,[55] Mr Justice Cobb reiterated that it was not just important but also essential that in this kind of case, the solicitor or counsel instructed should prepare a note of the hearing and circulate it to the respondents forthwith following the hearing. The Judge reminded practitioners of the view of Munby J (as he then was) expressed in *C v C (Without Notice Orders)*[56] that the applicant's legal representatives should respond forthwith to any reasonable request from the party injuncted or his legal representatives either for copies of the materials read by the judge or for information about what took place at the hearing.

## GROUNDS FOR MAKING AN ORDER

### Health, safety and well-being

**6.54**  An FGM protection order may be made by the court for the purposes of protecting a girl against the commission of a genital mutilation offence, or protecting a girl against whom any such offence has already been committed.

**6.55**  The evidence may vary enormously from case to case and the threshold for the making of an order is broadly drafted. In determining whether to make an FGM protection order and, if so, on what terms, the court must have regard to all the circumstances, including the need to secure the 'health, safety and well-being' of the girl to be protected.[57]

## TERMS OF THE ORDER

**6.56**  The language of FGM protection orders is modelled loosely on injunctive orders within the Family Law Act 1996 (so that practitioners and judges of all levels can deal with the injunctive provisions using the language that is already familiar and in circulation).

**6.57**  The terms of the FGM protection order typically state that the respondents should not subject the girl to be protected to the practice of FGM, or encourage anybody else to do so. The terms of the order can include further prohibitions, restrictions or any other requirements that the court considers appropriate for the purposes of the order and necessary to protect a girl at risk.[58]

---

[55]  [2014] EWHC 2042 (Fam) at para [299].
[56]  [2005] EWHC 2741 (Fam).
[57]  2003 Act, Sch 2, para 1(2).
[58]  2003 Act, Sch 2, para 1(3), as inserted by s 73 of the 2015 Act.

**6.58** Cases may involve girls being taken abroad for the purposes of being cut. The terms of an FGM protection order may relate to conduct outside England and Wales as well as (or instead of) conduct within England and Wales.[59]

**6.59** The order can stipulate that the respondent does not enter into any arrangements, in the UK or abroad, for FGM to be performed on the person to be protected. If the girl to be protected is at risk of being taken abroad the applicant may also seek ancillary orders order under the inherent jurisdiction of the High Court, including port alerts and orders for the surrender a person's passport.

## Other restrictions

**6.60** The terms of an FGM protection order can include further prohibitions, restrictions or any other requirements that the court considers appropriate for the purposes of the order and necessary to protect a girl at risk. This broad ranging provision is contained within paragraph 1(3) of Schedule 2.[60] In the matter of *Re E (Children) (Female Genital Mutilation Protection Orders)*[61] Mrs Justice Hogg made an FGM protection order and in exercise of her powers under paragraph 1(3) of Schedule 2, added to the terms of the order the following further restrictions:

> 'The respondent must not himself, or encourage, permit or cause any other people to:
>
> (a) use or threaten violence against the applicant or children;
> (b) intimidate, harass, threaten or pester the applicant or the children.'[62]

**6.61** When extending those restrictions at the subsequent hearing, Mr Justice Holman added a further restriction (under paragraph 1(3) of Schedule 2) prohibiting the respondent from going within 100 metres of the applicant's address and the children's school.[63]

**6.62** When doing so, Mr Justice Holman cautioned that the wide-ranging powers within paragraph 1(3) of Schedule 2 should only be for protection against FGM and not to offer more general protection to an individual, for which there exists other legislation such as (but not limited to) the provisions for injunctive orders with the Family Law Act 1996.[64]

**6.63** The judgment of Mr Justice Holman stated:

---

[59]  2003 Act, Sch 2, para 1(4)(a).
[60]  2003 Act, Sch 2, para 1(3) as inserted by s 73 of the 2015 Act.
[61]  [2015] EWHC 2275.
[62]  *Re E (Children) (Female Genital Mutilation Protection Orders)* [2015] EWHC 2275, at para 25.
[63]  *Re E (Children) (Female Genital Mutilation Protection Orders)* [2015] EWHC 2275, at para 26.
[64]  *Re E (Children) (Female Genital Mutilation Protection Orders)* [2015] EWHC 2275, at para 27.

'[27] ... it is extremely important that the courts do not allow their powers under the Female Genital Mutilation Act 2003, which are very wide ones, to get stretched to providing protection for somebody such as the mother herself in this case. She says that she has suffered great violence at the hands of her former husband. But if she in her own right needs protection from him, she has a different statutory remedy under the Family Law Act 1996, as amended. I wish to make very, very clear that, in adding, as I will, those restrictions against the respondent father from coming within 100 metres of the home or the children's school, I am doing so purely for the purposes of protecting these three girls from female genital mutilation, and not for the purpose of protecting the mother from any feared violence from the father. But it does seem to me, on the facts and in the circumstances of this case, that simply to prohibit the father from himself or by others practising enforced genital mutilation upon these girls is not sufficient. He must, for the time being, be prohibited altogether from coming within a restricted radius of their home and, when they return there next term, their school.

[28] For those reasons, I will add provisions to that effect to the underlying order which was made by Hogg J on 22nd July 2015.'

## Duration of the order

**6.64** Where the court determines that the evidence and circumstances require the making of an order, it has wide powers as to the terms and duration of the FGM protection order it may make. The order may be made for a specified period or until varied or discharged.[65]

# RESPONDENTS

**6.65** The order can be made against named respondents who are identified in the evidence. The order can relate to respondents who are, or may become, involved in other respects.[66] As well as respondents, the order can also relate to other persons who are, or may become, involved for example by: (a) aiding, abetting, counselling, procuring, encouraging or assisting another person to commit, or attempt to commit, a genital mutilation offence against a girl; or (b) conspiring to commit, or to attempt to commit, such an offence.[67]

**6.66** That orders may be made against people who are not named in the application underscores the complexity of the issues and the numbers of people who might be involved in the wider community.

# JURISDICTIONAL REACH OF ORDERS

**6.67** Cases may involve girls being taken abroad for the purposes of being cut. Paragraph 1(4)(a) of Schedule 2 of the 2003 Act specifically provides that the

[65] 2003 Act, Sch 2, para 1(3) and 1(6).
[66] 2003 Act, Sch 2, para 1(4)(b).
[67] 2003 Act, Sch 2, para 1(5).

terms of an FGM protection order may relate to conduct outside England and Wales as well as (or instead of) conduct within England and Wales.[68]

**6.68** Offences of FGM generally committed abroad by or against those who at the time are habitually resident in the UK, irrespective of whether they are subject to immigration restrictions, are therefore covered by the 2003 Act.

**6.69** This extension of extra-territorial jurisdiction is provided for by s 70(1) of the 2015 Act which amends s 4 of the 2003 Act so that the extra-territorial jurisdiction extends to prohibited acts done outside the UK by a UK national or a person who is resident in the UK. Consistent with that change, s 70(1) also amends s 3 of the 2003 Act (offence of assisting a non-UK person to mutilate overseas a girl's genitalia) so it extends to acts of FGM done to a UK national or a person who is resident in the UK.

**6.70** 'UK resident' is defined as an individual who is habitually resident in the UK. The term 'habitually resident' covers a person's ordinary residence, as opposed to a short, temporary stay in a country.[69] Whether an individual habitually resident in the UK is a matter for the courts to determine on the facts of individual cases.

## DESIGNATED COURTS

**6.71** In England and Wales an FGM protection order may be made by the High Court, the Family Court[70] or where applicable a court in criminal proceedings.[71] Twenty-three courts have been designated as specialist centres to deal with applications. These courts have been selected to build up expertise in this area and given the specialist nature of these cases.

**6.72** Currently the following courts have been designated as court centres where applications for FGM protection orders can be made:[72]

**Birmingham Civil and Family Justice Centre**
Priory Courts 33 Bull Street
Birmingham
West Midlands
England B4 6DS
Phone: 0300 123 1751
Email: family@birmingham.countycourt.gsi.gov.uk
or e-filing@birmingham.countycourt.gsi.gov.uk

---

[68]  2003 Act, para 1(4)(a), Sch 2.
[69]  2015 Act, s 70(1)(c).
[70]  2003 Act, para 17(1) of Sch 2 as inserted by s 73 of the 2015 Act. Also as observed by Mr Justice Holman at para 13, *Re E (Children) (Female Genital Mutilation Protection Orders)* [2015] EWHC 2275.
[71]  2003 Act, para 17(2) of Sch 2 as inserted by s 73 of the 2015 Act.
[72]  https://formfinder.hmctsformfinder.justice.gov.uk/fgm700-eng.pdf.

**Bradford Combined Court**
Exchange Square
Drake Street
Bradford
West Yorkshire
England BD1 1JA
Phone: 01274 840274
Email: family@bradford.countycourt.gsi.gov.uk
or e-filing@bradford.countycourt.gsi.gov.uk

**Brighton Family Court Hearing Centre**
1 Edward Street
Brighton
East Sussex
England BN2 0JD
Phone: 01273 811 333
Email: sussexfamily@hmcts.gsi.gov.uk

**Bristol Civil and Family Justice Centre**
2 Redcliff Street
Bristol
England BS1 6GR
Phone: 0117 366 4880
Email: family@bristol.countycourt.gsi.gov.uk

**Cardiff Civil and Family Justice Centre**
2 Park Street
Cardiff
South Wales CF10 1ET
Phone: 029 2037 6400
Email: enquiries@cardiff.countycourt.gsi.gov.uk

**Central Family Court**
First Avenue House
42–49 High Holborn
London
England WC1V 6NP
Phone: 020 7421 8594
Email: cfc.privatelaw@hmcts.gsi.gov.uk

**Derby Combined Court**
Morledge
Derby
Derbyshire
England DE1 2XE
Phone: 01332 622600
Email: family@derby.countycourt.gsi.gov.uk

**East London Family Court**
6th and 7th Floor
11 Westferry Circus
London
England E14 4HD
Phone: 020 3197 2886
Email: eastlondonfamilyenquiries@hmcts.gsi.gov.uk

**Leeds Combined Court**
The Court House
1 Oxford Row Leeds
West Yorkshire
England LS1 3BG
Phone: 0113 306 2800
Email: leedsdfcprivatelawgeneralenquiries@hmcts.gsi.gov.uk
or leedspubliclawissue@hmcts.gsi.gov.uk

**Leicester County Court and Family Court**
90 Wellington Street
Leicester
Leicestershire
England LE1 6HG
Phone: 0116 222 5700
Email: family@leicester.countycourt.gsi.gov.uk

**Liverpool Civil and Family Court Hearing Centre**
35 Vernon Street
Liverpool
Merseyside
England L2 2BX
Phone: 0151 296 2607
Email: family@liverpool.countycourt.gsi.gov.uk

**Luton County Court and Family Court**
2nd Floor, Cresta House Alma Street
Luton
Bedfordshire
England LU1 2PU
Phone: 0300 123 5577
Email: enquiries@luton.countycourt.gsi.gov.uk

**Manchester County Court and Family Court**
1 Bridge Street West
Manchester
Greater Manchester
England M60 9DJ
Phone: 0161 240 5420
Email: familyapplications.manchester@hmcts.gsi.gov.uk

**Newcastle upon Tyne Combined Court Centre**
The Quayside
Newcastle-upon-Tyne
Tyne & Wear
England NE1 3LA
Phone: 0191 201 2000
Email: COPNewcastle@newcastle.countycourt.gsi.gov.uk

**Norwich Combined Court and Family Hearing Centre**
Bishopgate Norwich
Norfolk
England NR3 1UR
Phone: 0344 892 4000
Email: family@norwich.countycourt.gsi.gov.uk
or e-filing@norwich.countycourt.gsi.gov.uk

**Oxford Combined Court and Family Court Hearing Centre**
St Aldates
Oxford
Oxfordshire England OX1 1TL
Phone: 01865 264 200
Email: family@oxford.countycourt.gsi.gov.uk

**Plymouth Combined Court**
10 Armada Way
Plymouth Devon
England
PL1 2ER
Phone: 01752 677 400
Email: family@plymouth.countycourt.gsi.gov.uk

**Portsmouth Combined Court Centre**
Winston Churchill Avenue
Portsmouth
Hampshire
England PO1 2EB
Phone: 02392 893 000
Email: family@portsmouth.countycourt.gsi.gov.uk

**Preston Family Court**
Sessions House
Lancaster Road
Preston
Lancashire
England PR1 2PD
Phone: 01772 844 700
Email: prestonSFCissue@hmcts.gsi.gov.uk

**Reading County Court and Family Court Hearing Centre**
160–163 Friar Street
Reading
Berkshire
England RG1 1HE
Phone: 0118 987 0500
Email: family@reading.countycourt.gsi.gov.uk

**Sheffield Combined Court Centre**
50 West Bar Sheffield
South Yorkshire
England S3 8PH
Phone: 0114 2812400
Email: family@sheffield.countycourt.gsi.gov.uk

**Teesside Combined Court**
Russell Street
Middlesbrough
Cleveland
England TS1 2AE
Phone: 01642 340 000
Email: family@middlesbrough.countycourt.gsi.gov.uk

**West London Family Court**
Gloucester House
4 Dukes Green Avenue
Feltham
Middlesex
England TW14 0LR
Phone: 020 8831 3500
Email: westlondonfamilyenquiries@hmcts.gsi.gov.uk

## Family Division of the High Court

**6.73** An application may also be made at the High Court if the case has an international element and orders may be required under the inherent jurisdiction of the High Court. Where there is evidence that a girl has already been taken out of the jurisdiction for FGM to be undertaken then the High Court is most likely to be the correct forum.

## Urgent cases

**6.74** Where an urgent application is required, an application should be made where possible within court hours. It is key that in such situation, early liaison with the Clerk of the Rules occurs in order that they can attempt to accommodate such requests.

**6.75**   When it is not possible to apply for an urgent order within court hours and the urgent out of hours procedure should be followed,[73] contact should be made with the security office at the Royal Courts of Justice (020 7947 6000 or 020 7947 6260), who will refer the matter to the urgent business officer. The urgent business officer can contact the duty judge. The judge may agree to hold a hearing, either convened at court or elsewhere, or by telephone.

## UNDERTAKINGS

**6.76**   Where an application is made for an FGM protection order, the court may accept an undertaking if the parties are in agreement and if the court is satisfied that a full hearing and findings of fact are not necessary to protect an individual.

## DRAFT ORDER(S)

**6.77**   There remains no formal pro forma order and the terms of the order will vary according to the circumstances of each case.

**6.78**   The wording of orders is modelled on the Family Law Act 1996 injunctive orders (so that practitioners and judges of all levels can readily adopt the language they are used to). Two examples of draft orders are reproduced here:

---

[73]   See courts out of hours procedure, r 12.36(1) of the Family Procedure Rules 2010, SI 2010/2955. Also see FPR Practice Direction 12E (Urgent Business).

## Example order 1

BEFORE the Honourable _____ sitting at the Royal Courts of Justice on _____

UPON HEARING Counsel for the Applicant Local Authority _____ and

_____.

AND UPON the Court making this Order on a without prejudice to the Respondent and underlining to the Father the importance him receiving legal advice.

UPON CONSIDERING the documents supplied by the Applicant on notice to the Respondent _____.

AND UPON the Court noting that the terms of an FGM protection order may, in particular, relate to conduct outside England and Wales as well as conduct within England and Wales

### AND UPON IT BEING RECORDED THAT:

1.   The Respondent _____ confirmed at Court today that the Respondent Mother has also been subjected to FGM.

### AND UPON THE COURT MAKING AN FGM PROTECTION ORDER IN THE BELOW TERMS:

1.   The Respondent _____ is forbidden, whether by himself or by aiding, abetting, counselling, procuring, encouraging or assisting any other person from:
     a.   taking any steps to cause _____ (D.O.B _____) to undergo female genital mutilation;
     b.   causing or permitting _____ (D.O.B _____) to undergo female genital mutilation;
     c.   forcing, or attempting to force, _____ (D.O.B _____) to undergo female genital mutilation;
     d.   conspiring to force, or attempting to force _____, (D.O.B _____) to undergo female genital mutilation;
     e.   using or threatening to use violence against _____, (D.O.B _____);
     f.   using or threatening to use violence against any other person known to _____ with a view to causing them to subject her to female genital mutilation.
2.   Paragraph 1 of the FGM protection order above is remains in force until 4pm on Respondent _____.

3.  There is liberty to the Respondent _____ to apply to vary or discharge the above FGM protection order with 48 hours' notice to the Applicant.

**IT IS FURTHER ORDERED BY CONSENT:**

1.  The Respondent, _____ shall surrender his own passport and the passport of his children _____ to Respondent _____ no later than Respondent _____.

**AND IT IS ORDERED:**

1.  The Applicant shall issue its application for a FGM protection order forthwith.
2.  The Respondent _____ back to the jurisdiction of England and Wales no later than Respondent _____.
3.  The Respondent _____ shall notify Respondent _____ of the Metropolitan Police Service by telephone and email forthwith upon arrangement being made for the return of the person to be protected to the jurisdiction of England and Wales to include details of the booking reference, flight number, date and time of departure and arrival and the name of the airports in Guinea and the UK.
4.  The Applicant shall by 4pm on Respondent _____ write to the FGM Lead at the Forced Marriage Unit to ascertain what assistance they may be able to provide in securing the return of the subject children to this jurisdiction.
5.  There is leave to the Applicant to serve a copy of this Order on the FGM Lead at the Forced Marriage Unit.
6.  The Applicant shall by 4pm on _____:
    a.  Write to the Embassy of Respondent _____ with a copy of this Order, to inform them of these proceedings, given that the Respondent _____ has indicated that both he and the children are Respondent _____ nationals.
    b.  Write to the Embassy of the Netherlands to ascertain what assistance they may be able to provide in securing the return of the subject children to this jurisdiction.
7.  The Applicant shall file and serve a paginated bundle by 1100 on 30th June 2016.
8.  The matter is listed for a return hearing at 10.30 on 1st July 2016 [listed for 30 minutes] before a Judge of the Family Division sitting at the Royal Courts of Justice. The parties to attend court at 09.30 for pre-hearing discussions.
9.  This order is to take effect pending it being sealed.
10. No order as to costs.

**Example order 2**

## IN THE HIGH COURT OF JUSTICE

### FAMILY DIVISION

Case number:

---

Female Genital Mutilation (FGM) Protection Order

Part 1 of Schedule 2 to the Female Genital Mutilation Act 2003

_____ Applicant

_____ First Respondent

_____ Second Respondent

UPON HEARING Counsel for the Applicant Local Authority, Counsel for the 1st Respondent Mother and the 2nd Respondent Father in person.

AND UPON the Court noting that the terms of an FGM protection order may, in particular, relate to conduct outside England and Wales as well as (or instead of) conduct within England and Wales.

AND UPON the Court noting the Mother is currently cooperating with the Local Authority and the Father in arranging the return of the children to this jurisdiction. In the circumstances the Court will dismiss the application for committal.

Notice   To:

Address:

---

**Warning**

You must obey this order. You should read this order carefully. If you do not understand anything in this order you should go to a solicitor, Legal Advice Centre or Citizens Advice Bureau. You have a right to apply to the court to change or cancel the order.

Failure to obey this order is a serious criminal offence under paragraph 4, Part 1 of Schedule 2 to the Female Genital Mutilation Act 2003, for which you could face a maximum penalty of 5 years' imprisonment. Alternatively, you

**could be found guilty of contempt of court under paragraph 15, Part 1 of Schedule 2 to the Female Genital Mutilation Act 2003 and face a maximum penalty of 2 years' imprisonment.**

Terms of the Order   Date of hearing

Name of person to be protected

_____

The court makes a Female Genital Mutilation Protection Order in the following terms:

1.   The Respondent Mother shall, whether by herself or by permitting, encouraging, assisting or agreeing with any other person whatsoever, be forbidden from entering into any arrangements in relation to genital mutilation of Respondent _____.

2.   The Respondent Mother shall inform the court if she is aware of any current plans for to be subjected to any form of genital mutilation and shall take immediate steps to prevent the same.

3.   The matter is hereby listed for a return hearing on notice to all parties, at 10.30am on_____ time estimate 1 hour, before a Judge of the Division sitting at the Royal Courts of Justice, Strand, London WC2A 2LL, subject to confirmation with the Clerk of the Rules.

4.   This order is made until further order.

5.   No order as to costs.

Duration of Order:

This order is made until further notice.

Notice of further hearing:

The court will reconsider the application and whether the order should continue at a further hearing.

Place: Royal Courts of Justice, Strand, London WC2A 2LL

Date: _____ Time: 10.30am

If you do not attend at the time shown the court may make an order in your absence

This order is made with notice to the respondents

Ordered by Mr Justice _____ On _____

## VARIATION AND DISCHARGE OF ORDERS

**6.79**  An application can be made to extend, change ('vary') or cancel ('discharge') an FGM protection order at any time. An application to vary or discharge the order needs to be made using form FGM003.[74] The court may vary or discharge an FGM protection order on an application by:

(a)  any party to the proceedings for the order;

(b)  the girl being protected by the order (if not a party to the proceedings for the order); or

(c)  any person affected by the order.[75]

**6.80**  In the case of an order made in criminal proceedings both the prosecution and the defendant are able to make applications to vary or discharge an FGM protection order.[76] The court may vary or discharge an FGM protection order of its own volition notwithstanding the absence of an application being made.[77]

**6.81**  An application can also be made to add people to the terms of the order if it is contended that they are also at risk of FGM, or remove people if they are no longer at risk. An application to add or remove people from the terms of the order needs to be made using form FGM007.[78]

## BREACH AND ENFORCEMENT

### Breach of an order

**6.82**  The breach of an FGM protection order is a criminal offence.[79] Paragraph 4(1) of Schedule 2 to the 2003 Act states that:

> 'A person who without reasonable excuse does anything that the person is prohibited from doing by an FGM protection order is guilty of an offence.'

**6.83**  A person guilty of breaching an FGM protection order is liable:

(a)  on conviction on indictment, to imprisonment for a term not exceeding five years, or a fine, or both;

(b)  on summary conviction, to imprisonment for a term not exceeding 12 months, or a fine, or both.[80]

---

[74]   https://formfinder.hmctsformfinder.justice.gov.uk/fgm003-eng.pdf.
[75]   2003 Act, Sch 2, para 6(1).
[76]   2003 Act, Sch 2, para 6(2).
[77]   2003 Act, Sch 2, para 6(3).
[78]   https://formfinder.hmctsformfinder.justice.gov.uk/fgm007-eng.pdf.
[79]   2003 Act, Sch 2, para 4(1).
[80]   2003 Act, Sch 2, para 4(5).

**6.84**  As an alternative to prosecution, breach of an FGM protection order may be dealt with by the civil route as contempt of court. The maximum penalty for contempt of court is up to two years' imprisonment. In the case of an FGM protection order made at an ex parte hearing a person can only be guilty of an offence in respect of conduct engaged in at a time when the person was aware of the existence of the order.[81]

## Arrest under warrant

**6.85**  An interested party may apply to the relevant judge for the issue of a warrant for the arrest of a person if the interested party considers that the person has failed to comply with an FGM protection order or is otherwise in contempt of court in relation to such an order.[82]

**6.86**  An 'interested party' is defined as:

(a)  the girl being protected by the order;

(b)  (if a different person) the person who applied for the order; or

(c)  any other person with the leave of the relevant judge.[83]

**6.87**  The relevant judge must not issue a warrant on an application unless:

(a)  the application is substantiated on oath; and

(b)  the relevant judge has reasonable grounds for believing that the person to be arrested has failed to comply with the order or is otherwise in contempt of court in relation to the order.[84]

## *Remand*

**6.88**  The court before which an arrested person is brought by virtue of a warrant under paragraph 7 may, if the matter is not then disposed of immediately, remand the person concerned.[85] If remanded in custody, the person is to be brought before the court at the end of the period of remand, or at such earlier time as the court may require.[86]

**6.89**  The court may remand a person on bail:

(a)  by taking from the person a recognizance (with or without sureties) conditioned as provided in paragraph 11; or

---

[81]  2003 Act, Sch 2, para 4(2).
[82]  2003 Act, Sch 2, para 7(1).
[83]  2003 Act, Sch 2, para 7(3).
[84]  2003 Act, Sch 2, para 7(2).
[85]  2003 Act, Sch 2, para 8(1).
[86]  2003 Act, Sch 2, para 10(2).

(b)  by fixing the amount of the recognizances with a view to their being taken subsequently in accordance with paragraph 14 and, in the meantime, committing the person to custody.[87]

**6.90**  Where a person is brought before the court after remand the court may further remand the person.[88] The court may not remand a person for a period exceeding eight clear days unless:

(a)  the court adjourns a case under paragraph 9(1); or

(b)  the person is remanded on bail and both that person and the other party to the proceedings (or, in the case of criminal proceedings, the prosecution) consent.[89]

**6.91**  Where the court has power to remand a person in custody, the person may be committed to the custody of a constable if the remand is for a period not exceeding three clear days.[90] Paragraphs 9 to 14 of Schedule 2 contain further provision about the powers of a court to remand a person.[91]

## The contempt of court route and committal proceedings

**6.92**  As an alternative to prosecution, the breach of an FGM protection order may be dealt with by the civil route as contempt of court.[92] Where a person has already been convicted for breaching an FGM protection order, he cannot then be punished for the same conduct through the contempt of court route.[93] Further, a person cannot be convicted for the offence of breaching an order for any conduct which has been punished as a contempt of court.[94]

**6.93**  The spectre of committal proceedings has also been used by the courts to facilitate compliance with urgent court orders and to secure the return of children at risk of FGM who may already be missing.[95]

## SERVICE OF THE ORDER ON OTHER BODIES

**6.94**  Where an agency has obtained an FGM protection order it should consider which, if any, other agencies need to be aware of the order, for example those not served with a copy of the order by the court, and whether it is necessary for that information to be shared in order to secure the protection

---

[87]  2003 Act, Sch 2, para 10(3).
[88]  2003 Act, Sch 2, para 10(4).
[89]  2003 Act, Sch 2, para 12(1).
[90]  2003 Act, Sch 2, para 12(3).
[91]  2003 Act, Sch 2, para 12(3), paras 9–14.
[92]  2003 Act, Sch 2, para 15.
[93]  2003 Act, Sch 2, para 4(3).
[94]  2003 Act, Sch 2, para 4(4).
[95]  See *Re F and X (Children)* [2015] EWHC 2653 (Fam).

of the girl at risk.[96] The multi-agency guidance advises that care should be exercised in sharing information, particularly if it could have the adverse effect of leading to reprisals for the victim and/or other members of their family.[97]

**6.95** When the court has made an order, the applicant or the court (where requested or if the court makes an order of its own initiative) should serve a copy of the order on the police, together with a statement showing that the respondents and/or any other persons directed by the court have been served with the order or informed of its terms. The order and statement should be delivered to the police station for the address of the person being protected by the order, unless the court specifies another police station.[98]

## EVIDENTIAL CONSIDERATIONS AND THE USE OF EXPERTS

**6.96** FGM can occur at different ages and in different forms from tribe to tribe and from country to country. The consequences of the wrong decision being made by the court can have life-long implications for the health and wellbeing of the potential victim. Accordingly, it is essential that the court is provided with the best possible evidence upon which to make its decision.

**6.97** These cases often involve complex cultural issues, often with an international dimension. It may be necessary for the court to require the assistance of an anthropologist or cultural expert for the court to be have the best evidence before it. The court may also take into account statistics (for example data from UNICEF and the OHCHR) in relation to FGM pertaining to a particular community and sub-community.

**6.98** In cases where the allegations of risk of harm are denied, children may be made parties to the proceedings. Often if allegations are contested and/or the necessity of the making of an order is contested, the court will need the best information to be placed before it as possible in order to make a finding of risk.

## Necessity

**6.99** The court may only permit expert evidence to be adduced if it believes the evidence is 'necessary to assist the court to resolve the proceedings justly'.[99] In *Re H-L (Expert Evidence: Test For Permission)*[100] the Court of Appeal held that the word 'necessary' should be construed as lying 'somewhere between

---

[96] Multi-agency statutory guidance on female genital mutilation, HM Government (April 2016), para 3.3.4.
[97] Multi-agency statutory guidance on female genital mutilation, HM Government (April 2016), para 3.3.4.
[98] Multi-agency statutory guidance on female genital mutilation, HM Government (April 2016), para 3.3.4.
[99] Children and Families Act 2014, s 13(6) and Family Procedure Rules 2010, r 25.4(3).
[100] [2013] EWCA Civ 655, [2013] 2 FLR 1434.

"indispensible" on the one hand and "useful", or "reasonable" or "desirable" on the other hand, having the connation of the imperative, what is demanded rather than what is merely optional or reasonable or desirable'.

## The application for permission to instruct an expert

**6.100**  A party wishing to instruct an expert in accordance with s 13 of the Children and Families Act 2014 and FPR 2010, Part 25 must apply for the court's permission as soon as possible. In public law proceeding this should be done no later than the Case Management Hearing (CMH).

**6.101**  The legal provisions in relation to FGM introduced by the 2015 Act are in their infancy and there remains a dearth of expertise before the courts. Choosing the appropriate expert to provide a report is crucial to a case, and to avoid delay. It is crucial at the outset to identify appropriate experts with specific training and experience.

**6.102**  Practitioners should check CVs carefully for specific training, education and experience in relation to FGM issues. Careful consideration should be given to the specific questions to be asked of the expert and on his/her suitability to answer those questions. For instance, in relation to medical experts, are they still working as clinicians? If the expert has not until now being doing court work – are they able to meet the expert standards?

## National standards for expert witnesses

**6.103**  With effect from 1 October 2014, an annex has been inserted into FPR 2010, PD25B, which sets out national standards expected of experts within family proceedings. These are as follows:

'1.  The expert's area of competence is appropriate to the issue(s) upon which the court has identified that an opinion is required, and relevant experience is evidenced in their CV.

2.  The expert has been active in the area of work or practice (as a practitioner or an academic who is subject to peer appraisal), has sufficient experience of the issues relevant to the instant case, and is familiar with the breadth of current practice or opinion.

3.  The expert has working knowledge of the social, developmental, cultural norms and accepted legal principles applicable to the case presented at initial enquiry, and has the cultural competence skills to deal with the circumstances of the case.

4.  The expert is up-to-date with Continuing Professional Development appropriate to their discipline and expertise, and is in continued engagement with accepted supervisory mechanisms relevant to their practice.

5.  If the expert's current professional practice is regulated by a UK statutory body (See Appendix 1 [to PD25B]) they are in possession of a current licence to practise or equivalent.

6.  If the expert's area of professional practice is not subject to statutory registration (e.g. child psychotherapy, systemic family therapy, mediation, and experts in exclusively academic appointments) the expert should

demonstrate appropriate qualifications and/or registration with a relevant professional body on a case by case basis. Registering bodies usually provide a code of conduct and professional standards and should be accredited by the Professional Standards Authority for Health and Social Care (See Appendix 2 [to PD25B]). If the expertise is academic in nature (eg regarding evidence of cultural influences) then no statutory registration is required (even if this includes direct contact or interviews with individuals) but consideration should be given to appropriate professional accountability.

7.    The expert is compliant with any necessary safeguarding requirements, information security expectations, and carries professional indemnity insurance.

8.    If the expert's current professional practice is outside the UK they can demonstrate that they are compliant with the FJC 'Guidelines for the instruction of medical experts from overseas in family cases' [December 2011].

9.    The expert has undertaken appropriate training, updating or quality assurance activity – including actively seeking feedback from cases in which they have provided evidence-relevant to the role of expert in the family courts in England and Wales within the last year.

10.   The expert has a working knowledge of, and complies with, the requirements of Practice Directions relevant to providing reports for and giving evidence to the family courts in England and Wales. This includes compliance with the requirement to identify where their opinion on the instant case lies in relation to other accepted mainstream views and the overall spectrum of opinion in the UK.

11.   The expert should state their hourly rate in advance of agreeing to accept instruction, and give an estimate of the number of hours the report is likely to take. This will assist the legal representative to apply expeditiously to the Legal Aid Agency if prior authority is to be sought in a publicly funded case.'

## Risk assessments

**6.104** Whether the court is dealing with FGM protection order or FGM within wider care proceedings, it is usually necessary for the court to have a forensic assessment of risk of FGM posed within a family.

**6.105** In *Re Z (A Child: Independent Social Work Assessment)*[101] HHJ Bellamy, sitting as a High Court judge, held:

'In any case in which a local authority applies to the court for a care order, the assessment of the parent is of critical importance. That assessment will be a key piece of the evidential jigsaw, which informs the local authority's decision-making, in particular with respect to the formulation of its care plan. If the assessment is deficient then it is likely to undermine the reliability of the decision-making process. It follows from there, that any assessment of a parent must be, and must be seen to be, fair, robust and thorough'.

**6.106** A risk assessment should be undertaken by an expert, often an independent social worker, with experience of such assessments, and it should

---

[101]  [2014] EWHC 729.

ideally be an individual with specific expertise on the type of FGM and the nuances of the practice in the part of the world with which the court may be concerned. It is therefore imperative for the court to be furnished with relevant CVs of appropriate experts.

**6.107** Risk assessment in FGM cases can be accompanied by educational and/or therapeutic intervention work with girls thought to be at risk and their family members. The educational element of the risk assessment work often focuses on teaching not only about the adverse health consequences of FGM but also on equipping girls with the advice on how to protect themselves should they be at imminent risk either in the UK or overseas. For example, the Barnado's National FGM Centre offers risk assessment at the beginning of an intervention and at the end of an intervention to assess whether the risk has been decreased. In between this, intensive work is done with the family unit as a whole to increase their understanding of FGM and the risks associated with it.

**6.108** The intention of the targeted interventions is to ensure families have a sound understanding of safeguarding as a whole and particularly in terms of FGM. For children, it is to ensure they understand how to identify risk and protect themselves from it, and for parents to be able to identify risk and protect themselves and their daughters from it. The risk assessments offered by the National FGM Centre range from between 2–4 weeks ideally with between 2–6 sessions.

**6.109** The National FGM Centre RAM risk assessment matrix encompasses significant risk factors, potential risk factors, complicating factors, protective/safety factors. Risk assessment tools are not exhaustive, they should be adapted to incorporate knowledge of working within a particular community if there is a specific risk factor. Any assessment should include professional judgement and not be a tick box exercise. Professionals should take into account dynamics within families and recognise that the mother, who may be the survivor of FGM, may not make the decisions within the family unit. The influence of other family members, including the extended family, should also be considered when assessing risk.

**6.110** Examples of individuals and organisations that have offered expert evidence are listed below (this is not intended to be an exhaustive list):

FORWARD (Foundation for Women's Health Research and Development)

Offers expertise on FGM, Child Marriage and Obstetric Fistula
Registered charity number: 292403
Suite 2.1 Chandelier Building
8 Scrubs Lane
London NW10 6RB
Telephone: +44 (0)20 8960 4000
E-mail: forward@forwarduk.org.uk

Leyla Hussein

Leyla's Therapy and Consultancy
Working Towards Ending Violence Against Women And Girls
Psychotherapist/Lead Campaigner and Consultant
Co-Founder Of Daughters Of Eve, Hawa's Haven and Dahlia's Project
www.leylahussein.com
Email: see http://leylahussein.com/contact-leyla/

Africans Unite against Child Abuse (AFRUCA)

Head Office London
Unit 3D/F Leroy House 436 Essex Road
London N1 3QP
Telephone: 0207 704 2261
Fax: 0207 704 2266

Manchester
AFRUCA Centre for Children and Families
Phoenix Mill, 20 Piercy Street, Ancoats
Manchester M4 7HY
Telephone: 0161 205 9274
Fax: 0161 205 2156

New Step for African Community (NESTAC)

237 Newstead
Lower Falinge
Rochdale OL12 6RQ
Telephone: 01706 868993
Email: see http://www.nestac.org/contact/contact.html

FGM National Clinical Group

A multidisciplinary group of healthcare professionals, advisors and academia
Website: http://www.fgmresource.com
Telephone: +44 (0)779 146 2415
Email: info@fgmnationalgroup.org

The Dhalia Project

Manor Gardens Centre
6-9 Manor Gardens
London N7 6LA
Telephone: 020 7561 5263
Email: admin@manorgardenscentre.org

FGM National Clinical Group

Telephone: +44 (0)779 146 2415
Email: info@fgmnationalgroup.org

**6.111** Practitioners may also wish to be aware of the following academic experts:

Dr Anita Schroven

Research Fellow, the Max Planck Institute for Social Anthropology (Germany)
Expertise on West Africa (Guinea, Sierra Leone, Liberia)
Telephone: +49 (0) 345 29 27 180
Email: schroven@eth.mpg.de
Website: http://www.eth.mpg.de/schroven

Dexter Dias QC

Garden Court Chambers
57–60 Lincoln's Inn Fields
London, WC2A 3LJ
Telephone: 020 7993 7600
dexterdiasqc@gmail.com

Professor Alison Macfarlane

Professor of Perinatal Health
City University London
Northampton Square
London EC1V 0HB
Telephone: +44 (0)207 040 5832
A.J.Macfarlane@city.ac.uk

Academic researchers the Multisectorial Academic Program to prevent and combat female Genital Mutilation (FGM/C)

http://mapfgm.eu/researchers/

## The expert's report

**6.112** The duties of an expert are set out in FPR 2010, Part 25, supplemented by PD25B. The contents of the expert's report are prescribed by PD25B, para 9.1. An expert instructed in children proceedings has 'an overriding duty to the court that takes precedence over any obligation to the person from whom the expert takes instructions or by whom the expert is paid', PD25B, para 3.1.

PD25B, para 4.1 states that among any other duties an expert may have, an expert shall have regard to the following duties:

'(a)   to assist the court in accordance with the overriding duty;

(aa)   to comply with the Standards for Expert Witnesses in Children Proceedings in the Family Court, which are set out in the Annex to PD25B;

(b)    to provide advice to the court that conforms to the best practice of the expert's profession;

(c)    to answer the questions about which the expert is required to give an opinion (in children proceedings, those questions will be set out in the order of the court giving permission for an expert to be instructed, a child to be examined or otherwise assessed or expert evidence to be put before the court);

(d)    to provide an opinion that is independent of the party or parties instructing the expert;

(e)    to confine the opinion to matters material to the issues in the case and in relation only to questions that are within the expert's expertise (skill and experience);

(f)    where a question has been put which falls outside the expert's expertise, to state this at the earliest opportunity and to volunteer an opinion as to whether another expert is required to bring expertise not possessed by those already involved or, in the rare case, as to whether a second opinion is required on a key issue and, if possible, what questions should be asked of the second expert;

(g)    in expressing an opinion, to take into consideration all of the material facts including any relevant factors arising from ethnic, cultural, religious or linguistic contexts at the time the opinion is expressed;

(h)    to inform those instructing the expert without delay of any change in the opinion and of the reason for the change.'

## CASE-LAW AND PRACTICAL CONSIDERATIONS

**6.113**   In *Fornah v Secretary of State for the Home Department*,[102] Lord Justice Auld described FGM as an internationally condemned practice that clearly violates Article 3 of the European Convention for the Protection of Human Rights and Fundament Freedoms 1950. The judgment was in respect of an appeal against the Secretary of State's refusal to grant asylum. Lord Justice Auld went on to observe that FGM is not peculiar to Sierra Leone but is so 'widespread there and so bound up in the culture and traditions of that country at all levels that it causes difficulties in claims for asylum by young Sierra Leonean girls who fear it'.[103]

## Inherent jurisdiction and wardship

**6.114**   Paragraph 16 of Schedule 2 to the 2003 Act recognises that the none of the provisions in the 2003 Act interfere with the inherent jurisdiction of the High Court. The multi-agency statutory guidance recognises the ongoing use of the inherent jurisdiction of the High Court is cases in which orders under that jurisdiction may be necessary.[104]

---

[102]  [2005] 2 FLR 1085 at para 1.
[103]  [2005] 2 FLR 1085 at para 1.
[104]  Multi-agency statutory guidance on female genital mutilation, HM Government (April 2016).

**6.115** A local authority may only apply for an order under the High Court's inherent jurisdiction if it has permission from the court to do so (under s 100 of the Children Act 1989). Leave to apply may only be granted by the court if it is satisfied that the result the local authority wishes to achieve could not be attained through the making of any order, other than one under the court's inherent jurisdiction. A local authority is entitled to apply for this where they have reasonable cause to believe that if the court's inherent jurisdiction is not exercised, the child is likely to suffer significant harm.

**6.116** Orders under the inherent jurisdiction are flexible and wide-ranging, and an order may be sought where there is a real risk of a child being subjected to FGM. A children's social care department or any person with a genuine interest in the child can apply to have a child made a ward of court.

**6.117** In international cases, where the girl to be protected is at risk of being taken overseas or has already been taken out of the jurisdiction, the inherent jurisdiction of the High Court has continued to be used alongside the civil protection orders in order to protect girls at risk. Upon making the FGM protection order within the inherent jurisdiction proceedings, the High Court may go on to consider other ancillary orders such as Tipstaff passport orders, location orders, telecoms orders and orders against public bodies.

**6.118** Where necessary the court can also exercise its wardship jurisdiction. Where there is a fear that a child may be taken overseas for the purpose of FGM, an order for the surrender of their passport may be made as well as an order that the child may not leave the jurisdiction without the court's permission. Once a young person has left the country, there are fewer legal options open to police, social services, other agencies or another person to recover the young person and bring them back to the UK. Orders for the immediate return of the child or young person can be obtained and can be enforced on family members or extended family members. The orders are in the form of injunctions with penal notices attached.

**6.119** One course of action is to seek the return of the young person to the jurisdiction of England and Wales by making them a ward of court. Making a child a ward of court falls within the inherent jurisdiction of the High Court. An application for wardship is made to the High Court Family Division, and may be made by a relative, friend close to the child or young person or CAFCASS/CAFCASS CYMRU legal services department or any interested party.

## The Foreign & Commonwealth Office and the Forced Marriage Unit

**6.120** The UK's Forced Marriage Unit (FMU), based within the Foreign & Commonwealth Office (FCO) has seen cases involving 90 countries since 2005 and helped 1,200 individuals in 2015.[105] The experience and expertise of the FMU continues to play a crucial role in international cases. The FMU has now appointed a Lead on FGM.[106] The advice of the FMU should be sought in such cases and particularly in circumstances where individuals at risk may be taken out of the jurisdiction or may already be overseas.

**6.121**  Where liaison with an embassy or consulate is required, practitioners should consult the relevant guidance from the President of the Family Division.[107]

## Liaison with embassies

**6.122**  If the girl to be protected is not a British national, or if there is no British diplomatic assistance available in the country of concern, a further step which should be considered is liaising with an appropriate foreign embassy to seek assistance as appropriate. Where liaison with an embassy or consulate is required, practitioners should consult the relevant guidance from the President of the Family Division.[108]

**6.123**  The multi-agency statutory guidance on FGM makes clear that when a British national seeks assistance at a British Embassy or High Commission overseas and wishes to return to the UK, the FCO will do all it can to repatriate and facilitate the individual's return to the United Kingdom. The FCO may assist in providing emergency travel documents, in some exceptional circumstances helping to arrange flights and, where possible, by helping to find temporary safe accommodation while the victim is overseas. However, the FCO does not pay for repatriation.[109]

**6.124**  They will normally ask the person or trusted friends to fund the cost of repatriation. In some cases, repatriation has been funded by schools or social services. However, this should never delay the process of getting the individual to safety.[110]

**6.125**  Sometimes the FCO may ask the police or social services for assistance when a British national is being repatriated to the UK from overseas.[111] The

---

[105] http://uksaysnomore.org/fgm-forced-marriage-summer-holidays-support/.
[106] Ms Sophie Lotte.
[107] 'Liaison between Courts in England and Wales and British Embassies and High Commissions Abroad', *Guidance from the President's Office* (April 2016).
[108] 'Liaison between Courts in England and Wales and British Embassies and High Commissions Abroad', *Guidance from the President's Office* (April 2016).
[109] Multi-agency statutory guidance on female genital mutilation, HM Government (April 2016), para E6.
[110] Multi-agency statutory guidance on female genital mutilation, HM Government (April 2016), para E6.
[111] Multi-agency statutory guidance on female genital mutilation, HM Government (April 2016), para E6.

FCO or social services may ask the police to meet the person on arrival, in case family members try to abduct them at the airport.[112]

**6.126**  In many cases a victim of FGM may be extremely vulnerable, because of their age, the country in which they are located or their personal circumstance. If the FCO is able to repatriate them, it may not be able to give the police or social services much, if any, notice of the person's arrival due to the urgency of the situation.[113] Sometimes a person may have risked their life to escape and their family may go to considerable lengths to find them. She may be extremely traumatised and frightened. These factors can make individuals particularly vulnerable when they return to the UK and it is likely that urgent multi-agency consideration of the level of risk faced by a victim of FGM will be appropriate.[114]

**6.127**  Many FGM cases involve children under the age of 16. In such cases, to assist the victim to return to the UK, the support and assistance of UK agencies (such as police and social services) will be essential and assistance from overseas authorities seized with safeguarding duties is also likely to be necessary. In some countries this could be the police, but in others it may be the Ministry for Children or even Health. Supporting repatriation of FGM victims under 16 without the support of at least one person with parental responsibility or the safeguarding authorities in-country may be very difficult and drawn out.

## Office of International Family Justice

**6.128**  In certain circumstances, particularly where practitioners are dealing with a country that is not party to the Hague Convention[115] and enquiries need to be made in respect of enforceability and/or the provision of mirror orders, an approach may be made in the first instance to the Office of International Family Justice.[116] This may assist in establishing whether there is a liaison judge in the country where a person at risk may be. The office can be contacted by email: ifjoffice@hmcts.gsi.gov.uk. The legal adviser to the Head of International Family Justice can be contacted by telephone: 020 7947 7197.

**6.129**  Lady Justice Black was appointed Head of International Family Justice for England and Wales in 2013. The Office deals with a range of legal queries and correspondence from both internal and external sources (judges in this country and abroad, practitioners, officials in the field of international family law and academics). It liaises directly with European Judicial Network and Hague Network judicial contacts, for the purposes of assisting, where possible,

---

[112] Multi-agency statutory guidance on female genital mutilation, HM Government (April 2016), para E6.
[113] Multi-agency statutory guidance on female genital mutilation, HM Government (April 2016), para E6.
[114] Multi-agency statutory guidance on female genital mutilation, HM Government (April 2016), para E6.
[115] 1980 Hague Convention on the Civil Aspects of International Child Abduction.
[116] HM Courts and Tribunals, International Family Justice:https://www.judiciary.gov.uk/about-the-judiciary/international/international-family-justice/.

in the smooth-running of cross-border cases. It also liaises with the Ministry of Justice, the Foreign & Commonwealth Office, and the International Child Abduction and Contact Unit, as well as European and International bodies. The work of the Office involves providing assistance of various sorts, on a range of matters. These include:

(a)   international family law issues arising in individual cases, including in cross-border public law (care) cases relating to children, and in international child abduction and relocation cases;

(b)   issues arising under Brussels IIA, the 1980 Hague Convention and the 1996 Hague Convention as well as other European regulations and international conventions;

(c)   the shaping of developments in European and international family law, practice and policy;

(d)   domestic and international seminars/conferences.


## INTERNATIONAL CASES

**6.130**   *Re F and X (Children)*[117] concerned F (a girl) and X (a boy) who had been taken from the United Kingdom, where they had spent their entire lives to date, to the Sudan at the beginning of their summer holidays in 2015. The mother returned to the jurisdiction at the end of August without the children, against the wishes of their father who remained in UK. The children had been left with the mother's maternal family and enrolled in school in Sudan.

**6.131**   The matter was drawn to the attention of the local authority, Kent County Council, by F's schoolteacher, following an email from the subject girl from Sudan expressing that she was concerned that she had not returned with her mother at the end of the summer holidays as had been planned.[118]

**6.132**   The father had grave concerns that there were plans for F to be subjected to FGM and he further stated that all of the women in the maternal family in Sudan had been cut. According to statistical data from UNICEF, the percentage of girls and women aged 15–49 years who have undergone FGM (between 2004–2015) is 87%.[119]

**6.133**   The local authority, Kent County Council, made an application under the inherent jurisdiction and under the 2003 Act, contending that if F remained in the Sudan she would be subject to FGM.

**6.134**   Mr Justice Baker found that on the evidence placed before the court by the local authority and the respondent father, there were real grounds of

---

[117]   [2015] EWHC 2653 (Fam).
[118]   Judge makes new-style FGM order to protect girl (13), *The Independent*, 10 September 2015.
[119]   http://www.unicef.org/media/files/FGMC_2016_brochure_final_UNICEF_SPREAD.pdf.

concern that F would be subject to FGM.[120] Mr Justice Baker therefore made an FGM protection order, as well as an order for the children to be made Wards of the High Court. The respondent mother, having accepted that she had unlawfully retained the children in Sudan, was initially directed to take all reasonable steps to arrange for the children's return to this jurisdiction.[121] The mother was also directed to arrange for the children to be presented as soon as possible to the British Embassy in Khartoum.[122] When those directions were not complied with, the local authority sought to initiate committal proceedings but with the clear indication that the application would be significantly affected by the mother's response to the orders of the court.[123]

**6.135** As the postscript to the judgment reflects, the children were returned on 2 October 2015. The short judgment demonstrates the effectiveness of the targeted use of FGM protection orders alongside the jurisdiction of the High Court. The case also underlines the important role of school teachers in reporting matters to the authorities without delay. In that regard it also reflects the importance of the new rules on mandatory reporting as regulated by the Education Workforce Council.[124]

**6.136** The international aspects of FGM were drawn into sharp focus in the matter of Re FGMPO; diplomatic immunity.[125] The High Court ordered that the baby daughter of a West African diplomat based in London must not be removed from England after her mother reported that she was at risk of being subjected to genital cutting.

**6.137** The mother, who was herself subjected to FGM at the age of 12, told the court that a relative's baby had died after enduring the practice. She also stated: 'I just want my child to be safe. Right now my family has disowned me. They ask, "Why did you go to the police?" They are laughing at me'.[126]

**6.138** Mr Justice Keehan approved the protection order to remain enacted until a full hearing. The child was made a Ward of the High Court. Mr Justice Keehan requested the Secretary of State to issue a certificate under s 4 of the Diplomatic Privileges Act 1964, confirming that the respondent father had entitlement to immunity. The applicant local authority requested the United Kingdom government to seek a waiver of the diplomat's immunity; the request was subsequently granted.

**6.139** In the matter of *Re E (Female Genital Mutilation and Permission to Remove)*,[127] Mr Justice MacDonald heard a mother's application for FGM

---

[120] [2015] EWHC 2653 (Fam) at para 3.
[121] [2015] EWHC 2653 (Fam) at para 4.
[122] [2015] EWHC 2653 (Fam) at para 4.
[123] [2015] EWHC 2653 (Fam) at para 9.
[124] 2003 Act (n 2) s 5B(2)(a), (11) and (12).
[125] *The Times*, 1 March 2016.
[126] *The Times*, 1 March 2016.
[127] [2016] EWHC 1052 (Fam).

protection orders in relation to her three children: SE (13), FE (10) and CE (7), alongside the father's application for permission for the children to relocate in Nigeria. Mr Justice MacDonald presided over the fact-finding and welfare hearing in respect of both applications. The parties married in Nigeria in 2001. The mother is a member of the Igbo ethnic group in Nigeria. The father is a member of a sub-group of the Igbo known as the Delta Igbo in Nigeria. In December 2012 they travelled to the United Kingdom (UK) with their children under a two year visitors' visa. The father returned soon after. The mother later sought to secure her immigration status in the UK.

**6.140**   On 21 January 2014 she applied for leave to remain on the basis of EU national spousal rights, having allegedly married a Lithuanian national. Her purported marriage was found to be a sham marriage, designed to help her secure her immigration status in the UK. Her application was therefore rejected. The mother's subsequent appeal was rejected on 26 June 2015 and shortly afterwards on 15 July 2015 she raised allegations of FGM against the father. At the same time she suspended contact between the father and the children.

**6.141**   The Mother secured an FGM protection order for all three children having made an ex parte application before Mrs Justice Hogg on 22 July 2015. The FGM protection order was renewed on 24 July 2015 by Mr Justice Holman at hearing. The father did not attend and was not represented. Mr Justice Holman relied on the mother's sworn evidence, which alleged that she had been forced into marriage and that she and the children had been subjected to extensive abuse by the father. The mother also alleged that the father sought to subject the children to FGM. Within his judgment, set out in *Re E (Children) (Female Genital Mutilation Protection Orders)*[128] Holman J noted:

> 'I stress, of course, that at the moment this is simply the one-sided account of the mother, and the respondent father may in due course file and serve different and contradictory evidence. But clearly, if what the mother says is true or substantially true, there is currently a very high risk indeed to one or more of these three vulnerable girls that they may be forced, just as their mother was, into undergoing some form of genital mutilation.'

**6.142**   It was in that context that the matter fell for final determination by Mr Justice MacDonald. In defining 'female genital mutilation' MacDonald J adopted the classification system from the World Health Organisation as had been the example set by the President of the Family Division in *Re B and G (Children) (No 2)*.[129]

**6.143**   After hearing all the evidence from both parties Mr Justice MacDonald determined that the mother's allegations, including the allegations of forced marriage and abuse, had not been proven and that her evidence lacked

---

[128] [2015] EWHC 2275 (Fam).
[129] [2015] EWFC 3. See *Re E (Female Genital Mutilation and Permission to Remove)* [2016] EWHC 1052 (Fam) at para 58.

credibility. In relation to FGM, Mr Justice MacDonald found that the father did not intend to subject the children to FGM in Nigeria.[130]

**6.144**   The judge examined statistics detailing the prevalence of FGM in Nigeria. In particular the judge considered the UNICEF Nigeria FGM/C Country Profile (UNICEF 2003), UNICEF *Statistical profile on female genital mutilation/Cutting* (2013).[131] Mr Justice MacDonald noted:

> 'Care must, of course, be taken with statistics. It is important that the court decides the case on the evidence before it in relation to the subject child or children in question. However, treated with appropriate caution, statistics can help to provide context and, in some circumstances, can serve to corroborate or undermine certain evidence. Within this context I note that the aforementioned statistical surveys indicate that Nigeria has the lowest level of FGM performed after the age of 14 years (16 per cent) and that over 90 per cent of Igbo girls on whom FGM is performed have it performed in early infancy (there appears to be no data in respect of the sub-group of Delta Igbo).'[132]

**6.145**   After considering all the evidence Mr Justice MacDonald found that there was no evidence to support the mother's allegation that the father intended to subject the children to FGM in Nigeria.[133] She had entered into a sham marriage and made false claims of FGM to support her asylum application.[134] Whilst it was not determinative, the judge also noted the family originate from an area of Nigeria that was one of the first to experience campaigns against FGM and that the practice is now a criminal offence in Nigeria pursuant to the Violence against Persons Prohibition Act 2015.[135]

**6.146**   The practice of FGM amongst the father's community was decreasing and although his own mother had been subjected to it, his sister had not (contrary to the mother's allegation). The current age of the children further mitigated any risk of FGM. The evidence before the court was that Nigeria had the lowest level of FGM performed after the age of four years (16%).[136]

**6.147**   The judge also considered the Department of Health *Female Genital Mutilation Risk and Safeguarding Guidance for Professionals* and the chapter on FGM in the 5th edition of *London Safeguarding Children Board London Child Protection Procedures* (2015). The judge paid close regard to the indices of risk set out in those publications.[137]

**6.148**   The judge found that the mother had not been subjected to FGM at the hands of the paternal family. The mother had claimed that she was a victim of

---

[130]   [2016] EWHC 1052 (Fam) at para 93.
[131]   UNICEF *Statistical profile on female genital mutilation/Cutting* (2013).
[132]   [2016] EWHC 1052 (Fam) at para 55.
[133]   [2016] EWHC 1052 (Fam) at para 93.
[134]   [2016] EWHC 1052 (Fam) at para 111.
[135]   [2016] EWHC 1052 (Fam) at para 93.
[136]   [2016] EWHC 1052 (Fam) at para 99.
[137]   [2016] EWHC 1052 (Fam) at para 56.

Type II FGM but was inconsistent as to whether this had taken place prior to or after the marriage. Independent medical evidence was that she had been subject to a less severe form of FGM (Type I). The court accepted the father's evidence that this had not been perpetrated by him or his family.[138]

**6.149**  Finally, pursuant to s 13(1)(b) of the Children Act 1989, Mr Justice MacDonald granted the father's application to permanently remove the children to Nigeria.[139]

[138] [2016] EWHC 1052 (Fam) at para 94.
[139] [2016] EWHC 1052 (Fam) at para 118.

# CHAPTER 7

# MANDATORY REPORTING

**7.1**    The Serious Crime Act 2015 (the 2015 Act) imposed a mandatory duty on health and social care professionals and teachers to report to the police 'known' cases of FGM.[1]

**7.2**    The new duty places an obligation on regulated professionals who discover a known case of FGM in the course of their work to report such a discovery to the police. The duty is applicable only in cases where the FGM is discovered in girls under the age of 18. Mandatory reporting applies only in England and Wales and came into force on 31 October 2014. To assist regulated professionals in interpreting their obligations under the Act, the Home Office has published a helpful report, Mandatory Reporting of Female Genital Mutilation – Procedural Information, referred to below as the Home Office Report.

**7.3**    The legislation clarifies professionals' responsibility with respect to reporting cases, as well as aiding police in their investigation of FGM to increase the prosecution of its perpetrators. Mandatory reporting is intended to supplement and strengthen the existing safeguarding framework. It does not replace any safeguarding responsibilities, as professionals are still obliged to undertake safeguarding actions as required.[2]

**7.4**    The professional is only under a duty to report the 'known' case to the police in two circumstances. First, 'where the girl informs the person that an act of female genital mutilation (however described) has been carried out on her.'[3] Alternatively, the duty arises where: (a) the person observes physical signs on the girl appearing to show an act of female genital mutilation has been carried out on her, and (b) the person has no reason to believe that the act was, or was part of, a legitimate surgical operation.[4]

---

[1]    In December 2014, Government launched a consultation on the introduction of mandatory reporting of FGM. It ran until 30 September 2015. See HM Government, *Summary of responses, Consultation on the draft statutory multi-agency practice guidance on Female Genital Mutilation (FGM)* (April 2016), p 2.
[2]    Jon Rouse, Department of Health, NCAS Conference 2015.
[3]    2003 Act, Sch 2, para 2; s 5B(3) (as inserted by s 73 of the 2015 Act).
[4]    2003 Act, Sch 2, para 2; s 5B(4) (as inserted by s 73 of the 2015 Act).

# REGULATED PROFESSIONALS

**7.5**    The duty applies to all regulated professionals (as defined in s 5B(2)(a), (11) and (12) of the 2003 Act) working within health or social care, and the teaching profession.

**7.6**    The duty covers health and social care professionals regulated by a body overseen by the Professional Standards Authority for Health and Social Care, including the General Chiropractic Council, General Dental Council General Medical Council, General Optical Council, General Osteopathic Council, General Pharmaceutical Council, Nursing and Midwifery Council, Health and Care Professions Council, whose role includes the regulation of social workers in England. All social workers in Wales are covered by the legislation.[5]

**7.7**    There is also an obligation on all qualified teachers or persons employed or engaged in carrying out teaching work in schools and other institutions.[6] In Wales, the obligation extends to all educational practitioners regulated by the Education Workforce Council.[7]

**7.8**    The duty applies to professionals regardless of whether they are employed in the private or public sector, as long as they are working as a regulated professional. As the mandatory reporting duty applies only in England and Wales, health or social care professionals and teachers working in Scotland and Northern Ireland are not affected by this legislation.

## A legal duty to report

**7.9**    The 2003 Act, as amended by the 2015 Act, places a legal duty on health and social care professionals and teachers in England and Wales to notify the police when, in the course of their work:

> '5B(2)(b) a person discovers that an act of female genital mutilation appears to have been carried out on a girl in either of the following two cases.

> (3)    The first case is where the girl informs the person that an act of female genital mutilation (however described) has been carried out on her.
> (4)    The second case is where—
>     (a)    The person observes physical signs on the girl appearing to show that an act of female genital mutilation has been carried out on her, and

---

[5]    2003 Act, Sch 2, para 2; s 5B(11) (as inserted by s 73 of the 2015 Act) defines a 'social care worker' as a person registered in a register maintained by the Care Council for Wales under s 56 of the Care Standards Act 2000.

[6]    2003 Act, Sch 2, para 2; s 5B(11)(a) (as inserted by s 73 of the 2015 Act) defines a 'teacher' as a person within s 141A(1) of the Education Act 2002 (persons employed or engaged to carry out teaching work at schools and other institutions in England).

[7]    2003 Act, Sch 2, para 2; s 5B(11)(b) (as inserted by s 73 of the 2015 Act) defines a teacher as a person who falls within a category listed in the table in para 1 of Sch 2 to the Education (Wales) Act 2014 (anaw 5) (categories of registration for purposes of Part 2 of that Act) or any other person employed or engaged as a teacher at a school (within the meaning of the Education Act 1996) in Wales.

(b)  The person has no reason to believe that the act was, or was part of, a surgical operation within section 1(2)(a) or (b).'[8]

**7.10**  A regulated professional is placed under a personal duty. It requires the professional himself or herself to notify the police following the discovery that an act of FGM appears to have been carried out. The duty to report cannot be transferred to another, not even the professional's designated safeguarding lead. However, there is no need to make a duplicative report if someone else in the profession has already made one.

**7.11**  Importantly, in making a report, the professional cannot be held in breach of any confidentiality requirements or restrictions on disclosure.[9]

**7.12**  The girl is considered an under-18 for the purposes of the mandatory reporting duty if she is under 18 at the time of the disclosure or identification of the FGM.[10] In other words, it does not apply where a woman aged over 18 discloses that she had FGM when she was under 18. Nor does the duty apply where a sibling, parent or guardian discloses that a girl has had FGM.[11] In each of these circumstances, the professional should handle the disclosure in line with their wider safeguarding responsibilities. A record of the discussion should be kept and the information shared with the Multi-Agency Safeguarding Hub, if available.[12] In Wales, the disclosure would be referred to the local authority.[13]

**7.13**  Alongside the mandatory reporting duty, healthcare professionals in England must also place an indicator on the girl's health record using the FGM Risk Indication System (FGM RIS). 'This indicator will be accessible to all healthcare professionals throughout childhood, highlighting that they need to consider the potential risk of FGM as and when they provide care, as well as whether they need to take any action in this regard.'[14] Finally, the healthcare professional must notify his or her organisation in order for the information to be included in the national FGM Enhanced Dataset collated by the Health and Social Care Information Centre. The dataset is only published in aggregate form in order to ensure that a woman or child's personal data remain confidential. Importantly 'the collection of this data will not trigger individual criminal investigations.'[15]

---

[8]  2003 Act, Sch 2, para 2; s 5B(2)–(4) (as inserted by s 73 of the 2015 Act).

[9]  2003 Act, Sch 2, para 2; s 5B(7) (as inserted by s 73 of the 2015 Act).

[10]  2003 Act, Sch 2, para 2; s 5B(1) (as inserted by s 73 of the 2015 Act).

[11]  2003 Act, Sch 2, para 2; s 5B(3) (as inserted by s 73 of the 2015 Act).

[12]  Multi-agency statutory guidance on female genital mutilation, HM Government (April 2016), pp 49–50.

[13]  Multi-agency statutory guidance on female genital mutilation, HM Government (April 2016), pp 49–50.

[14]  Department of Health, *Female genital mutilation risk and safeguarding, guidance for professionals* (May 2016), p 17.

[15]  Department of Health, *Female genital mutilation prevention programme, understanding the FGM Enhanced dataset, updated guidance and clarification to support implementation* (September 2015), p 3.

## Identifying 'physical signs'

**7.14**  The duty only applies to regulated professionals who discover cases in the course of their work. If a professional does not currently undertake genital examinations in the course of their work, then the law does not require them to start doing so. The Home Office report recognises that professionals will only find physical signs that appear to be FGM 'as a secondary result of undertaking another action.'[16]

**7.15**  The duty arises where healthcare professionals see physical signs that appear to show a child has undergone FGM. The Home Office guidance makes clear that practitioners are not expected to be 100% certain that FGM has been carried out, and that it is not necessary to carry out a full clinical diagnosis confirming FGM before a report is made.[17]

**7.16**  For teachers and social workers, the circumstances where physical signs are identified will be far more limited. It is possible that a nursery teacher helping a child in the toilet or changing a nappy may see physical signs that appear to show that FGM may have taken place. In such circumstances, the teacher must make a report under the duty, but should not conduct any further examination of the child's genitals.[18]

## THE REPORT

**7.17**  A regulated professional under a duty to report (having been told by a child that FGM has been carried out on her, or having identified physical signs that appear to show FGM has occurred) must notify the police force from the area where the girl lives.

**7.18**  The Home Office Report suggests that the regulated professional call the non-emergency number, 101.[19] Information regarding the name, profession, and contact details of the person making the report, as well as the name, age, and address of the girl should be given to the police force.

**7.19**  It may also be relevant to tell the police force of any safeguarding actions that have been undertaken or will be undertaken with regards to the girl and any other children who may be at risk.

---

[16]  Home Office, *Mandatory reporting of female genital mutilation: procedural information* (October 2015), p 5.

[17]  Home Office, *Mandatory reporting of female genital mutilation: procedural information* (October 2015), p 5.

[18]  Home Office, *Mandatory reporting of female genital mutilation: procedural information* (October 2015), p 5.

[19]  Home Office, *Mandatory reporting of female genital mutilation: procedural information* (October 2015), p 6.

## When to report

**7.20** The police should be notified as soon as possible after a case is discovered. The Home Office Report considers 'best practice' as making the report 'by the close of the next working day' and advises that practitioners act 'with at least the same urgency as is required by your local safeguarding processes'.[20]

**7.21** However, the 2015 Act allows for a report to be made a maximum of one month from the time of the discovery in exceptional cases.[21] A case will be considered exceptional if 'a professional has concerns that a report to the police is likely to result in an immediate safeguarding risk to the child (or another child, eg a sibling) and considers that consultation with colleagues or other agencies is necessary prior to the report being made'.[22]

**7.22** Practitioners are advised to keep a written record of circumstances surrounding the initial disclosure or identification of signs consistent with FGM having occurred, as well as any subsequent discussions or decisions. This is particularly important when a decision is made to delay reporting a case to the police, and practitioners may want to seek out their designated safeguard lead before taking such a decision.[23]

## Telling the child's family

**7.23** Consistent with standard safeguarding practice, the girl and her family/guardian should be informed in advance of or simultaneously with the report being made. The Multi-Agency Statutory Guidance sets out a framework for professionals preparing to speak to women or girls affected by FGM, or their family members. Professionals are encouraged to 'understand the appropriate language to use and maintain a professional and non-judgmental approach to engage with the individual in what may be a challenging and upsetting situation.'[24] Using culturally sensitive language and having an awareness of the different terms for FGM in different communities is considered particularly important.[25] Accredited female interpreters should be used whenever possible, and not family members or anyone known to the family.[26]

---

[20]   Home Office, *Mandatory reporting of female genital mutilation: procedural information* (October 2015), p 6.

[21]   2003 Act, Sch 2, para 2; s 5B(5)(c) (as inserted by s 73 of the 2015 Act).

[22]   Home Office, *Mandatory reporting of female genital mutilation: procedural information* (October 2015), p 6.

[23]   Home Office, *Mandatory reporting of female genital mutilation: procedural information* (October 2015), p 6.

[24]   Multi-agency statutory guidance on female genital mutilation, HM Government (April 2016), p 44.

[25]   Multi-agency statutory guidance on female genital mutilation, HM Government (April 2016), p 44.

[26]   Multi-agency statutory guidance on female genital mutilation, HM Government (April 2016), p 44.

**7.24**  If the professional considers that talking to the child's family would place the girl or anyone else at risk of serious harm, then the information should not be disclosed.[27]

## CONTINUING RESPONSIBILITIES FOLLOWING THE REPORT

**7.25**  As discussed above, the mandatory reporting duty operates in conjunction with safeguarding processes and other professional standards. Following a report, the professional will still be expected to act in accordance with these processes and may need to contribute to any multi-agency responses following the report.

**7.26**  Regulated practitioners in Wales should also be mindful of complying with the protocols adopted by all safeguarding boards in Wales, which include a detailed protocol on FGM. Section 130 of the Social Services and Well-being (Wales) Act 2014 also applies to cases where the mandatory reporting duty arises. From April 2016, the local authority in the area where a child is at risk must be informed by where they have reasonable cause to suspect that a child is at risk of abuse, neglect, or other kinds of harm and has need of care and support.[28] This means that professionals who identify cases that fall within the FGM mandatory reporting duty will also need to make a report to the local police force and to the local authority.

**7.27**  This legislation places an obligation on a wide range of professionals, including police officers, probation services and those involved in offender management, as well as teachers and health professionals.[29]

## THE ROLE OF THE POLICE FOLLOWING THE REPORT

**7.28**  Following notification, the police will initiate a multi-agency response. While procedures may vary across the country, children's social care will be consulted prior to the police taking action. The police will have lead responsibility for any criminal investigation, while healthcare services will lead in providing care for the girl's health and wellbeing and social services will be responsible for protecting the girl and any other children identified as being at risk of harm.[30]

---

[27]  Home Office, *Mandatory reporting of female genital mutilation: procedural information* (October 2015), p 8.

[28]  Home Office, *Mandatory reporting of female genital mutilation: procedural information* (October 2015), p 9.

[29]  Social Services and Well-being (Wales) Act 2014, s 162(4).

[30]  Home Office, *Mandatory reporting of female genital mutilation: procedural information* (October 2015), p 10.

**7.29** An option available to the police or local authority is to apply to the court for an FGM Protection Order. As described in chapter 6, this is a civil order aimed at protecting a girl at risk of FGM or a girl on whom an FGM offence has been committed.

## Failure to comply with the duty

**7.30** Where a registered professional fails to comply with the duty to report under the 2003 Act, they will be referred to their professional regulator. As proclaimed by the Home Office Report 'FGM is child abuse, and employers and professional regulators are expected to pay due regard to the seriousness of breaches of the duty.'[31]

## HEALTH AND SOCIAL CARE PROFESSIONALS

**7.31** In the health and social care sector, the failure to comply with the mandatory duty to report FGM will be considered by the relevant professional regulatory body through a Fitness to Practice proceeding. By looking at the case as a whole, the regulator will consider whether the practitioner did not make a report on behalf of a patient who is later identified as having had FGM because he or she did not recognise the physical signs. Ultimately, the regulator will have to consider whether it is appropriate that the professional continue to practice or whether further training or supervision should be put in place.

**7.32** The Home Office Report suggests that regulators issue guidance as to how to act and what action may be taken for failure to report.[32] A recent review of the three largest regulators in the health and social care sector shows that each has issued a statement informing their members of the legislation, but all are light on detail regarding what would occur if a practitioner failed to comply with the reporting duty.

**7.33** The Nursing and Midwifery Council published a statement on their website encouraging their members to review the Home Office Report and warning that 'failure to comply with the duty may result in an investigation of the nurse or midwife's fitness to practice.'[33] The statement also signals that the Nursing and Midwifery Council (NMC) will consider a failure to report as a breach of the requirement 'to take all reasonable steps to protect people who are vulnerable or at risk from harm, neglect or abuse.'[34]

---

[31] Home Office, *Mandatory reporting of female genital mutilation: procedural information* (October 2015), p 11.

[32] Home Office, *Mandatory reporting of female genital mutilation: procedural information* (October 2015), p 3.

[33] Nursing & Midwifery Council, *Additional information on female genital mutilation cases* (October 2015), p 1.

[34] Nursing and Midwifery Council, *Professional standards of practice and behaviour for nurses and midwives* (March 2015), para 17.1.

**7.34** The General Medical Council (GMC) also issued an online 'update' about the new legislation and advised doctors that their new duty to report fits within previously issued guidance on Confidentiality and Protecting Children and Young People.[35] The GMC goes one step further than the NMC, telling its members that failure to follow their 'guidance may put a doctor's registration at risk', meaning a doctor may no longer be able to practice medicine.[36]

**7.35** The Health & Care Professions Council published a statement on their website informing their registrants about the mandatory reporting duty, linking to the Home Office Report and to a package of information developed by the Department of Health.[37] The statement contained no mention of what action would be taken if professionals fail to uphold their mandatory duty to report.

## TEACHING PROFESSIONALS

**7.36** Teachers who fail to comply with the duty to report may face disciplinary action in accordance with their school's staff disciplinary procedures. The duty attaches to anyone who is employed or engaged in carrying out 'teaching work' in the following activities: planning and preparing lessons and courses for pupils; delivering lessons to pupils; and assessing and/or reporting on the development, progress and attainment of pupils.[38]

**7.37** The Home Office Report states that if this results in a teacher being dismissed, or where the teacher resigns prior to being dismissed, the school 'must consider whether to refer the matter to professional regulators, the National College of Teaching and Leadership (NCTL) in England or the Education Workforce Council (EWC) in Wales.'

**7.38** Similar to health and social care regulators, the NCTL and EWC will consider the whole case against the professional to decide whether his or her actions 'amount to unacceptable professional conduct or conduct likely to bring the profession into disrepute' and, if so, will make a prohibition order, preventing the professional from carrying out any teaching work.[39]

**7.39** The Department of Education issued guidance on the mandatory reporting duty in its publication entitled 'Keeping children safe in education'. Noting that it will be 'rare' that teachers see physical signs of FGM, and that teachers should generally not be conducting physical examinations of pupils, the guidelines state that teachers may discover through disclosure by the girl

---

[35]  General Medical Council, *What advice does the does the GMC give* (September 2016), p 1.
[36]  General Medical Council, *What advice does the does the GMC give* (September 2016), p 1.
[37]  Health & Care Professions Council, *Mandatory duty to report female genital mutilation in England and Wales* (October 2015), p 1.
[38]  Home Office, *Mandatory reporting of female genital mutilation: procedural information* (October 2015), p 14. See also the 2003 Act, Sch 2, para 2; s 5B(11) (as inserted by s 73 of the 2015 Act).
[39]  Home Office, *Mandatory reporting of female genital mutilation: procedural information* (October 2015), p 11.

that she has been subjected to FGM. The guidance informs teachers that those who fail 'to report such cases will face disciplinary sanctions'.[40]

## Schools, colleges and universities: additional considerations

**7.40**　The statutory duties on schools and colleges are set out in *Working Together to Safeguard Children* (for England) and *Safeguarding Children – Working Together under the Children's Act 2004* (for Wales) and *Keeping Children Safe in Education* or *Keeping Learners Safe* in Wales. These apply to FGM as to any other form of abuse.

## MANDATORY REPORTING – FIT FOR PURPOSE?

**7.41**　The introduction of mandatory reporting in England and Wales was intended to follow the proactive example set by France, where there has been an intensive campaign of education and girls are systematically examined for signs of FGM during health checks carried out on babies.[41] In the early 1980s, analysis of the examinations showed that if a mother had been 'excised', there was an 80% chance that her daughter would also have been subjected to FGM. A survey in 2007 suggested this had been reduced to 11%.[42]

**7.42**　Despite the progress and new initiatives, research suggests that there is still a long way to go. A 2015 study was undertaken at a district general hospital in London with a high prevalence of patients originating from countries where FGM is practised.[43] The research aimed to assess healthcare professionals' knowledge and confidence in managing FGM, as this underpins their ability to respond adequately to the medical needs of patients with FGM and safeguard girls and young women from the practice. Over 150 healthcare professionals responded to a confidential survey distributed within the hospital from January–March 2014. Over a third were midwives, 45% were doctors, and 19% were nursing staff.

**7.43**　Interestingly, 73% felt there were barriers that prevent healthcare professionals from speaking to patients about FGM. Lack of knowledge of FGM was rated the most important barrier, followed by a language barrier and fear of cultural insensitivity. Over 70% thought they would benefit from further training, and only 21% of respondents said they would feel comfortable discussing FGM with patients. The authors of the research study highlighted the need for specialised communication training provided by those who are

---

[40]　Department of Education, *Keeping children safe in education, Statutory guidance for schools and colleges* (September 2016), p 55.

[41]　Roundtable Discussion on Female Genital Mutilation, House of Commons Home Affairs Select Committee, 6 July 2016, Question 37.

[42]　J Lichfield, 'The French way: a better approach to FGM?', *The Independent*, 15 December 2013.

[43]　R Gabrasadig, F Asamoah, N Wilson, 'Female genital mutilation: knowledge, training and experience of healthcare professionals at a London hospital' (2015) 100 *Archives of Disease in Childhood*, Supplement 3, A23–24.

already familiar with working with women who have suffered FGM.[44] It is possible that imposing a legal duty on healthcare, social care, and teaching professionals may encourage them to learn more about FGM and be less fearful of cultural sensitivities. It may improve the standard and efficacy of training on FGM for these professionals.

**7.44**  However, there continue to be hugely disparate opinions as to whether the introduction of mandatory reporting is an effective solution. Instead of looking to punish professionals, it is argued that specialist training should be provided to health workers on the issues surrounding FGM and that health workers should also educate at-risk women about FGM. It has also been suggested that mandatory screening for FGM risk factors should be incorporated into antenatal care.

**7.45**  The additional difficulty with mandatory reporting provisions is that it remains unclear what additional sanctions a professional would face if he or she failed to make a report contrary to the 2003 Act. The failure to make a report in the circumstances mandated under the Act would mean the professional would also be in breach of current safeguarding procedures. The failure to act in accordance with safeguarding procedures would often lead to the professional facing disciplinary action, so it is hard to know what impact the new legislation will have.

**7.46**  This approach is reflected in the guidance issued by the regulatory bodies, most of who venture little further than reminding their members that the failure to report may result in them being investigated by the regulator. However, it is hard to criticise the regulators for taking such a stance, as the mandatory reporting requirements stop short of imposing criminal sanctions on professionals who fail to report. It is unsurprising then that Janet Fyle, the FGM lead at the Nursing and Midwifery Council, believes that the current iteration of mandatory reporting is not working as 'professionals believe they don't have to do it' and have 'franchised it out to community groups'.[45]

**7.47**  If Fyle is correct, then the mandatory reporting duty will do little to change the attitude of health and social care professionals and teachers towards FGM and instances of FGM will remain undetected and perpetrators unprosecuted.

## INFORMATION SHARING

**7.48**  When dealing with FGM, organisations and professionals should continue to have regard to their wider responsibilities in relation to the

---

[44]  R Gabrasadig, F Asamoah, N Wilson, 'Female genital mutilation: knowledge, training and experience of healthcare professionals at a London hospital' (2015) 100 *Archives of Disease in Childhood* Supplement 3, A23–24.

[45]  Roundtable Discussion on Female Genital Mutilation, House of Commons Home Affairs Select Committee, 6 July 2016, Question 12.

handling and sharing of information. To safeguard children and vulnerable adults in line with relevant statutory requirements and guidance, it may be necessary to share information with other agencies or departments.

**7.49** Chief executives and professionals working in healthcare in England should have due regard to the FGM Enhanced Dataset Information Standard (SCCI2026) which instructs all clinicians on how and what to record in health records when a patient with FGM is identified, including additional details, for example the type of FGM. The standard also instructs upon standardised information sharing protocols to support safeguarding against FGM.

**7.50** The FGM Enhanced Dataset Information Standard also instructs NHS acute and mental health trusts and GP practices on how they should submit data about patients who have FGM to the Health and Social Care Information Centre (HSCIC). HSCIC collects and publishes anonymised statistics on behalf of the Department of Health and NHS England. The information is used nationally and locally to improve the NHS response to FGM and to help commission the services to support women who have experienced FGM and safeguard women and girls at risk of FGM.

**7.51** Personal information held and collected under the FGM Enhanced Dataset Information Standard is not released to anyone outside of HSCIC. If these arrangements were to change, any information which was held prior to such a change would continue to be protected under the current arrangements.

**7.52** Guidance on the recording of FGM and the FGM Enhanced dataset standard is available at www.hscic.gov.uk/fgm.

# CHAPTER 8

# PUBLIC LAW INTERVENTION AND SAFEGUARDING RESPONSIBILITIES

**8.1**   Paragraph 16 of Schedule 2 to the FGM Act 2003 makes it clear the provisions of that Act have no effect on any protection or assistance under the Children Act 1989. Professionals should have regard to their wider safeguarding responsibilities in relation to FGM as well as to the statutory duty in s 5A of the 2003 Act.[1]

**8.2**   In appropriate cases, care proceedings may be issued under the Children Act 1989 when FGM is thought to have been carried out or if a girl is at risk. This may be done either with or without an ancillary FGM protection order.

## RISK FACTORS

**8.3**   The most significant factor to consider when deciding whether a girl or woman may be at risk of FGM is whether her family has a history of practising FGM. In addition, it is important to consider whether FGM is known to be practised in her community or country of origin. The age at which girls undergo FGM varies enormously according to the community. The procedure may be carried out when the girl is newborn, during childhood or adolescence, at marriage or during a first pregnancy.

**8.4**   There are a number of factors in addition to a girl's or woman's community, country of origin and family history, that could indicate she is at risk of being subjected to FGM. Potential risk factors may include:[2]

- a female child is born to a woman who has undergone FGM;
- a female child has an older sibling or cousin who has undergone FGM;
- a female child's father comes from a community known to practise FGM;
- the family indicate that there are strong levels of influence held by elders and/or elders are involved in bringing up female children;
- a woman/family believe FGM is integral to cultural or religious identity;

---

[1]   Multi-agency statutory guidance on female genital mutilation, HM Government (April 2016), section 3.1.5.
[2]   Multi-agency statutory guidance on female genital mutilation, HM Government (April 2016), para B.1.

- a girl/family has limited level of integration within UK community;
- parents have limited access to information about FGM and do not know about the harmful effects of FGM or UK law;
- a girl confides to a professional that she is to have a 'special procedure' or to attend a special occasion to 'become a woman';
- a girl talks about a long holiday to her country of origin or another country where the practice is prevalent;
- parents state that they or a relative will take the girl out of the country for a prolonged period;
- a parent or family member expresses concern that FGM may be carried out on the girl;
- a family is not engaging with professionals (health, education or other);
- a family is already known to social care in relation to other safeguarding issues;
- a girl requests help from a teacher or another adult because she is aware or suspects that she is at immediate risk of FGM;
- a girl talks about FGM in conversation, for example, a girl may tell other children about it. It is important to take into account the context of the discussion;
- a girl from a practising community is withdrawn from Personal, Social, Health and Economic (PSHE) education or its equivalent;
- a girl is unexpectedly absent from school;
- sections are missing from a girl's Red book; and/or
- a girl has attended a travel clinic or equivalent for vaccinations/anti-malarials.

**8.5**    The above is not an exhaustive list of risk factors. There may be additional risk factors specific to particular communities. For example, in certain communities FGM is closely associated to when a girl reaches a particular age.

**8.6**    In the matter of *A London Borough v B and Ors (Female Genital Mutilation: FGM)* HHJ Tolson QC made supervision orders and FGM protection orders at the conclusion of care proceedings involving two girls, one aged 13 and one aged 5. The case came to light when the mother informed a friend of hers that she was concerned as to a trip to Guinea Conakry from where the family originates. The elder child gave an ABE interview to the police, the terms of which were deeply concerning as to the intention which underpinned the trip to Guinea. The concern formulated in the minds of the authorities that the girls were at serious risk of FGM and proceedings were therefore issued.[3]

---

[3]    *A London Borough v B and Ors (Female Genital Mutilation: FGM)* [2016] EWFC B111 (18 October 2016).

**8.7**   Professionals should not assume that all women and girls from a particular community are supportive of, or at risk of FGM. Women who recognise that their ongoing physical and/or psychological problems are a result of having had FGM and women who are involved or highly supportive of FGM advocacy work and eradication programmes may be less likely to support or carry out FGM on their own children. However, any woman may be under pressure from her husband, partner or other family members to allow or arrange for her daughter to undergo FGM. Wider family engagement and discussions with both parents, and potentially wider family members, may be appropriate.[4]

**8.8**   In addition it is important that professionals look out for signs that FGM has already taken place so that the girl or woman receives the care and support she needs to deal with its effects and enquiries can be made about other female family members who may need to be safeguarded from harm.[5]

## MANAGING RISK

**8.9**   The multi-agency statutory guidance reminds practitioners that being born to a mother who has undergone FGM may mean a female child is at greater risk of FGM. This risk can usually be identified at birth as, through ante-natal care and delivery of the child, NHS professionals can and should have identified that the mother has had FGM. Guidance for healthcare professionals on FGM risk and safeguarding is available at: www.gov.uk/government/publications/safeguarding-women-and-girls-at-risk-of-fgm.

**8.10**   FGM can be carried out at any age, so identifying that a girl is at risk of FGM at birth means that safeguarding measures adopted may need to remain in place for a number of years over the course of her childhood.[6] This differs from other forms of harm, and this difference in approach should be recognised when putting in place policies and procedures to protect against FGM.[7]

**8.11**   If the only risk indicator is that a girl's mother has undergone FGM, referral to children's social care may not be appropriate, but other local multi-agency arrangements may be relevant. In such cases, monitoring is important to ensure that agencies respond appropriately if circumstances change and other risk factors arise. Where there is a specific risk, the case should be referred to social care.

---

[4]   Multi-agency statutory guidance on female genital mutilation, HM Government (April 2016), para B.1.

[5]   Multi-agency statutory guidance on female genital mutilation, HM Government (April 2016), para B.1.2

[6]   Multi-agency statutory guidance on female genital mutilation, HM Government (April 2016), para D.1–D.2.

[7]   Multi-agency statutory guidance on female genital mutilation, HM Government (April 2016), para D.1–D.2.

**8.12**   Where a girl or woman, given her individual circumstances, is identified as being at risk of FGM, but the current situation does not indicate that the risk is imminent or significant, appropriate safeguarding actions should be taken, making sure that this information is shared appropriately. This will help to make sure that, if other agencies or professionals have a wider scope or understanding of the child's or woman's circumstances, they will be able to use the most up to date information to consider the risk the girl or woman currently faces.[8]

**8.13**   A girl at risk of FGM may need to be safeguarded over a significant proportion of her childhood, and it is therefore essential that agencies work together to determine the most appropriate safeguarding response.[9] Health professionals and relevant organisations in England, should have regard to the Department of Health guidance for professionals, Female Genital Mutilation Risk and Safeguarding.[10]

## Other family members

**8.14**   Whenever a woman is identified as having had, or being at risk of FGM, consideration must be given not only to whether she is at risk of further harm, but also to whether there are other girls or women in her family or wider unit who may be at risk of FGM.[11] Issues to consider may include the potential need to:

- share information about an adult related to or known to the child or vulnerable adult in relation to whom safeguarding action is being taken;
- share information about a girl or young woman who the professional does not have a direct relationship with, eg the elder daughter of a pregnant woman who a midwife is treating.

---

[8]   Multi-agency statutory guidance on female genital mutilation, HM Government (April 2016), para D.2.2
[9]   Multi-agency statutory guidance on female genital mutilation, HM Government (April 2016), para D.1–D.2.
[10]   www.gov.uk/government/publications/safeguarding-women-and-girls-at-risk-of-fgm.
[11]   Multi-agency statutory guidance on female genital mutilation, HM Government (April 2016), para D.2.7.

## POLICE PROTECTION

**8.15**   A local authority concerned about the possible risk of FGM on a child may seek a joint investigation with the police.[12] This can be particularly effective where it is thought that a girl or young woman is at immediate risk of FGM.[13]

**8.16**   Where there is reasonable cause to believe that a child would otherwise be likely to suffer significant harm, a police officer may remove that child from the parent(s) and use the powers for 'police protection' for up to 72 hours. The police must inform children's social care who must assist in finding safe and secure accommodation for the girl or young woman if requested to do so.[14]

**8.17**   Children's social care must assist the police, by arranging a placement for the child or young person in a place of safety, taking into account risk management and safety planning, whether this is in local authority accommodation provided by children's social care, on their behalf, or in a refuge. Local authority children's social care must commence child protection enquiries under s 47 of the Children Act 1989 when they are informed that a child who lives, or is found in their area, is in police protection.[15] They must also do so if they are told that the child is the subject of an emergency protection order, or they have reasonable cause to suspect that a child who lives, or is found, in their area is suffering or likely to suffer significant harm.

## EMERGENCY PROTECTION ORDERS

**8.18**   In urgent cases the court is able to make an Emergency Protection Order (EPO) under s 44 of the Children Act 1989. An application for an EPO can be made by anyone including local authorities, police, youth workers, advocates or friends of the girl or young woman. In practice it is usually made by the local authority.

**8.19**   An EPO authorises the applicant to remove the girl and keep her in safe accommodation, but this power can only be exercised in order to safeguard the girl's welfare. In addition, the EPO operates to require any person in a position to do so to comply with any request to produce the child to the applicant.

**8.20**   The multi-agency statutory guidance makes clear that an EPO may also include directions as to the medical examination of the child (or that such

---

[12]   The way in which this is to be handled should be covered in the procedures prepared by the Local Safeguarding Children Board and in accordance with *Working Together to Safeguard Children (for England) and Safeguarding Children – Working Together under the Children's Act 2004* (for Wales).

[13]   Multi-agency statutory guidance on female genital mutilation, HM Government (April 2016), para E.1.

[14]   Children Act 1989, s 46.

[15]   Children Act 1989, s 47(1)(a)(ii).

examinations should not take place), although if the child is of sufficient understanding to make an informed decision, she may refuse to submit to such an examination.

**8.21** An EPO lasts for a period not exceeding eight days, but it may be renewed for up to a further seven days.

## CARE ORDERS AND SUPERVISION ORDERS

**8.22** The multi-agency statutory guidance endorses the use of Care Orders or Supervision Orders (ss 31 and 38 of the Children Act 1989) in appropriate FGM cases.[16]

**8.23** Without either a Care Order or an Interim Care Order, once the EPO has lapsed, the local authority will no longer have parental responsibility.

**8.24** Care proceedings may be issued with or without an ancillary FGM Protection Order. Whilst the 2003 Act defines girls to include adult, for the purpose of the Children Act's jurisdiction to make care or supervision orders, no care order or supervision order may be made with respect to a child who has reached the age of seventeen (or sixteen, in the case of a child who is married).[17]

**8.25** When a Care Order or Supervision Order is not available due to the age of the child, children's social care should be aware of the opportunities presented by an FGM Protection Order or by making a child a ward of court, under the inherent jurisdiction of the High Court. A Ward of Court Order is available up to 18 years old. A child who is the subject of a Care Order cannot be made a ward of court.[18]

## Actual or likely significant harm

**8.26** Section 31 of the Children Act 1989 sets out the legal basis or the 'threshold criteria' on which a Family Court can make a Care Order or Supervision Order to a designated Local Authority in relation to a child. Section 31(2) states that:

> 'A court may only make a care order or supervision order if it is satisfied:
>
> (a)    that the child concerned is suffering, or is likely to suffer, significant harm; and
> (b)    that the harm, or likelihood of harm, is attributable to:

---

[16]    Multi-agency statutory guidance on female genital mutilation, HM Government (April 2016), Section 3.1.5.
[17]    Children Act 1989, s 31(3).
[18]    Multi-agency statutory guidance on female genital mutilation, HM Government (April 2016), Section 3.1.5.

(i)     the care given to the child, or likely to be given to him if the order were not made, not being what it would be reasonable to expect a parent to give to him; or

(ii)    the child's being beyond parental control.'

**8.27**  The Children Act 1989 defines 'harm' as 'ill-treatment or the impairment of health or development'. 'Development' means physical, intellectual, emotional, social or behavioural development; 'health' means physical or mental health; and 'ill-treatment' includes sexual abuse and forms of ill-treatment which are not physical.[19]

**8.28**  It has been determined in the Family Court that in applying the WHO definition of FGM to the care proceedings, all types of FGM (including Type IV) may constitute 'significant harm'.[20]

## USE OF EXPERTS

**8.29**  For commentary on evidential considerations and expert evidence, please see chapter 6 on FGM protection orders.

## USE OF INTERPRETERS

**8.30**  Within any proceedings in which FGM is an issue, whether that be care proceedings or proceedings for an FGM protection order, it is recommended that practitioners should not use as an interpreter family members, anyone known to the individual or any person with influence in the community.[21]

**8.31**  It is also recommended that an accredited female interpreter be used and where possible someone with an understanding of FGM. Care must be taken to ensure that if possible the interpreter is available at services supporting women with FGM, as this is likely to be required for many appointments relating to FGM.[22]

**8.32**  The Legal Aid Agency expects HM Courts & Tribunal Service to provide interpreters for within hearings when requested (as per the Legal Aid Agency's Guidance on the Remuneration of Expert Witnesses). If the court service is unable to provide a suitable interpreter, practitioners should consider applying for prior authority to incur the costs and/or have it recorded on the face of the order that this is a necessary disbursement under the circumstances.

---

[19]   Children Act 1989, s 31(9).

[20]   *B and G (Children) (No 2)* [2015] EWFC 3.

[21]   Multi-agency statutory guidance on female genital mutilation, HM Government (April 2016), C.2.1.

[22]   Multi-agency statutory guidance on female genital mutilation, HM Government (April 2016), C.2.1.

## RESOLUTION TOOLKIT

**8.33** FGM is often one of a range of issues that the client will be presented with, including honour based violence as well as all other forms of domestic abuse. The organisation Resolution has developed a toolkit for professionals which offers advice on assessment and screening questions.[23] The Resolution Toolkit is available online at the following address: http://www.resolution. uk/site_content_files/files/fgm_toolkit.pdf.

**8.34** The Resolution toolkit aims to support family lawyers in raising the issue of FGM with their clients. Potential victims may only have one chance to ask for help. The toolkit also gives guidance to those representing clients who may be victims in terms of opening up a conversation, asking key questions and signposting clients to dedicated support services available.

## *B AND G (CHILDREN) (NO 2)* [2015] EWFC 3

**8.35** In the case of *B and G (Children) (No 2)*[24] the President of the Family Division, Sir James Munby, gave a detailed judgment giving guidance on FGM in the context of care proceedings.

### Summary

**8.36** The case concerned proceedings brought by Leeds County Council, in respect of two children, B and G, aged 3 and 4 respectively. The care proceedings were initiated following an incident where the mother seemingly abandoned G in the street.[25]

**8.37** Against this background, the main issues for the court's consideration were whether G had been subjected to FGM (FGM WHO Type IV),[26] and whether this constituted significant harm[27] within the meaning of the Children Act 1989. Whilst disputed by both parents, three medical experts investigated the claims and gave written and oral evidence to the court.

**8.38** The court found that the local authority had failed to prove that FGM had been conducted on G. This was the first reported case in care proceedings in which FGM was the sole issue in the case and the President took the opportunity to make observations concerning FGM in the context of s 31 of the Children Act 1989, whilst also providing useful guidance to medical

---

[23]  FGM Toolkit, Resolution, 2016.
[24]  [2015] EWFC 3.
[25]  *B and G (Children) (No 2)* [2015] EWFC 3 at 1.
[26]  World Health Organisation (WHO), *Eliminating Female genital mutilation: an Interagency Statement* (2008, NLM classification: WP 660), http://www.un.org/womenwatch/daw/csw/csw52/statements_missions/Interagency_Statement_on_Eliminating_FGM.pdf, accessed 7 August 2016.
[27]  Children Act 1989, s 31.

practitioners undertaking examinations and reporting to the court.[28] The judgment included a comparative analysis of the legal treatment of FGM and male circumcision.

## Facts

**8.39** Both parents were Muslims of African origin, but the mother was born and raised in a Scandinavian country.[29] Suspicions of FGM first arose when blood was found in G's nappy (November 2012), but on subsequent medical examination, no such findings of FGM were confirmed. Since then, doubts arose again (November 2013, when G's foster carer reported her 'irregular genitalia'.[30]

**8.40** The court undertook an extensive review of reports and oral evidence given by experts S, M and C to make its findings. All three agreed that in the event that G had been subject to FGM, it took the form of a scar adjacent to G's left clitoral hood.[31]

**8.41** At issue was whether there was any evidence of any such scar.[32] On this point, a considerable amount of disagreement and discrepancy existed regarding both the reported findings of the examination, as well as the typology or classification for identifying FGM.[33]

## Whether G was subjected to FGM as alleged?

**8.42** After a forensic review, the court held that based on S and M's evidence, it could not reliably be established that G had been subjected to FGM.[34]

**8.43** The President gave detailed guidance in relation to medical examinations and expert evidence to the court in such cases (as is further explored in chapter 9 on Medical Examinations). The President was critical of the experts in the case and emphasised the vital role of experienced professionals to report to in FGM cases for the court to make well-informed findings.

## If G was subjected to FGM as alleged, did this amount to significant harm?

**8.44** Notably, whilst addressing this issue, Sir James Munby distinguished the court's position on FGM generally from that of FGM within care proceedings, the latter involving additional key considerations. To begin with, he reiterated

---

[28] *B and G (Children) (No 2)* [2015] EWFC 3 at 1 at 79.
[29] *Re B (Children) (No 3)* [2015] EWFC 27.
[30] *B and G (Children) (No 2)* [2015] EWFC 3 at 14.
[31] *B and G (Children) (No 2)* [2015] EWFC 3 at 21, taken from Dr Share's examination recorded on DVD using a video-colposcope, report dated 13 February 2014.
[32] *B and G (Children) (No 2)* [2015] EWFC 3 at 30.
[33] *B and G (Children) (No 2)* [2015] EWFC 3 at [32]–[36].
[34] *B and G (Children) (No 2)* [2015] EWFC 3 at 39.

that FGM was generally considered a criminal offence under the 2003 Act, as well as a recognised human rights abuse. Citing *Singh v Entry Clearance Officer*[35] and *Fornah v Secretary of State for the Home Department*,[36] he noted that the practice was repulsive,[37] barbarous,[38] 'deleterious to women's health'[39] and in violation of Article 3 of the ECHR. Further, referring to case-law related to forced marriage in which he previously gave judgment,[40] he emphasised that in the same way that no justification, whether socio-cultural or religious, can exist for the gross human rights abuse that is forced marriage,[41] the same rationale applies equally to FGM.

## Overall welfare evaluation

**8.45**  It could not be established that G had in fact been subjected to FGM, or was at any future risk of the same. The President noted in general terms that balancing welfare arguments is often complex, and that both local authorities and judges should be cautious when deciding whether proven FGM should necessarily result in adoption.[42]

## Male circumcision

**8.46**  In examining the factual matrix of the case the court noted that FGM Type IV brought with it the need to address the comparable context of male circumcision. This becomes material in the context of care proceedings in that the local authority initiated these proceedings with the ultimate suggestion of placing both children for adoption if issues (I) and (II) were answered in the affirmative.[43] The court also considered whether these measures were wholly proportionate.

**8.47**  As detailed in the judgment, 'male circumcision involves the removal of a significant amount of tissue', a procedure that often alters the appearance of the genitals, leaving an identifiable scar.[44] Usually involving the removal of the foreskin, it was noted that the procedure often includes removal of the tissue connecting the foreskin to the glans, but with the genitals left intact.[45]

**8.48**  Understanding the procedure becomes particularly relevant in assessing the degree of invasiveness involved in comparison to FGM scenarios. For instance, Type I, II and III FGM are in most cases more invasive than male

---

[35]  [2004] EWCA Civ 1075, [2004] INLR 515.
[36]  [2005] EWCA Civ 680, [2005] 1 WLR 3773.
[37]  *Fornah v Secretary of State for the Home Department* (n 36) per Arden LJ at [58].
[38]  *Singh v Entry Clearance Officer* (n 35) at 68
[39]  *Fornah* (n 36) per Arden LJ at [58].
[40]  *NS v MI* [2006] EWHC 1646, [2007] 1 LFR 444 (Fam).
[41]  *B and G (Children) (No 2)* [2015] EWFC 3 at 79 at 3.
[42]  *B and G (Children) (No 2)* [2015] EWFC 3 at para 77.
[43]  *Re B and G (Children) (No 1)*.
[44]  *B and G (Children) (No 2)* [2015] EWFC 3 at 59.
[45]  *B and G (Children) (No 2)* [2015] EWFC 3 at 59.

circumcision, but often Type IV, characterised most commonly by 'pricking, piercing, and incising'[46] is considerably less invasive.[47]

**8.49** The President added in a footnote that there is a possible qualification in relation to FGM Type Ia, which, although apparently very rare, is physiologically somewhat analogous to male circumcision.

**8.50** With reference to the manner in which male circumcision is treated under the law, it was noted that the practice seems to be performed, in many cases, for non-therapeutic reasons, most commonly either religious, sociocultural, or customary. The arguments put forward in favour of male circumcision within the therapeutic context are disputed,[48] and often not the primary justification for the practice. Academic opinion on whether a 'medically indicated circumcision' results in health benefits is divided.[49]

**8.51** Looking at the jurisprudence, the President pointed out that circumcision does not, on its own, generally give rise to care proceedings.[50] On the contrary, local authorities are able to rely on FGM Type IV or on the threat thereof, according to the 2003 Act, if proven, to initiate such care proceedings.

**8.52** Although not at issue on the facts, Sir Munby noted that B, the younger boy, may be equally susceptible to or may already have undergone male circumcision. Although it was emphasised that this was a hypothetical assumption based on the child's background, it brought into focus the difficulties involved in reconciling the differential legal treatment of FGM and male circumcision in accordance with s 31 of the Children Act 1989. If the court were to reach an opinion to the effect that G had been or was under threat of being subjected to FGM, this would allow local authorities to bring proceedings 'justifying the adoption of both children'.[51]

**8.53** Due to the lack of equivalent treatment of male and female circumcision under the law, the court used a statutory threshold required under s 31(2) of the Act to determine whether the criteria for the care order had successfully been met. The court first considered whether G had suffered or was likely to suffer significant harm.[52] On this question, 'significant' related to that parental care which was not reasonable to expect of a parent.[53] Following from *Re B (Care*

---

46    *B and G (Children) (No 2)* [2015] EWFC 3 at 59, 60.
47    *B and G (Children) (No 2)* [2015] EWFC 3 at 59, 61.
48    Christopher Price, 'Male Circumcision: An Ethical and Legal Affront' (1997) 128 *Bull Med Ethics* 13–19.
49    Christopher Price, 'Male Circumcision: An Ethical and Legal Affront' (1997) 128 *Bull Med Ethics* 14–15.
50    *Re J (Specific Issue Orders: Child's Religious Upbringing and Circumcision)* [1999] 2 FLR 678.
51    *Re B and G (Children) (No 1)* at 62.
52    Children Act 1989, s 31(2)(a).
53    Children Act 1989, s 31(2)(a).

*Proceedings: Appeal)*,[54] it had already been clearly established by Baroness Hale that 'any form of FGM, including FGM WHO Type IV amounted to significant harm'.[55] The court noted:

> 'What emerges from the case is the confirmation of the distinction between FGM and male circumcision. Whereas it can never be reasonable parenting to inflict any form of FGM on a child, the position is quite different with male circumcision. Society and the law, including family law, are prepared to tolerate non-therapeutic male circumcision performed for religious or even for purely cultural or conventional reasons, while no longer being willing to tolerate FGM in any of its forms. FGM in any form will suffice to establish "threshold" in accordance with section 31 of the Children Act 1989; male circumcision without more will not.'[56]

## *A (A CHILD: FGM)* [2016] EWFC B103

**8.54**  Inconclusive medical evidence or medical evidence that does not positively point towards FGM, does not itself rule out a FGM Type IV procedure having taken place. The court must take into account all the evidence as a whole.

**8.55**  This was demonstrated very clearly in the matter of *A (A Child: FGM)*.[57] Her Honour Judge Mayer heard care proceedings involving A (5 years old). She and her siblings (the third respondents) were represented through their Children's Guardian. Her siblings were B, aged 7, C aged 4 (both males) and D, a female, aged 2 months. Their mother, M was the first respondent. The second respondent was the father, F. The parents both had parental responsibility in respect of all four children.[58]

**8.56**  The applicant local authority applied for orders pursuant to s 31 of the Children Act 1989 in respect of the three older children. On 31 August 2016 they applied for similar orders in respect of D. D had never been removed from her mother.[59] The issue before the court was whether A had undergone a FGM procedure.

### Background

**8.57**  Both parents, who were both from Somalia, had separated. The mother had undergone FGM herself. A few days before 28 March 2016 A told AS, her class teacher, that her willy hurt when she went to the toilet. Ms S reported this to the mother, and suggested she went to the chemist to treat a possible infection.[60]

---

[54]  [2013] UKSC 33, [2013] 1 WLR 1911 (Baroness Hale).
[55]  [2013] UKSC 33, [2013] 1 WLR 1911 (Baroness Hale).
[56]  *B and G (Children) (No 2)* [2015] EWFC 3 at paras 72–73.
[57]  [2016] EWFC B103.
[58]  *A (A Child: FGM)* [2016] EWFC B103, paras 1–89.
[59]  *A (A Child: FGM)* [2016] EWFC B103, paras 1–89.
[60]  *A (A Child: FGM)* [2016] EWFC B103, paras 1–89.

**8.58** On 28 March 2016 A told several members of staff at her school that her willy hurt and she mentioned two boys hurting her willy at her sister's house. Other than the father, apparently, everybody in the case knew that A called her vagina 'willy'. On 31 March A spoke to MP, a teaching assistant, about her willy hurting, giving a very concerning account. JO, the school's pastoral manager, was informed forthwith, and spoke to the mother at the end of the school day, telling her to take A to her GP. There was a dispute as to the reason given to the mother for taking A to the GP; but there was no dispute about the mother telling the GP that A had discomfort in her lower abdomen. A's genitals were neither mentioned nor examined.[61]

**8.59** Between the very end of March and 10 June, A complained, from time to time, about her willy hurting, without giving any detail. On 10 June 2016 she gave a very specific account about her mummy cutting her willy. In between these two dates, on 21 April 2016, A was asked what she did over the Easter holidays. She said her mother told her not to tell the teachers anything, because it was 'private'. Consequent upon her account on 10 June 2016, A was taken to see Dr H, a Consultant Paediatrician, at Barnet General hospital, for a child protection medical. Dr H considered that A was missing her labia majora. She considered that the physical finding, together with the account A gave her before the examination, indicated FGM. All three children were taken into police protection.[62]

**8.60** On 11 June the mother was interviewed under caution. She refused to answer any questions, but provided a statement claiming that A became itchy in her genital area when she ate bananas and she washed her 'down there'. She informed the police that she did not know where the father was, nor was she able to give a contact number for him. This was at a time when he was apparently staying in the family home two–three nights a week.[63]

**8.61** On 15 June the local authority successfully applied for interim care orders. On 20 June 2016 the social worker and the Children's Guardian visited the boys, who were placed with a maternal aunt. B said he saw private parts of girls being cut on the computer, at home. His verbatim account was repeated in the Guardian's report. Forensic examination of the family computer did not reveal any material relevant to cutting vaginas or any other type of FGM, although it revealed access to adult pornography. On 1 July 2016 A was ABE interviewed but did not repeat any of her accounts about her willy being cut.[64]

**8.62** On 4 July 2016 A was seen by Dr Hodes and Professor Creighton. This was organised by the police. The two doctors disagreed with Dr H's diagnosis, and concluded that A's labia majora were intact, and other than a small shortening of the clitoral hood, which could be a normal variant, did not necessarily identify physical evidence of FGM. This, they explained, did not

---

[61]   *A (A Child: FGM)* [2016] EWFC B103, paras 1–89.
[62]   *A (A Child: FGM)* [2016] EWFC B103, paras 1–89.
[63]   *A (A Child: FGM)* [2016] EWFC B103, paras 1–89.
[64]   *A (A Child: FGM)* [2016] EWFC B103, paras 1–89.

exclude the possibility of Type IV FGM, as this could heal without leaving any physical signs. Dr H indicated, by a letter of 15 July, that she deferred to the expertise of Dr Hodes and Professor Creighton, and accepted their views. On 11 July 2016 the ICOs in respect of the boys were discharged and they went home.[65]

**8.63** With the above background, the Family Court embarked on a fact-finding hearing. In light of B's account of watching a video of cutting female genitalia, the court gave permission for Dr A, a consultant child and adolescent psychiatrist, to consider A's accounts.

## Fact-finding

**8.64** At the fact-finding hearing evidence was heard over three days, from two social workers, from Professor Creighton, Dr H, from four members of the school staff, from DC JR, Child Protection officer, from LG, A's foster carer, from Dr A and from the parents.

**8.65** In relation to the medical evidence Her Honour Judge Mayer noted that both Dr Creighton and Dr Hodes were established experts on FGM. They had conducted the medical examination at the behest of the police, as part of child protection procedure.[66]

**8.66** Although Dr Creighton, who gave oral evidence to the court, was not formally appointed as an expert in the care proceedings, she was treated as one by the court. Dr Creighton explained that it was not uncommon for there to be no visible injury to confirm that FGM had taken place. The methods used by those who subscribe to this cultural belief have been adapted because of increasing international focus on the practice and the possibility of criminal prosecution. Girls are being 'done' much younger than previously and often they are cut very slightly or pricked in the genital area to draw blood.[67]

**8.67** The two doctors found that A's labia majora were intact. In her written conclusion Dr Creighton stated:[68]

> 'There were no physical signs which confirm recent or historic FGM. There was no evidence of any recent trauma or scarring to the genitals and FGM has not been performed within the last three months. The slightly shortened clitoral hood may be consistent with normal congenital variation or with removal of a small piece of the clitoral hood as in type 1 FGM. In addition we are unable to exclude type 4 FGM which may consist of a small cut or prick as this can heal without leaving any physical signs. These examination findings do not exclude the possibility that

[65] *A (A Child: FGM)* [2016] EWFC B103, paras 1–89.
[66] *A (A Child: FGM)* [2016] EWFC B103, paras 90–121.
[67] *A (A Child: FGM)* [2016] EWFC B103, paras 90–121.
[68] *A (A Child: FGM)* [2016] EWFC B103, paras 90–121.

A underwent a type 1 or type 4 FGM which has healed without trace. This may have been performed during A's visit ...'[69]

**8.68** In her judgment Her Honour Judge Mayer noted the following observations made by Dr Creighton during her evidence:

'96. i. Type IV FGM will often not leave any physical evidence at all. It has a vast range of procedures – cutting, pricking, nicking, burning and others. In the course of seeing 88 girls, since 2014, who were referred with suspected FGM, 42 have undergone FGM. Some parents come from countries such as Indonesia and Malaysia, with certificates in support of the procedure having been done, and admit it readily, even though there are no physical signs; in their countries, it is not a criminal offence. I bear in mind that in type 4 FGM, where there are no physical signs, is unlikely to trigger criminal prosecution here either, due to the mutilation element missing.

ii. The slightly shortened clitoral hood is more likely to be a normal variant than evidence of cutting; if there had been cutting, a scar would have been likely to have been visible. Altogether, more damage would have been expected having regard to A's description. I accept this evidence as support for a finding that on the balance of probabilities it is unlikely that A's clitoral hood has been shortened, and concentrate on type IV FGM.

iii. Type IV FGM is often inferred and diagnosed based on accounts of parents or children, including siblings of girls who undergo the procedure.

iv. According to UNICEFF, about 50% of all FGM procedures are carried out on girls between birth and 5 years of age.

v. Although there are little comparative data, it would appear that type IV FGM is increasingly common.

vi. Although in Somalia type III used to be more prevalent, Somalia appears to be moving to type 4, because it is harder to detect.

vii. Professor Creighton has not come across a case where a mother performed FGM on her own child.'[70]

# Ruling

**8.69** Turning to the parents' evidence, the judge found a number of conflicting accounts between the father and the mother. After considering all the evidence together in some detail and unpicking the parties accounts the judge concluded:

---

[69] *A (A Child: FGM)* [2016] EWFC B103, paras 90–121.
[70] *A (A Child: FGM)* [2016] EWFC B103, paras 90–121.

'140.

… A has undergone a procedure to her genitalia which is more likely than not to be type 4 FGM. I cannot say who did it, and what exactly was done. It could be a little cut, or a nick, or a prick; none have left a mark, but some blood was involved. It is possible that if her mother did not do it, she was there, and was involved in soothing her. I cannot say whether the father was involved in the procedure. I am satisfied that he knows that it has taken place.

141. I find that there is no evidence at this stage to suggest that A is at risk of suffering a further procedure of FGM.

142. I also find that D is at risk of undergoing the same procedure as her sister.'[71]

**8.70**  The reasoned judgment serves as a reminder that medical evidence that does not positively point towards FGM does not itself rule out the possibility of a FGM Type IV procedure having taken place. As Her Honour Judge Mayer stated:

'122. I have considered the expert evidence, A's and B's accounts, the veracity of the parents, the behaviour of the mother and the additional risk factors identified by Professor Creighton. They all form part of the wider canvas, the basis on of which I have to make findings.

123. The absence of physical evidence of FGM is no evidence that type IV FGM did not take place. By way of analogy, in cases of child sexual abuse, physical evidence is absent from a great deal of cases. It makes the evidential basis more difficult, but by no means impossible, to resolve.'[72]

**8.71**  Her Honour Judge Mayer concluded:

'137. Dr A said that children's accounts tend to drift away with time, and the fact that A's account to him verged, in part, on fantasy, did not negate for him the importance of her original accounts. Interestingly, the only aspect that really concerned him, and the foster carer, was her reaction to the question whether her mother's willy has been cut. It was the only time when A changed her demeanour and appeared distressed.

138. I take into account that her mother has undergone FGM, and that she visited Somalia for 8 weeks in the summer of 2015. These are 2 risk factors, identified by Professor Creighton. On their own, they would be meaningless; as part of the wider canvass, they fit in with the rest of my analysis.

139. It may be that on the basis of A's accounts only I might, I emphasise might, have hesitated about making positive findings of FGM. The behaviour of the

---

[71]  *A (A Child: FGM)* [2016] EWFC B103, paras 140–142.
[72]  *A (A Child: FGM)* [2016] EWFC B103, paras 122–123.

parents which I consider to be part of the wider canvass, together with the evidence of Dr A, permit me to make the finding below on the balance of probability.'[73]

## ADULT WHO HAS HAD FGM

**8.72**  There is no requirement for automatic referral of adult women with FGM to adult social services or the police. Professionals should be aware that any disclosure may be the first time that a woman has ever discussed her FGM with anyone. The multi-agency statutory guidance suggests that a referral to the police should not be an automatic response for all adult women who are identified as having undergone FGM. Cases must be individually assessed.[74] Professionals should seek to support women by referring them to appropriate services and should also consider whether the individual and/or her family are known to social services, and whether there are any existing safeguarding arrangements in place.[75]

---

[73]  *A (A Child: FGM)* [2016] EWFC B103, paras 137–139.

[74]  HM Government, *Multi-agency statutory guidance on female genital mutilation* (April 2016), Section 3.1.5, para D.2.5.

[75]  HM Government, *Multi-agency statutory guidance on female genital mutilation* (April 2016), Section 3.1.5, para D.2.5.

# CHAPTER 9

# MEDICAL EXAMINATIONS AND SPECIALIST SERVICES

**9.1** Medical examinations to ascertain if an individual has been subjected to FGM are now commonplace in family proceedings as well as in criminal investigations.

**9.2** The statutory guidance states that where there are concerns that a girl or women may have been subjected to FGM, corroborative evidence should be sought through a medical examination conducted by a qualified medical professional trained in identifying the different types of FGM. In all cases involving children, an experienced pediatrician should be involved in setting up the medical examination. It is vital to ensure that a holistic assessment (which explores any other medical, support and safeguarding needs of the girl or young woman) is offered and that appropriate referrals are made as necessary.[1]

**9.3** Knowledge and understanding of the classification and categorisation of the various types of FGM is key for any expert instructed. Before an expert is instructed, it is essential that practitioners should consider the expert's experience in examining victims in a paediatric context and of the age of child subject to the proceedings. When the medical examination is conducted, it is vital that clear and detailed notes are made, recording (with the use of appropriate drawings or diagrams) exactly what is observed.

**9.4** Type IV FGM performed in infancy is easily missed on examination and so vigilance in assessing children with suspected FGM is essential.[2]

## LEAVE OF THE COURT

**9.5** The court's leave is required before an expert may be instructed and before a child is medically or psychiatrically examined for the purposes of the

---

[1] Multi-agency statutory guidance on female genital mutilation, HM Government (April 2016), p 58.

[2] D Hodes, A Armitage, K Robinson, S Creighton, 'Female genital mutilation in children presenting to a London safeguarding clinic: a case series', *Arch Dis Child* doi:10.1136/archdischild-2015-308243, 27 July 2015 – see https://www.ncbi.nlm.nih.gov/pubmed/26216833.

provision of expert evidence. If the court's permission is not sought, the evidence resulting from the instruction or examination is inadmissible unless the court rules that it is admissible.[3]

## USE OF SPECIFIC ISSUE ORDERS – IN THE MATTER OF *B AND OTHERS*

**9.6**　In the matter of *A London Borough v B and Ors (Female Genital Mutilation: FGM)* HHJ Tolson QC gave judgment in care proceedings involving the risk of harm to two girls, one aged 13 and one aged 5. The girls had been in foster care. The parties agreed that the girls should return to the care of their mother and father. It was an outcome in accordance with the two experts who have looked at the case and offered an opinion as well as the children's guardian.[4]

**9.7**　The judge approved a written agreement covering a wide range of areas as to the steps that would be in place in order to protect the girls in the future. The court ruled that the risk was such that there should be regular medical examinations of the girls.[5]

**9.8**　In coming to that view the court examined the history of the matter. The case came to light in circumstances which involved the mother informing a friend of hers that she was concerned as to a trip to Guinea Conakry from where the family originates. This was without warning, it was said, at the instigation of the father.[6]

**9.9**　Subsequently, the parents were to give different versions of events about the circumstances which led to the suggestion that the girls might be taken to Guinea in the near future. The elder child gave an ABE interview to the police, the terms of which were deeply concerning as to the intention which underpinned the trip to Guinea. The idea formulated in the minds of the authorities that the girls were at serious risk of FGM.[7]

**9.10**　It was therefore considered too uncertain to leave it to some future child protection referral to the local authority to trigger such a medical examination. HHJ Tolson QC went on to make a specific issue order in the following terms:[8]

---

[3]　Children and Families Act 2014, s 13(1).
[4]　[2016] EWFC B111 (18 October 2016).
[5]　*A London Borough v B and Ors (Female Genital Mutilation: FGM)* [2016] EWFC B111 (18 October 2016).
[6]　*A London Borough v B and Ors (Female Genital Mutilation: FGM)* [2016] EWFC B111 (18 October 2016).
[7]　*A London Borough v B and Ors (Female Genital Mutilation: FGM)* [2016] EWFC B111 (18 October 2016).
[8]　*A London Borough v B and Ors (Female Genital Mutilation: FGM)* [2016] EWFC B111 (18 October 2016).

'As a specific issue as to the exercise of parental responsibility in respect of the two girls, the parents shall, subject to the consent of any competent child, arrange a medical examination at the request of the Local Authority but not more frequently than annually to demonstrate that the children have not undergone female genital mutilation. The parents shall provide independent evidence of the result to the Local Authority. The medical practitioner concerned should be one which attracts the approval of the Authority.'[9]

**9.11** In considering whether such a medical examination would be disproportionate as an interference with the ECHR, Article 8 rights of the two girls, the court noted that the reality of this case was that a likelihood of risk had been demonstrated in the past and the facts of the case suggested that it was not a risk which could in any sense be said to have somehow vanished with the conclusion of those proceedings.[10]

## GUIDANCE FOR EXPERTS: *B AND G (CHILDREN) (NO 2)*[11]

**9.12** The understandable reliance on expert medical evidence in FGM cases is vital to making well-informed findings and the detailed guidance from the court is partially directed at discouraging sub-standard evidence, both during examinations and its delivery.

**9.13** In the matter of *B and G (Children) (No 2)*[12] the court gave detailed guidance on the provision of expert medical examinations in FGM cases. In considering whether G had been subjected to FGM, three medical experts investigated the claims gave written and oral evidence to the court. The experts were as follows:

(1)   Dr Alison Share (S), a Consultant Community Paediatrician at St James's University Hospital (Leeds); her expertise covered child sexual abuse but was limited in relation to female genitalia assessment within an FGM context.[13]

(2)   Dr Comfort Momoh (M), a Registered Midwife at Guy's and St Thomas Hospital NHS Foundation Trust (London); her experience covered reproductive health and multiple aspects of FGM. Notwithstanding, as a midwife her 'primary expertise'[14] related to pregnant women who had been subjected to FGM, but was significantly limited with respect to 'very young girls.'[15]

---

9    *A London Borough v B and Ors (Female Genital Mutilation: FGM)* [2016] EWFC B111 (18 October 2016).
10   *A London Borough v B and Ors (Female Genital Mutilation: FGM)* [2016] EWFC B111 (18 October 2016).
11   [2015] EWFC 3.
12   [2015] EWFC 3.
13   *B and G (Children) (No 2)* [2015] EWFC 3 at 17.
14   *B and G (Children) (No 2)* [2015] EWFC 3 at 18.
15   *B and G (Children) (No 2)* [2015] EWFC 3 at 19.

(3)   Professor Sarah Creighton (C), Consultant Obstetrician and Gynaecologist at University College Hospital (London), who established the African Woman Clinic for women with specialist FGM advice. This clinic notably stands out as the first specialist paediatric FGM clinic in the country. Her primary focus was on 'paediatric and adolescent gynaecology, reconstructive genital surgery, and Female Genital Mutilation (FGM)'.[16] Further, she was actively involved as Chair of the FGM Clinical National Group and had prior experience in advising the DPP, Home Office, NHS London, and NHS England on the issue of FGM at a strategic level.

## Expert evidence of whether G was subjected to FGM

**9.14**   After a careful analysis of the evidence the court concluded that based on S and M's evidence, it could not reliably be established that G had been subjected to FGM.[17] Both S and M examined G personally. S reported a scar close to G's left clitoral hood, but with considerable confusion as to whether it constituted Type I or possibly Type II FGM on initial inspection, but finalised that it was Type IV FGM when she reviewed the DVD repeatedly after returning to her office.[18] In two different places, there was an attempt to classify the scar using divergent typologies – UNICEF as well as WHO classifications.[19] Additionally, she also identified more than one variant of FGM within the WHO classification itself when filling in parts B and C of her report.[20] In summary, there were unsatisfactory variants in her report.

**9.15**   M, the second expert, simply concluded that G had been subjected to some form of FGM, without identifying any typology for classifying her own findings, which she attributed to an abnormal vulva.[21] There was no correlation between S and M's description of the scar, with the former observing it was 'curved and raised',[22] whilst the latter noted it was 'straight'.[23] M was also unable to provide a satisfactory justification for not reviewing the scar more closely, when it had been agreed upon previously in joint discussions between S and M.

**9.16**   C, on the other hand, 'could not confirm the presence of a scar',[24] although it was noted that she reviewed DVDs from S and M's examinations, but had not seen G personally. S's oral evidence was 'clear and measured,[25] and the court noted that it carried conviction.[26] The court made allowance for the

---

[16]   *B and G (Children) (No 2)* [2015] EWFC 3 at 19.
[17]   *B and G (Children) (No 2)* [2015] EWFC 3 at 39.
[18]   *B and G (Children) (No 2)* [2015] EWFC 3 at 21.
[19]   *B and G (Children) (No 2)* [2015] EWFC 3 at 22.
[20]   *B and G (Children) (No 2)* [2015] EWFC 3 at 23.
[21]   *B and G (Children) (No 2)* [2015] EWFC 3 at 27, report dated 23 April 2014 from examination conducted on 7 April 2014.
[22]   *B and G (Children) (No 2)* [2015] EWFC 3 at 49.
[23]   *B and G (Children) (No 2)* [2015] EWFC 3.
[24]   *B and G (Children) (No 2)* [2015] EWFC 3 at 30.
[25]   *B and G (Children) (No 2)* [2015] EWFC 3 at 39.
[26]   *B and G (Children) (No 2)* [2015] EWFC 3 at 46.

fact that C did not have the benefit of the naked eye, but her experience of FGM in a paediatric context made her an appropriate expert to make such a determination. Coupled with an inconsistent account from S and M, the court was unable to find sufficient evidence solely based on the presence of a disputed scar, and could not conclude that G had been, or was at the risk of being, subjected to FGM. It was noted that the local authority had not made an argument based on any such continued or future risk, and thus evidence on the facts, remained minimal.

**9.17** With the exception of Professor Sarah Creighton, the President was critical of the experts in the case and emphasised the vital role of experienced professionals to report in FGM cases in order for the court to make well-informed findings.

**9.18** Although Dr Share (S) was recognised as a well-respected medical practitioner, and known most notably for her experience in child protection investigations, her oral and written evidence with regards to the present case was identified as 'well below the standard required of an expert witness'.[27] This was in reference to initially identifying removal of G's tissue as FGM Type I and possibly Type II, but concluding that it took the form of a scar, most close to Type IV FGM.[28] In summary, her evidence was labelled as 'confused, contradictory, and wholly unreliable'.[29] Despite this, her frank and open admission of errors was appreciated and the court noted that she did not put herself out as being an expert on FGM, less so in a paediatric context.

**9.19** The court found Dr Momoh (M) 'merited the harsh criticism'[30] expressed by the respondent's counsel.[31] It was noted that her expertise in relation to young children was extremely limited and her report was labelled a 'shoddy piece of work'.[32] This followed from her vague diagnosis of FGM with no clear reference to any typology or linkage with the scar.[33] In part, this determination also stemmed from her inability to explain matters material to the case at the witness box. When asked why there was no reference to any scarring in both her handwritten notes or in those of the final examination, she was unable to give an explanation in response.

## Policy based change and future guidance for practitioners

**9.20** Sir James Munby, drawing on the technical deficiency in both S and M's findings, and with reference to useful suggestions made by C in the course of her oral evidence, laid out significant suggestions for dealing with future FGM cases. This broadly covered policy objectives as well as practical guidance for

---

[27]  *B and G (Children) (No 2)* [2015] EWFC 3 at 46.
[28]  *B and G (Children) (No 2)* [2015] EWFC 3 at 42.
[29]  *B and G (Children) (No 2)* [2015] EWFC 3 at 42.
[30]  *B and G (Children) (No 2)* [2015] EWFC 3 at 45.
[31]  *B and G (Children) (No 2)* [2015] EWFC 3 at 45.
[32]  *B and G (Children) (No 2)* [2015] EWFC 3 at 45.
[33]  *B and G (Children) (No 2)* [2015] EWFC 3 at 45.

conducting examinations of the required standard. He started with noting the 'dearth of medical experts in this area, particularly in relation to FGM in young children'.[34] In response to this, he called for more specific training that caters to increased paediatric expertise. Evidencing this, he pointed out that only 12 clinics across the country offer specialist FGM support, out of which UCL Hospital is the only one that is considered a 'specialist paediatric FGM clinic'.[35]

**9.21**  It was also suggested that an increased awareness of the classification of the numerous types of FGM must be encouraged, and that for forensic purposes, the WHO classification is the preferred definition to follow for forensic purposes.[36] Given the difficulties caused due to mixing of typologies, the reports and oral evidence produced a seemingly contradictory and unclear result, causing unnecessary confusion. Without adequate consensus, the court found it more difficult to determine whether G had in fact been subjected to FGM.

## Practical guidance on conducting examinations

**9.22**  It was emphasised that the planning process for an examination must ensure that an expert of 'an appropriate level of relevant experience' is available at the early stages.[37] It was also recommended that referrals be made to specialist FGM clinics, as referenced by C.

**9.23**  In the event that this is not possible, a safeguarding consultant paediatrician of the required skill should carry out an examination with the use of a colposcopy, so that the situation may be reviewed again. In relation to notes made during an examination, they must be clear and detailed. It is also necessary that the type of FGM must be categorised where such cases are identified. This must be supported by clear and precise evidence, and must cross-reference the recording.[38]

## COMMUNICATING ABOUT FGM

**9.24**  Good communication is essential when talking to individuals who have had FGM, may be at risk of FGM, or are affected by the practice. Professionals should ensure that they enquire sensitively about FGM. The topic of FGM may arise in a variety of settings, including a GP's surgery as part of a medical consultation, a home environment during a health visitor's post-natal visit, or at school. Conversations may take place with the girl or woman who may be affected by FGM, a parent or other family member. How the conversation is opened and the language used will vary according to the setting and who the

---

[34]  *B and G (Children) (No 2)* [2015] EWFC 3 at 79.
[35]  *B and G (Children) (No 2)* [2015] EWFC 3 at 19.
[36]  *B and G (Children) (No 2)* [2015] EWFC 3 at 79.
[37]  *B and G (Children) (No 2)* [2015] EWFC 3 at 79.
[38]  *B and G (Children) (No 2)* [2015] EWFC 3 at 79.

conversation is with. Key principles which should apply in all cases are set out within Annex C of the statutory guidance.[39]

## SPECIALIST FGM CLINICS AND HEALTH SERVICES

**9.25**   The following health services have extensive experience in dealing with FGM and understand the cultural reasons behind FGM. Several drop-in clinics are available for girls and women to access, in order to address any health concerns they have. De-infibulation is also offered at some of the clinics, and no referral is required from the GP or midwife.

## Specialist services for FGM

**9.26   LONDON:**

**1. African Women's Clinic**

University College London Hospitals
NHS Foundation Trust

Description: FGM clinic and an affiliation with the urogynaecology service. Links with the paediatric clinic running on Fridays, and plans to do a joint clinic monthly in future.

Address:
Elizabeth Garrett Anderson Wing
UCLH Lower Ground Floor
25 Grafton Way
London, WC1E 6DB

Dr Lata Kamble – FGM Clinical Lead and Obstetrician Mrs Yvonne Saruchera – Midwifery Lead

Dr Sohier Elneil – Urogynaecology Support

Dr Hodes – Lead Paediatrician

Open: Run three clinics every month at present. They have a procedure list which happens on the first Monday of the month and the other clinics take place on the third and fourth Mondays of the month.

Email: For complex cases sohier.elneil@uclh.nhs.uk or fgmsupport@uclh.nhs.uk

Telephone: 07944 241992

---

[39]   Multi-agency statutory guidance on female genital mutilation, HM Government (April 2016), Annex C.

For Dr Hodes contact 02034475241 or email Kirsty.phillips2@uclh.nhs.uk and renara.begum@uclh.nhs.uk for an appointment.

Dr Hodes takes referrals in her clinic on Fridays when there is a suspicion of FGM or a history of having had FGM.

At present children under 18 and women are seen in separate clinics – the clinic is working towards making it joined up but at the moment under 18s go to the pediatric addresses and over 18s go to the African Woman's Clinic.

**2. Acton African Well Woman Clinic: Imperial College Healthcare NHS Trust**

A partnership project funded by Ealing Hospital NHS Trust community services and Imperial College Healthcare NHS Trust. This service is for pregnant and non-pregnant women. They aim to see women within two weeks of contact. They provide counselling and support for women with FGM, a de-infibulation service for women with Type III FGM using local anaesthetic and a referral service for women with complex perineal trauma as a result of FGM.

Address:

Acton Health Centre 35–61 Church Road London, W3 8QE

Open: Monday to Friday 9am – 5pm

Project Lead – Juliet Albert (Specialist FGM Midwife) Health Advocates – Deqa Dirie and Mushtag Kahin Counsellor – Melanie Mendel

Telephone: 07956 001 065 or 0208 383 8761 or 07730970738

**3. Queen Charlotte's & Chelsea Hospital African Well Woman Clinic Imperial College Healthcare NHS Trust**

This service is for pregnant and non-pregnant women. They aim to see women within two weeks of contact. They provide counselling and support for women with FGM, a de-infibulation service for women with Type III FGM using local anaesthetic and a referral service for women with complex perineal trauma as a result of FGM.

Address:

Du Cane Road, London W12 0HS

Open: Monday to Friday 9am – 5pm

Telephone: 07956 001 065 or 0208 383 8761 or 07730970738

Health Advocates – Deqa Dirie and Mushtag Kahin Project Lead – Juliet Albert (Specialist FGM Midwife) Counsellor – Melanie Mendel

**4. West London African Women's Service – Chelsea and Westminster Hospital NHS Trust**

Provides sexual health, maternity and gynaecology advice and treatment for women affected by FGM. No GP referral required. This service is for pregnant and non-pregnant women. They aim to see women within two weeks of contact. The service can see children/young women aged 13 and above. They can be seen in the same clinic. Alternatively, they can be seen in a confidential walk-in Young People's Service held every Monday, Tuesday and Thursday 2:30 pm to 5:00 pm at the West London Centre for Sexual Health.

Two sites:

Chelsea and Westminster Hospital
369 Fulham Road
London, SW10 9NH

and

West London Centre for Sexual Health
Charing Cross Hospital (South Wing) Fulham Palace Road
London, W6 8RF

Sexual health:

West London Centre for Sexual Health

Telephone: 0208 846 1579 (Health Advisors)

Fax: 0203 311 7582

Clinic times:

Thursday 10am – 12pm

Maternity/Gynaecology

Chelsea and Westminster Hospital & West London Centre for Sexual Health

Telephone: 020 3315 3344 (Debora Alcayde, Specialist FGM Midwife)

Clinic times:

Thursday 9:30am – 12:30pm – Chelsea and Westminster Hospital

Second and fourth Wednesday of every month 10:30am – 1:00pm – West London Centre for Sexual Health

Email enquires (all aspects of the service): caw-tr.fgmwestlondon@nhs.net

**5. St Marys Hospital: Imperial College Healthcare NHS Trust – Well Women Clinic**

These services are only available for those women who are formally booked at St Marys site.

Address:

Well Women Clinic
Gynaecology & Midwifery Department Praed St.
London, W2 1NY

Open: once a month from 9am – 5pm – structured appointments in mornings for consultation, and afternoon for procedures.

Telephone: 0207 886 6691 or 0207 886 1443

Helpline: 0203 312 6135

**6. African Well Women's Clinic – Whittington Hospital**

The clinic is midwifery led and gender specific. Both pregnant and non-pregnant women can access the clinic. Their aim is to see women within two weeks of their referral. The clinic offers advice, counselling, antenatal care and assessment, de-infibulation, post-surgery and postnatal follow up. Home visits are offered to women living in the borough of Islington and Haringey.

Address:

African Well Women's Clinic Kenwood Wing
Antenatal Clinic
Level 5
Highgate Hill
London, N19 5NF

Open: Open every Wednesday from 8:30am – 4:30pm

Telephone: 0207 2883482/3 or 07956257992 to make or change an appointment

Specialist Lead Joy Clarke: joy.clarke@nhs.net; Shamsa Ahmed: shamsa.ahmed@nhs.net http://www.whittington.nhs.uk/mini-apps/staff/staffpage.asp?StaffID=24&t=

## 7. African Well Women's Clinic – Guys & St Thomas' Hospital

Address:

Guy's & St Thomas's Hospital African Well Women's Clinic
8th Floor – c/o Antenatal Clinic
Lambeth Palace Rd
London, SE1 7EH

Open: Monday to Friday, 9am – 4pm

Telephone: 0207 188 6872

Dr Comfort Momoh MBE: comfort.momoh@gstt.nhs.uk

## 8. Mile End Hospital – Barts Health NHS Trust

Address:

Women's and Young People's Services Sylvia Pankhurst Health Centre
Third Floor, Bancroft road, London E1 4DG

Open: Monday–Thursday 12:00pm – 8:00pm, Friday 9:30am – 5:30pm

Telephone: 0207 377 7898, 0207 377 7870 or 0208 223 8322

Vanessa.apea@bartshealth.nhs.uk

www.bartsandthelondon.nhs.uk

## 9. Northwick Park Hospital & Central Middlesex Hospital – African Well Women's Clinic – North West London Hospitals NHS Trust

This clinic is held on Friday mornings. It is run by specialist midwives who will refer to a consultant if necessary.

Address:

African Well Women's Clinic – Antenatal Clinic
Watford Rd
Harrow
Middlesex, HA1 3UJ

Open: Friday mornings

Telephone:

Central Middlesex Hospital Park Royal Antenatal clinic: 020 8453 2108

Northwick Park Hospital Harrow Antenatal clinic: 020 8869 2880

nwlh-tr.PALS@nhs.net http://www.nwlh.nhs.uk/services/antenatal-care/

**10. Waltham Forest African Well Women's Services**

Oliver Road Polyclinics
Upper Ground Floor
75 Oliver Rd
Leyton
London, E10 5LG

Open: Drop-In Thursday 10am – 3pm

Telephone: 0208 430 7381

**NOTTINGHAM**

**11. Nottingham University Hospital – Nottingham University Hospitals NHS Trust: City Hospital Campus**

Address:

Antenatal Clinic Nottingham City Hospital
Hucknall Road
Nottingham, NG5 1PB

Open: (QMC) Thursday 13.30pm -17.00pm; (City) Thursday 9am – 12pm

Telephone: 0115 969 1169

Carol McCormick: Carol.mccormick@nuh.nhs.uk

**BRISTOL**

**12. Minority Ethnic Women's & Girl's Clinic – Bristol Charlotte Keel Centre**

Address:

Charlotte Keel Health Centre Seymour Road
Easton
Bristol, BS5 0UA

Open: Drop-In Last Weds of every month, 9:30am – 12pm

Telephone: 0117 9027138 0117 902 7111 (direct line); 0117 902 7100 (switchboard)

mgw@gp-L81092.nhs.uk www.eastonfamilypractice.co.uk

### 13. Bristol Community Rose Clinic at Lawrence Hill Health Centre

The Bristol Community Rose Clinic provides care and support for women who are experiencing problems as a result of FGM. This specialist service is staffed by an all-female team, who understand the sensitivity and complexity of issues relating to FGM.

Address:

Hassell Drive
Lawrence Hill
Bristol, BS2 0AN

Telephone: Contact Dr Katrina Darke at Lawrence Hill Heath Centre on: 07813016911 or talk to your GP regarding a referral.

Email: bristolroseclinic@nhs.net

http://www.bristolccg.nhs.uk/media/32270/bcrclinic_mulitilingual.pdf

### BIRMINGHAM

### 14. Birmingham Heartlands Hospital – Heart of England NHS Foundation Trust

Address:

Princess of Wales Women's Unit Heartlands Hospital
Bordesley Green
East Birmingham, B9 5SS

Open: Every Day

Telephone: 0121 424 3909

### LIVERPOOL

### 15. Link Clinic – Liverpool Women's Hospital

Staffed by a specialist midwife/coordinator, both community and Children's Centre midwives, and health link workers, the service offers a range of support aids including education and parenting classes, information leaflets and CDs. The clinic benefits from interpreters as well as a telephone interpreting service.

Address:

Antenatal Clinic
Crown St
Liverpool
Merseyside L8 7SS

Open: Mondays 9am and 1.30pm.

Telephone: 0151 702 4180 or 0151 702 4178

http://www.liverpoolwomens.nhs.uk/Our_Services/Maternity/Specialist_
antenatal_cli nics.aspx

## CARE AND SUPPORT SERVICES

### Health services

**9.27** Women and girls who have undergone FGM can have a variety of different needs for care and support, and may seek help from a range of places. The appropriate treatment will depend on the girl/woman's individual circumstances and an assessment of her needs. This will normally include considering her symptoms, type of FGM and whether she is pregnant. As with all health services, an individual care plan should be agreed with the patient and put in place to meet her specific needs.[40]

**9.28** When developing a new service or care pathway within an area, organisations are encouraged and advised to work with patient representatives and groups who can advise on the wishes and needs of service users.[41]

**9.29** For clinical guidelines on the care of women who have undergone FGM, please see *Female Genital Mutilation and its Management (Green-top Guideline No 53)*, published by Royal College of Obstetrics and Gynaecology.

**9.30** In Wales, there is a published FGM Care Pathway and any queries should be directed through the health board FGM lead: www.wales.nhs.uk/sitesplus/888/page/67421/.

### Counselling and psychological services

**9.31** All front line practitioners should give early consideration to signposting victims specialist counselling services. Case histories and personal accounts taken from women indicate that FGM can be an extremely traumatic

---

[40] Multi-agency statutory guidance on female genital mutilation, HM Government (April 2016), para F1.
[41] Multi-agency statutory guidance on female genital mutilation, HM Government (April 2016), para F1.

experience which stays with them for the rest of their lives. Young women receiving psychological counselling in the UK report feelings of betrayal by parents, incompleteness, regret, and anger.[42] There is increasing awareness of the severe psychological consequences of FGM for girls and women, which can become evident in mental health problems.[43]

---

[42]  Haseena Lockhat, *Female Genital Mutilation: Treating the Tears* (London: Middlesex University Press, 2004).

[43]  Multi-agency statutory guidance on female genital mutilation, HM Government (April 2016), para F2.

# CHAPTER 10

# IMMIGRATION AND ASYLUM ISSUES

*Jared Ficklin, Liverpool Law Clinic, School of Law and Social Justice,
University of Liverpool*

**10.1** The risk of FGM may be argued as the basis for a claim for international protection, usually described generically in the United Kingdom as a claim for asylum. It is not controversial that FGM amounts to 'serious harm'; the first essential element of an asylum claim. However, claimants often struggle to prove that the risk of FGM cannot be avoided by seeking protection from the police or other authorities in their home country, or that they cannot simply move to another part of the country where the risk may be avoided.

**10.2** Asylum, or international protection, are catch-all terms that in the UK currently encompass three overlapping legal frameworks. The most important of the three for these purposes is the Refugee Convention.[1] 'Refugee' is used colloquially to describe anyone fleeing war or disaster, and is often associated in lay-people's minds with political oppression. The legal definition is simultaneously broader in some respects, and narrower in others. Article 1 of the Refugee Convention contains the formal definition:

> 'A person who owing to a well-founded fear of being persecuted for reasons of race, religion, nationality, membership of a particular social group or political opinion, is outside the country of his nationality and is unable or, owing to such fear, is unwilling to avail himself of the protection of that country; or who, not having a nationality and being outside the country of his former habitual residence as a result of such events, is unable or, owing to such fear, is unwilling to return to it.'

**10.3** A successful claim for recognition[2] as a refugee must fulfil all of the elements of Article 1.

---

[1] The 'Refugee Convention' is actually shorthand for the combined effect of the 1951 Convention Relating to the Status of Refugees, which entailed temporal and geographic restrictions and was drafted with post-WWII Europe in mind, and the 1967 Protocol Relating to the Status of Refugees that removed those limitations. The UK is a signatory to both.

[2] Formally, refugees are recognised, not made. A finding by the Home Office or a court is declaratory in nature, and recognises that the claimant was a refugee from the moment all the criteria of Art 1 were met. This used to be recognised in the UK in a practical way by backdating some benefit entitlement to the date of claim if it ultimately succeeded. This practice ended in 2007.

**10.4**   There are two other layers of international protection that apply in different circumstances.[3] The second is Council Directive 2004/83/EC, known as the Qualification Directive,[4] and it sets out a definition of a refugee[5] that is effectively identical to that of the Refugee Convention as a minimum standard for European Union Member States. But it also provides for 'subsidiary protection', applied in the UK as 'Humanitarian Protection', in cases where the risk of serious harm is not based on a characteristic such as race, religion, political beliefs etc,[6] thus providing a second layer of protection if a claimant falls outside the Refugee Convention. These bases of risk are specific to recognition under the Refugee Convention and are known as the claimant's 'Convention Reason'. Since the case of *Fornah*[7] and the acceptance that women and girls at risk of FGM are members of a Particular Social Group, there is unlikely to be a need to resort to Humanitarian Protection in an FGM-based asylum claim.

**10.5**   Article 3 of the European Convention on Human Rights[8] is the third layer and also protects claimants from 'inhuman or degrading treatment' which is synonymous with *persecution* under the Refugee Convention and *serious harm* under the Qualification Directive. Asylum lawyers often refer to the 'Article 3 threshold' to describe the level of harm that the claimant fears, but it could equally be called the 'Convention' or 'Directive' threshold. Similarly, for all three layers a claimant must show a reasonable likelihood[9] of the harm taking place in the future, as well as a failure of protection (usually by the state), and the lack of a reasonable internal relocation alternative. Most of the definition presents no problems for an FGM claimant. FGM is accepted by the Home Office and courts to be a form of persecution or serious harm.[10] The claimant must be outside her country of origin, and not be able to return to a different country to avoid the risk.

---

[3]   Since 1 December 2007, in accordance with the Procedures Directive (2005/85/EC) of 1 December 2005, any application for asylum is considered an application for protection under the applicable framework (Refugee Convention, Qualification Directive, or ECHR, Art 3). Applicants need not apply separately for the different forms of protection.

[4]   Directive 2004/83/EC of the Council of the European Union on minimum standards for the qualification and status of third country nationals or stateless persons as refugees or as persons who otherwise need international protection and the content of the protection granted, 2004 (the 'Qualification Directive'). Formally it is this Directive that underpins the UK Immigration Rules Part 11: Asylum, ie paras 326A–352H; see *Gekhang (Interaction of Directives and Rules)* [2016] UKUT 00374 (IAC). Due to a right of 'opt-in', the UK is not a signatory to the recast Qualification Directive, Council Directive 2011/95/EU, which requires enhanced procedural rights and better protection for successful claimants. The UK determined that such protections would 'weaken' the asylum system; see the February 2014 Review of the Balance of Competences between the United Kingdom and the European Union: Asylum & non-EU Migration.

[5]   Qualification Directive, Art 10.

[6]   Qualification Directive, Art 15.

[7]   [2006] UKHL 46.

[8]   ECHR, Art 3 states: 'No one shall be subjected to torture or to inhuman or degrading treatment or punishment.' Again, 'inhuman or degrading treatment' is synonymous with serious harm and persecution.

[9]   That is, that the fear is 'well-founded'.

[10]   See the Home Office Asylum Policy Instruction: Gender Issues in the Asylum Claim which

**10.6**   Finally, the Secretary of State or tribunal will consider if there are 'serious reasons' to believe the applicant has committed serious political or non-political crimes that should exclude her from protection. If there are, then the Refugee Convention and the Qualification Directive will not apply, but Article 3 of the ECHR will still protect the claimant from *refouler*; that is, being returned to a real risk of serious harm that cannot be obviated by protection or internal relocation.

## DEFINITION OF A 'REFUGEE'

### Convention reason

**10.7**   The Refugee Convention requires that a claimant's fear must be associated with a personal characteristic, ie the 'Convention Reasons' set out in Article 1. As Lord Bingham put it in *Fornah v Secretary of State for the Home Department*,[11] 'the [Refugee] Convention is concerned not with all cases of persecution but with persecution which is based on discrimination'. Particular Social Group, or PSG, is the most problematic of the 'Convention Reasons' because claimants must be members of a group united by an immutable feature that is distinguishable from the persecution itself. The UNHCR *Guidelines on International Protection* of 7 May 2002 state:

> 'a particular social group is a group of persons who share a common characteristic other than their risk of being persecuted, or who are perceived as a group by society. The characteristic will often be one which is innate, unchangeable, or which is otherwise fundamental to identity, conscience or the exercise of one's human rights.'

**10.8**   This need for a 'common characteristic other than their risk of being persecuted' proved to be a significant conceptual barrier for the UK courts. Despite the various legal and informal systems of enforced gender inequality around the world, gender as a basis for persecution was only conclusively established in 1999 in *Shah and Islam*.[12] Before *Fornah*, UK courts sometimes pieced together a PSG out of a combination of social norms that tolerated violence toward women and girls with unequal status before the law.

**10.9**   In *P and M v Secretary of State for the Home Department*,[13] two Kenyan women argued that they were at risk from family members who would inflict serious harm on them (FGM, in M's case) and that the legal system in Kenya would not protect them due to entrenched discrimination against women and ineffective police. Their inferior societal position and the failure of state

---

states unequivocally: 'FGM, for example, is widely practised in some societies but it is a form of gender-based violence that inflicts severe harm, both mental and physical, and amounts to persecution.'

[11]   Para 13.

[12]   *Islam v Secretary of State for the Home Department Immigration Appeal Tribunal and Another, ex parte Shah, R v* [1999] UKHL 20.

[13]   [2004] EWCA Civ 1640.

protection were both direct consequences of being women, irrespective of their risk of serious harm. Discrimination against them and their inability to enforce their rights in Kenya was based on their gender, so the persecution feared was not the defining feature of the group, and the Court of Appeal accepted their claim of being members of a PSG.

**10.10**   By contrast, a later Court of Appeal rejected Ms Fornah's[14] claim to a PSG despite some similarities: a young woman who had not yet been cut in a country (Sierra Leone) that discriminated against women and which provided no effective state protection. The Secretary of State's arguments warrant quotation at length:[15]

> 'The main thrust of Mr Tam's submissions on that issue was that ... female genital mutilation in Sierra Leone, which Miss Fornah fears, is a deeply-embedded part of that country's culture and traditions. It is performed by women on women, and there is evidence suggesting that the vast majority of women undergo it willingly as an initiation into womanhood and membership of women's societies. In consequence, he maintained that the practice is a 'rite of passage' commonly accepted by the society in question – namely the men and women of Sierra Leone – not one of discrimination or cruelty to an unwilling section or 'particular social group' of that society. And, as to young Sierra Leonean women who have not yet undergone it, he noted that the evidence showed that, though some feared it, others welcomed it, making it difficult to identify a particular social grouping of them for this purpose.'

**10.11**   The lead judgment found that FGM in Sierra Leone 'is widespread and accepted as a normal route to womanhood for young girls'[16] and that the claim must fail since the proposed PSG was indistinguishable from those at risk of persecution.

**10.12**   The House of Lords resoundingly rejected this reasoning. Lord Bingham's dicta deserves equal length:[17]

> 'It is nothing to the point that FGM in Sierra Leone is carried out by women [...]. Most vicious initiatory rituals are in fact perpetuated by those who were themselves subject to the ritual as initiates and see no reason why others should not share their experience. Nor is it pertinent that a practice is widely practised and accepted [...]. ... FGM may ensure a young woman's acceptance in Sierra Leonean society, but she is accepted on the basis of institutionalised inferiority. I cannot, with respect, agree with Auld LJ that FGM "is not, in the circumstances in which it is practised in Sierra Leone, discriminatory in such a way as to set those who undergo it apart from society". As I have said, FGM is an extreme expression of the discrimination to which all women in Sierra Leone are subject, as much those who have already undergone the process as those who have not. I find no difficulty in recognising women in Sierra Leone as a particular social group [...].'

---

[14]   *Fornah v Secretary of State for the Home Department* [2005] EWCA Civ 680.
[15]   *P and M v Secretary of State for the Home Department* [2004] EWCA Civ 1640 at para 25.
[16]   *P and M v Secretary of State for the Home Department* [2004] EWCA Civ 1640 at para 42.
[17]   *K v Secretary of State for the Home Department* [2006] UKHL 46 at para 31.

**10.13** In addition to 'women in Sierra Leone', the House of Lords found further characteristics that could adequately define the PSG apart from the feared persecution, including women in Sierra Leone who had not been cut,[18] or women from an ethnic group that practised FGM.[19] In all formulations the inferior societal position of women in the country and legal discrimination against them were determinative, not the risk of harm feared. What constitutes an identifiable PSG in one country may not in another[20] based on the same fear of serious harm, depending on the societal and legal context.

**10.14** Before the Human Rights Act 1998 (HRA 1998) came into force in October 2000, if a woman or girl could not show that she had some other Convention Reason, the result was often an enforced return to the risk of FGM;[21] no doubt it was serious harm, but not inflicted for a reason for which the UK deigned to provide protection. Protection under Article 3 allowed the claimants to stay in the UK, but did not provide the level of integration support, duration of leave to remain, or right of family reunion afforded by the Refugee Convention. The Qualification Directive came into force for asylum claims made after 9 October 2006[22] and allowed grants of Humanitarian Protection, a distinctly stronger and longer variant of international protection than that granted under Article 3 of the ECHR. But *Fornah* was fortuitously promulgated on 18 October 2006 and generally brought FGM claimants within the scope of the Refugee Convention as it applied in the UK.

## Real risk

**10.15** The starting point for claimants is proving that their fear of FGM is well founded. Claimants often struggle to convey the level of threat to themselves or their daughters to the Home Office or the tribunal. Threats from family members or a local community are often hearsay, albeit generally backed by evidence of the FGM prevalence rate for that country, community or ethnicity. This is not unusual for asylum claims, which by their nature are often made by

---

[18] Lord Roger at para 80 of *Fornah*, 'the appellant belongs to the group of uninitiated intact women who face persecution by enforced mutilation. If I am wrong ... then I would, of course, accept that the appellant falls within the larger social group of women and girls who face enforced mutilation.'

[19] Baroness Hale at para 111 of *Fornah*, 'They share the immutable characteristics of being female, Sierra Leonean and members of the particular tribe to which they belong. They would share these characteristics even if FGM were not practised within their communities.'

[20] Lord Bingham at para 12 of *Fornah*, 'a particular social group may be recognisable as such in one country but not in another'.

[21] However, the SSHD could exercise discretion and grant what was then known as Exceptional Leave to Remain (ELR), which could and often did lead to Indefinite Leave to Remain albeit without recognition of the risk to the claimant. ELR was replaced from 1 April 2003 with either protection under the ECHR, Art 3 (then known as Humanitarian Protection until that term became associated with the Qualification Directive) or Discretionary Leave to Remain. See Immigration Directorates' Instructions, Leave Outside the Rules, April 2006, at https://www.gov.uk/government/uploads/system/uploads/attachment_data/file/262848/section14.pdf.

[22] As per The Refugee or Person in Need of International Protection (Qualification) Regulations 2006, SI 2006/2525.

people with no documentation and nothing material to 'prove' that they are at risk. When considering claims, the Home Office applies its own country-specific sources of background evidence,[23] coupled with its Asylum Policy Instructions[24] (APIs) depending on the nature of the case. The Immigration and Asylum Chamber is a 'specialist' tribunal; the expectation is that it is experienced, knowledgeable and sensitive to cultural practices and legal frameworks in a claimant's country of origin. The reality varies, but in theory this specialism and experience enables the tribunal to consider the claimant's account for consistency, both internal ie whether the account has been sufficiently detailed and consistent over the inevitable multiple re-telling required by the asylum process,[25] and external ie whether it accords with the background evidence relied upon by the Home Office and/or the claimant.[26]

**10.16**   The burden of proof is entirely on the claimant.[27] It is fundamental to asylum claims that the claimant is not seeking simply to prove what has happened in the past. The burden on the claimant is to show that there is a *future* risk. Events in the past may be the best indicator of future risk, especially in cases where a claimant fears government agents of persecution. A regime that has tortured a political activist, for example, may be reasonably likely to do so again.[28] In FGM cases, by contrast, the risk is generally a one-off event, albeit abuse or punishment for refusal to undergo FGM may be ongoing. For that reason, the serious harm and often life-long physical and psychological suffering of FGM victims is unlikely to be an indicator of future risk. However, past infliction of FGM on a woman may be evidence of a future risk for her daughter. This is particularly relevant when the claimant is from an ethnic group or cultural background with a high FGM prevalence rate. A high rate generally indicates high family or community pressure to undergo or inflict FGM and poor legal recourse or other available protection.

---

[23]   In the form of Country of Origin Information (COI), Operational Guidance Notes (OGNs) and County Information and Guidance reports (CIGs).

[24]   In particular, see *Asylum Policy Instruction: Assessing credibility and refugee status*, currently version 9.0 dated 6 January 2015. Other APIs may apply depending on the nature of the case; see also *Asylum Policy Instruction: Gender Issues in the Asylum Process*, 29 September 2010.

[25]   At a minimum, a claimant will give details of her claim at a screening interview, a substantive asylum interview, and at a tribunal hearing. Represented claimants will often also provide a witness statement and sometimes further witness statements clarifying or correcting the asylum interview record and in response to a Reasons for Refusal Letter.

[26]   The asylum jurisdiction utilises country-specific precedent cases that in theory comprehensively consider a particular issue or set of issues for the benefit of the tribunal and parties, and are designated as Country Guidance in the citation alongside the issue, eg *K and others (FGM) (CG)* [2013] UKUT 62 and *VM (FGM-risks-Mungiki-Kikuyu/Gikuyu) Kenya CG* [2008] UKAIT 00049. These cases are determined by panels of two or more Judges of the Upper Tribunal in the Immigration and Asylum Chamber, and are considered authoritative on an issue until the Upper Tribunal decides otherwise in a subsequently reported case.

[27]   An exception to this generality is where the Home Office positively asserts fraud or forgery, particularly in relation to documents, instead of simply putting the claimant to proof. This is called the Tanveer Ahmed principle after *Tanveer Ahmed v Secretary of State for the Home Department (Pakistan)* [2002] UKIAT 00439. For a slight gloss on the principle, see *MJ (Singh v Belgium: Tanveer Ahmed unaffected) Afghanistan* [2013] UKUT 253 (IAC).

[28]   This principle, that previous persecution or direct threats of such persecution is a 'serious indication of the person's well-founded fear' is codified in the Immigration Rules at para 339K.

**10.17** The standard of proof in asylum cases is lower than the civil standard. It is described variously, including simply 'the lower standard,' and not always clearly, but a useful formulation is 'a reasonable degree of likelihood'.[29] More recently the courts have preferred 'real risk'.[30] It was described by Sedley LJ,[31] as he then was, using the example of a choice of ten cars for a journey. If it was known that one car would have a fatal crash, but not which one, most people would understandably demur from the trip. That is not to say that the standard is a 10% likelihood, simply that the risk should be operative and genuine.

**10.18** The standard of proof is unaffected by glosses of language or the determination process. Two examples that required judicial clarification are s 8 of the Asylum and Immigration (Treatment of Claimants, etc) Act 2004, and the concept of 'benefit of the doubt.'

**10.19** Section 8(2) states that a claimant's credibility may be harmed by:

'... any behaviour by the claimant that the deciding authority thinks—

(a)   is designed or likely to conceal information,
(b)   is designed or likely to mislead, or
(c)   is designed or likely to obstruct or delay the handling or resolution of the claim or the taking of a decision in relation to the claimant.'

**10.20** Section 8 non-exhaustively lists various behaviours that may be considered damaging to credibility, including *inter alia* destroying one's travel documents, passing through a safe country *en route* to the UK or unreasonably delaying a claim for asylum after risk has arisen. In the context of risk of FGM, a claimant who may be in the UK as a student or for work may not consider that the risk to herself or her daughter has arisen until the end of her permitted leave to remain is imminent, or after an application to extend her stay is refused, and only then claim asylum. Or, despite her fear of FGM, a claimant without leave to remain may not wish to bring herself to the attention of the authorities[32] and so may claim only after detection and commencement of enforcement action against her. Despite the breadth of s 8 and due consideration given to it by the Home Office and the tribunal, none of this ultimately dictates a conclusion to the decision maker, nor does it affect the standard of proof. As leading counsel for the Secretary of State in *Y v Secretary of State for the Home Department*[33] accepted:

---

[29]   *Sivakumuran, R (on the application of) v Secretary of State for the Home Department* [1987] UKHL 1.
[30]   *PS (Sri Lanka) v Secretary of State for the Home Department* [2008] EWCA Civ 1213.
[31]   *Batayav v Secretary of State for the Home Department* [2003] EWCA 1489.
[32]   The UK's *Multi-agency statutory guidance on female genital mutilation* states at para D.2.8: 'Many individuals, especially women, may be frightened by contact with any statutory agency, as they may have been told that the authorities will deport them and/or take their parents or children from them.' It says that those who deal with such women should be 'extremely sensitive' because their insecure immigration status makes them 'particularly vulnerable'.
[33]   [2006] EWCA Civ 1223.

'The Secretary of State accepts that section 8 should not be interpreted as affecting the normal standard of proof in an asylum/human rights appeal. There is nothing in the wording of the Act that requires (or indeed permits) such a result. The effect of section 8 is simply to ensure that certain factors relating to personal credibility are taken into account when that standard of proof is applied. The weight and significance of those factors will vary according to the context and the precise circumstances of the behaviour.'

**10.21**    A related issue is the concept of 'benefit of the doubt'. This originates in the UNHCR *Handbook on Procedures and Criteria for Determining Refugee Status* which states:[34]

'it is hardly possible for a refugee to "prove" every part of his case and, indeed, if this were a requirement the majority of refugees would not be recognized. It is therefore frequently necessary to give the applicant the benefit of the doubt.'

**10.22**    However, the *Handbook* goes on that the benefit of the doubt should 'only be given when all available evidence has been obtained and checked and when the examiner is satisfied as to the applicant's general credibility.'[35]

**10.23**    The concept is imported into the Immigration Rules at paragraph 339L:

'Where aspects of the person's statements are not supported by documentary or other evidence, those aspects will not need confirmation when all of the following conditions are met:

(i)    the person has made a genuine effort to substantiate his asylum claim or establish that he is a person eligible for humanitarian protection or substantiate his human rights claim;

(ii)    all material factors at the person's disposal have been submitted, and a satisfactory explanation regarding any lack of other relevant material has been given;

(iii)    the person's statements are found to be coherent and plausible and do not run counter to available specific and general information relevant to the person's case;

(iv)    the person has made an asylum claim or sought to establish that he is a person eligible for humanitarian protection or made a human rights claim at the earliest possible time, unless the person can demonstrate good reason for not having done so; and

(v)    the general credibility of the person has been established.'

**10.24**    Despite this incorporation of the concept as a systematic approach, and further explication in an API,[36] the Upper Tribunal (IAC) has described the 'benefit of the doubt' thus:[37]

---

[34]  See para 203 of the 2011 re-issued UNHCR *Handbook*.
[35]  See para 204 of the 2011 re-issued UNHCR *Handbook*.
[36]  *Asylum Policy Instruction: Assessing credibility and refugee status*, version 9.0 dated 6 January 2015.
[37]  *KS (benefit of the doubt)* [2014] UKUT 552 (IAC).

'[The benefit of the doubt] is not to be regarded as a rule of law. It is a general guideline, expressed in the Handbook in defeasible and contingent terms. ...

What is involved is simply no more than an acceptance that in respect of every asserted fact when there is doubt, the lower standard entails that it should not be rejected and should rather continue to be kept in mind as a possibility at least until the end when the question of risk is posed in relation to the evidence in the round. ...

Correctly viewed, therefore, [the benefit of the doubt] adds nothing of substance to the lower standard of proof...'

**10.25** While the Secretary of State will rely on s 8 and claimants will rely on the benefit of the doubt, the ultimate question for the decision maker is whether there is a real risk of FGM. That is only the beginning of the process. If the claimant can establish a risk of FGM, further questions arise as set out below.

## Sufficiency of protection

**10.26** It is not enough for an asylum claimant to establish that there is a risk to her, ie that her fear of serious harm is well founded. She must also establish that there is insufficient protection for her in the country where she faces the risk. In *Horvath v Secretary of State for the Home Department*,[38] the House of Lords established that 'persecution' as defined in the Refugee Convention included two elements: both the real risk of serious harm and a failure of protection. In order for the UK to take responsibility for a claimant's protection, it had to be shown that claimant's state, or whoever controls her territory, had failed in the duty to protect its citizen, thus requiring the UK to step in as a surrogate. In general, where an asylum claimant has a well founded fear of the government itself, the police or other state agents, then the question of sufficiency of protection does not arise. Claims based on state persecution for political beliefs, opposition party activism, apostasy against a theocratic state etc generally do not require detailed consideration of the willingness of other state agents to provide protection, at least if that government's writ runs all the way to its borders and there is no other group of actors claiming to act with the authority of the state. But FGM claims are effectively always based on fear of non-state agents. Families and communities may seek to inflict FGM as a cultural or social norm. Even where that risk is established ('well founded') a claimant must also show that the state or other actors, usually but not necessarily in the form of the police, cannot provide that practical standard of protection.

**10.27** In *Horvath* it was found that the protection need not be absolute or even particularly good. Describing it as a 'practical standard' and observing that no police force can protect all citizens all the time and prevent all harm, Lord Hope stated:

---

[38] [2000] UKHL 37.

'The primary duty to provide the protection lies with the home state. It is its duty to establish and to operate a system of protection against the persecution of its own nationals. If that system is lacking the protection of the international community is available as a substitute. But the application of the surrogacy principle rests upon the assumption that, just as the substitute cannot achieve complete protection against isolated and random attacks, so also complete protection against such attacks is not to be expected of the home state. The standard to be applied is therefore not that which would eliminate all risk and would thus amount to a guarantee of protection in the home state. Rather it is a practical standard, which takes proper account of the duty which the state owes to all its own nationals.'

**10.28**   The generality of *Horvath* was focused in *R (Bagdanavicius) v Secretary of State for the Home Department*.[39] In that case the Court of Appeal drew together the authorities on the issue and clarified that a sufficiency of protection was to be assessed with regard to the facts of each case and the personal characteristics, circumstances and history of the particular claimant:

'An asylum seeker who claims to be in fear of persecution is entitled to asylum if he can show a well-founded fear of persecution for a Refugee Convention reason and that there would be insufficiency of state protection to meet it; Horvath.

...

Sufficiency of state protection, whether from state agents or non-state actors, means a willingness and ability on the part of the receiving state to provide through its legal system a reasonable level of protection from ill-treatment of which the claimant for asylum has a well-founded fear; Osman, Horvath, Dhima.

The effectiveness of the system provided is to be judged normally by its systemic ability to deter and/or to prevent the form of persecution of which there is a risk, not just punishment of it after the event; Horvath; Banomova. McPherson and Kinuthia.

Notwithstanding systemic sufficiency of state protection in the receiving state, a claimant may still have a well-founded fear of persecution if he can show that its authorities know or ought to know of circumstances particular to his case giving rise to his fear, but are unlikely to provide the additional protection his particular circumstances reasonably require; Osman.'

**10.29**   *Bagdanavicius* gives the impression that protection must be provided by a state, and that however much a state may aspire to provide protection, there must be at least some effectiveness in deterring the serious harm, not solely post-hoc punishment. But *Bagdanavicius* was decided before the Qualification Directive came into force in October 2006. Article 7(1)(b) of the Qualification Directive requires consideration of the potential for protection from 'parties or

---

[39]   [2005] EWCA Civ 1605, applied in *IM (Sufficiency of Protection) Malawi* [2007] UKAIT 00071 and *AW (Sufficiency of Protection) Pakistan* [2011] UKUT 31(IAC). Note that *Bagdanavicius* went to the House of Lords ([2005] UKHL 38) but the Court of Appeal's summary of guidance on sufficiency of protection and other asylum issues was not disturbed.

organisations, including international organisations, controlling the state or a substantial part of the territory of the states.'[40] The Qualification Directive goes on to clarify that the protection must be provided by parties 'operating an effective legal system for the detection, prosecution and punishment of acts constituting persecution or serious harm',[41] and that the claimant must have access to it. The Home Office's view on who can provide an 'effective legal system' may be surprising. Home Office guidance states:[42]

> 'A country which relies for its law and order functions on drug barons or armed militias may be less able to provide effective protection than one which can rely on those functions being performed by trained, resourced and accountable police or army personnel. But the question to be asked is a factual one, "Is protection afforded?"'

**10.30** In practice, application of the *Horvath* standard of protection in the UK presents a significant barrier in FGM claims, particularly when the Home Office prevents access to the tribunal. An example may be made of Nigeria, a country with a 25% FGM prevalence rate,[43] which rises to 55% for some ethnic groups,[44] and which has the largest absolute number of FGM victims in the world.[45] At least until recently, the Home Office routinely 'certified' FGM claims from Nigeria as 'clearly unfounded'[46] on the basis of the sufficiency of protection, which prevents an in-country appeal to the tribunal. The legal test for certification of an asylum claim, taking into account the background evidence and how much of the claim is capable of belief, has been stated as whether 'the claim cannot on any legitimate view succeed'.[47] Unless the certification is quashed by judicial review, a claimant may only appeal after returning to her country. If her fear of FGM is well founded, she or her daughter will be exposed to the risk while the tribunal hears the case in her absence and makes a determination.

**10.31** Nigeria has recently passed a national law[48] banning FGM throughout the country. Previously, FGM had been outlawed in a minority of Nigeria's 36 states.[49] Home Office guidance makes much of the new law, stating:[50]

---

[40] Qualification Directive, Art 7(1)(b).
[41] Qualification Directive, Art 7(2).
[42] *Asylum Policy Instruction: Assessing credibility and refugee status*, Version 9.0, 6 January 2015; section 8.1.
[43] Of women and girls aged 15–49, UNICEF, *Statistical Profile on Female Genital Mutilation/Cutting*: Nigeria, July 2014.
[44] UNICEF, *Statistical Profile on Female Genital Mutilation/Cutting*: Nigeria, July 2014.
[45] TC Okeke, USB Anyaehie, and CCK Ezenyeaku, 'An Overview of Female Genital Mutilation in Nigeria' (2012) 2(1) *Ann Med Health Sci Res* 70–73, https://www.ncbi.nlm.nih.gov/pmc/articles/PMC3507121/, accessed 27 October 2010.
[46] As per the Nationality, Immigration and Asylum Act 2002, s 94(2).
[47] *ZL & Anor v Secretary of State for the Home Department and Lord Chancellor's Department* [2003] EWCA Civ 25 at paras 56–57.
[48] Violence Against Persons (Prohibition) Act 2015, signed into law in May 2015 by outgoing President Goodluck Jonathan.
[49] FGM was banned in 12 Nigerian states as of 2012, according to the Home Office Country of

'This shows a determination to tackle violence against women, provides stiffer penalties for a number of gender-based offences such as FGM, and makes it easier for women to seek recourse and protection.'

**10.32** The guidance goes on to acknowledge serious problems with the Nigerian police, noting that only half of Nigerians surveyed would report a crime to them.[51] Women have even greater difficulty. Regarding gender based violence (GBV) generally, the guidance states:[52]

'There is widespread under-reporting and reluctance amongst women to report abuse to the authorities. This is because the police are perceived as being reluctant to take violence against women seriously and pursue allegations.'

**10.33**   And further:[53]

'police characteristically exhibit bias and discriminatory attitudes in their treatment of female victims of violence which is informed by cultural beliefs and notions which devalue and subjugate women, and often blame the victim.'

**10.34**   Despite this acknowledgment of the concerns and risks facing Nigerian women, the guidance makes clear that the starting point is that there is a sufficiency of protection:[54]

'In general, the Nigerian authorities are willing and able to provide protection from non-state agents, albeit women face greater difficulties in seeking and obtaining protection than men particularly for sexual- and gender-based violence. Each case will need to be considered on its particular circumstances taking into account factors such as their age, socio-economic circumstances, education and ethnicity. A person's reluctance to seek protection does not mean that effective protection is not available. The onus is on the person to demonstrate that the state is not willing and able to provide them with effective protection.'

**10.35**   Overall, the picture is complex, and like any other international protection claim, it is clear that a Nigerian FGM claim requires detailed consideration of the particular facts of the case.

---

Origin Information Report – Nigeria, 14 June 2013, section 23.75, quoting the US State Department Country Report on Human Rights Practices 2011: Nigeria, released on 24 May 2012.

[50] *Country Information and Guidance: Nigeria: Women fearing gender-based harm or violence*, Version 2.0, August 2016, section 2.4.1.

[51] *Country Information and Guidance: Nigeria: Women fearing gender-based harm or violence*, Version 2.0, August 2016, section 9.4.3, which cites A Global Observatory Report from July 2015.

[52] *Country Information and Guidance: Nigeria: Women fearing gender-based harm or violence*, Version 2.0, August 2016, sections 2.4.2–2.4.3.

[53] *Country Information and Guidance: Nigeria: Women fearing gender-based harm or violence*, Version 2.0, August 2016, section 5.1.1, citing The Canadian Immigration and Refugee Board, Nigeria: Domestic violence, including Lagos State; legislation, recourse, state protection and services available to victims (2011–October 2014), 10 November 2014.

[54] *Country Information and Guidance: Nigeria: Women fearing gender-based harm or violence*, Version 2.0, August 2016, section 2.4.4.

**10.36**  Between 2012–2014, nearly a third of asylum refusals (for all countries) were overturned at the tribunal,[55] illustrating the importance of the appeals process for the integrity of the asylum system. It might be reasonable to conclude that a Nigerian FGM case is usually inappropriate for certification as clearly unfounded, even considering the protection under the new law, and 'will need to be considered on its particular circumstances'.[56] But even prior to the passing of the new law in 2015 the Home Office regularly certified Nigerian FGM claims as clearly unfounded on the basis that whatever the failings of the police and legal system, they provided a practical standard of protection. At least until nearly the end of 2012, there had never been a prosecution for FGM in the Nigerian states that outlawed it.[57] Rather, the Home Office relied upon evidence of public education efforts[58] and the aspirations of the Nigerian government[59] to prevent such claims from troubling the tribunal.

**10.37**  This example illustrates that what constitutes sufficiency of protection must be looked at carefully. While there may be evidence of government or police opposition to FGM, whether that opposition amounts to a 'practical standard' or mere lip service is a matter of evidence based on the individual's circumstances vis-à-vis the state's (or some other actor's) capacity to provide protection in the country, or at least the claimant's home area in that country.

## Internal relocation

**10.38**  The asylum system is underpinned by the principle that the UK may act as a surrogate protector if a woman or girl at risk of FGM cannot be adequately protected in her home area. But it is not always the case that she is at risk everywhere in her country. It may be that the would-be persecutors are only active in one area, or that the police, drug barons or armed militia[60] somewhere else in the country are able to provide protection. If there is a part

---

[55]  From 2012–2014, 31% of asylum appeals were allowed (source Home Office, Immigration Statistics April to June 2016, Asylum Table as 06).

[56]  *Country Information and Guidance: Nigeria: Women fearing gender-based harm or violence*, Version 2.0, August 2016, section 2.4.4.

[57]  Landinfo: Norwegian Country of Origin Information Centre. Nigeria: Kjønnslemlestelse av kvinner. The Landinfo report states that 'no cases of legal prosecution of people who have subjected girls or women to FGM' have been documented in Nigeria (Norway 14 November 2012, 3).

[58]  US Department of State's Country Reports on Human Rights Practices 2013: Nigeria, released on 27 February 2014; the Nigerian Ministry of Health took part in sponsoring 'public awareness projects to educate communities about the health hazards of FGM/C'. Also Landinfo: Norwegian Country of Origin Information Centre. Nigeria: Kjønnslemlestelse av kvinner; '[p]rojects against FGM, run by both state authorities and NGOs, focus on information to the general public and consciousness building' (Norway 14 November 2012).

[59]  US Department of State's Country Reports on Human Rights Practices 2013: Nigeria, released on 27 February 2014, 'the federal government publicly opposed FGM/C but took no legal action to curb the practice'.

[60]  Drug barons and armed militia are examples of non-state actors who may be able to operate an effective legal system of protection, according to Home Office guidance; see the *Asylum Policy Instruction: Assessing credibility and refugee status*, Version 9.0, 6 January 2015; section 8.1.

of the claimant's country where she would not be at risk, she may be expected to return there instead of receiving international protection.

**10.39**   However, the absence of the real risk of serious harm[61] is not the only test for internal relocation. The House of Lords determined in *Januzi v Secretary of State for the Home Department*[62] that the proposed area must also be a reasonable place to live for the claimant. In the constant semantic battle in the tribunal between a claimant's lawyer and the Home Office Presenting Officer, the former still tend to refer to whether internal relocation is 'reasonable'[63] and the latter only to whether the circumstances would be 'unduly harsh'.[64] In *Januzi*, Lord Hope clarified that the difference was indeed semantic; the terms are aspects of the same thing:[65]

> 'As Linden JA put it in *Thirunavukkarasu v Canada (Minister of Employment and Immigration)* (1993) 109 DLR (4th) 682, 687, it is whether it would be unduly harsh to expect a claimant who is being persecuted for a Convention reason in one part of his country to move to a less hostile part before seeking refugee status abroad. The words "unduly harsh" set the standard that must be met for this to be regarded as unreasonable. If the claimant can live a relatively normal life there judged by the standards that prevail in his country of nationality generally, and if he can reach the less hostile part without undue hardship or undue difficulty, it will not be unreasonable to expect him to move there.'

**10.40**   As set out here, the standard of what is reasonable is not to be measured against circumstances in the UK, but against the prevailing conditions in the country of origin, and must take into account the characteristics and capabilities of the claimant. It may be fairly said that conditions of life in many countries from which claimants originate would be considered unreasonable or unduly harsh by UK standards. But as long as the conditions in the place of relocation do not cross the threshold of serious harm (are not inhuman and degrading) which would disqualify the area, the issue is whether the claimant and her dependants will reasonably be able to live there with reference to all relevant factors. In *Januzi* Lord Bingham cited UNHCR guidance[66] with approval regarding the scope of what must be considered:

> 'The socio-economic conditions in the proposed area will be relevant in this part of the analysis. If the situation is such that the claimant will be unable to earn a living

[61]   Recall that as per *Horvath v Secretary of State for the Home Department* [2000] UKHL 37, 'persecution' as defined in the Refugee Convention included two elements; both the real risk of serious harm and a failure of protection.
[62]   [2006] UKHL 5.
[63]   UNHCR *Handbook*, para 91. This language has also been incorporated into the Qualification Directive, Art 8(1).
[64]   One of the most important cases on IFA in the Commonwealth, and which was considered in *Januzi*, was the case of *Thirunavukkarasu v Minister of Employment and Immigration* [1993] 109 DLR (4th) 682, in the Canadian Federal Court.
[65]   [2006] UKHL 5, para 47.
[66]   UNHCR *Guidelines on International Protection*, No 4: 'Internal Flight or Relocation Alternative' within the Context of Art 1A(2) of the 1951 Convention and/or 1967 Protocol relating to the Status of Refugees, 23 July 2003.

or to access accommodation, or where medical care cannot be provided or is clearly inadequate, the area may not be a reasonable alternative. It would be unreasonable, including from a human rights perspective, to expect a person to relocate to face economic destitution or existence below at least an adequate level of subsistence. At the other end of the spectrum, a simple lowering of living standards or worsening of economic status may not be sufficient to reject a proposed area as unreasonable. Conditions in the area must be such that a relatively normal life can be led in the context of the country concerned. If, for instance, an individual would be without family links and unable to benefit from an informal social safety net, relocation may not be reasonable, unless the person would otherwise be able to sustain a relatively normal life at more than just a minimum subsistence level.

If the person would be denied access to land, resources and protection in the proposed area because he or she does not belong to the dominant clan, tribe, ethnic, religious and/or cultural group, relocation there would not be reasonable. For example, in many parts of Africa, Asia and elsewhere, common ethnic, tribal, religious and/or cultural factors enable access to land, resources and protection. In such situations, it would not be reasonable to expect someone who does not belong to the dominant group, to take up residence there. A person should also not be required to relocate to areas, such as the slums of an urban area, where they would be required to live in conditions of severe hardship.'

**10.41** Access to land, resources and protection, or the living conditions in the slums of an urban area may be particularly problematic for single women or female-headed households in many countries with high FGM prevalence.

**10.42** In the subsequent case of *AH (Sudan)*[67] Lord Bingham went further in expressing that there was no exhaustive list of what factors were to be included, stating:[68]

'... the enquiry must be directed to the situation of the particular applicant, whose age, gender, experience, health, skills and family ties may all be very relevant. There is no warrant for excluding, or giving priority to, consideration of the applicant's way of life in the place of persecution. There is no warrant for excluding, or giving priority to, consideration of conditions generally prevailing in the home country.'

**10.43** Baroness Hale gave the clearest guidance in *AH (Sudan)*, quoting directly from the UNCHR submissions as an intervener:[69]

'... the correct approach when considering the reasonableness of IRA [internal relocation alternative] is to assess all the circumstances of the individual's case holistically and with specific reference to the individual's personal circumstances (including past persecution or fear thereof, psychological and health condition,

---

[67] *Secretary of State for the Home Department (Appellant) v AH (Sudan) and others (FC) (Respondents)* [2007] UKHL 49.

[68] *Secretary of State for the Home Department (Appellant) v AH (Sudan) and others (FC) (Respondents)* [2007] UKHL 49, para 5.

[69] *Secretary of State for the Home Department (Appellant) v AH (Sudan) and others (FC) (Respondents)* [2007] UKHL 49, para 20.

family and social situation, and survival capacities). This assessment is to be made in the context of the conditions in the place of relocation (including basic human rights, security conditions, socio-economic conditions, accommodation, access to health care facilities), in order to determine the impact on that individual of settling in the proposed place of relocation and whether the individual could live a relatively normal life without undue hardship.'

**10.44** Article 8(2) of the Qualification Directive suggests that the UK should raise internal relocation at the time of the decision in the asylum refusal letter or not at all. Member States should consider the nexus between the personal characteristics of the claimant or her dependants and the conditions in the relocation area 'at the time of taking the decision on the application'. Tribunal caselaw supports this while clarifying that the burden of establishing the undue harshness lies with the claimant. In *AMM and others (conflict; humanitarian crisis; returnees; FGM) Somalia CG*[70] it was found that:

'The person who claims international protection bears the legal burden of proving that he or she is entitled to it. ... In practice, the issue of an internal relocation alternative needs to be raised by the Secretary of State, either in the letter of refusal or (subject to issues of procedural fairness) during the appellate proceedings. ... It will then be for the appellant to make good an assertion that ... it would not be reasonable to relocate there.'

**10.45** Countries with high FGM prevalence rates are also often places where women cannot reasonably internally relocate. Each case must be considered on its own facts, regardless of the tenor of the background evidence. But where a country has failed to curb FGM, or has not tried, other forms of gender-based violence and discrimination are often rife. 87% of Egyptian women and girls are subjected to FGM,[71] one of the highest rates in the world; the legal prohibition is ignored and unenforced.[72] It is not a coincidence that Egyptian women face particular difficulty both in accessing protection from serious harm and in relocating to avoid it. The Home Office internal guidance for asylum decision makers states:[73]

'... Women experience endemic sexual harassment, including sexual assault and rape. Inadequate legal provisions and government efforts to protect women from violence, together with a serious lack of police enforcement severely compromise women's access to effective protection. ...

...

---

[70]  [2011] UKUT 445 (IAC) at para 225 and headnote.
[71]  Of women and girls aged 15–49, UNICEF, *Statistical Profile on Female Genital Mutilation/Cutting: Egypt*, February 2016.
[72]  UNICEF, *Statistical Profile on Female Genital Mutilation/Cutting: Egypt*, February 2016. Egypt banned FGM nationally in 2008. Despite this the practice continues with impunity; 78% of cutters are 'health professionals' ie doctors and nurses.
[73]  Home Office, *Operational guidance note: Egypt*, 19 December 2013 (re-issued October 2014), sections 3.13.15–3.13.16.

Some applicants may be able to escape persecution by internally relocating to another area of Egypt. Independent travel will be difficult given the cultural milieu and the specific risks facing women in Egypt, but the evidence does not suggest a complete prohibition on women travelling unaccompanied. However it needs to be noted that women, especially single women with no support network, are likely to be vulnerable and may be subjected to destitution. The reasonableness of internal relocation must be assessed on a case by case basis taking full account of the individual circumstances of the particular claimant.'

**10.46** Somalia is even more extreme. 98% of Somali women and girls have been cut.[74] Gender-based violence of all types is ubiquitous and while cases always turn on their own facts, in most circumstances a woman with or without children who was unaccompanied by a man would be unable to internally relocate to avoid serious harm. Home Office guidance on gender-based violence[75] in Somalia is a shocking litany of abuse and impunity. A typical passage reads as follows:[76]

'Armed assailants, including members of state security forces, operating with complete impunity, sexually assault, rape, beat, shoot, and stab women and girls inside camps for the displaced and as they walk to market, tend to their fields, or forage for firewood.'

**10.47** Despite this, clearly there are parts of Somalia that are reasonable places to live for women, of course depending on their personal circumstances and access to a support network. Between 2007–2014, 39% of asylum appeals by Somali women were dismissed at the tribunal, only marginally fewer than were dismissed for men at 46%.[77]

**10.48** It is one thing for there to be a place of reasonable internal relocation, it may be another for the claimant to reach it. The Home Office long argued that there was no need for it, or indeed power for the courts, to consider anything but the elements of entitlement to international protection in the abstract. The practicalities of reaching the proposed areas of internal relocation, it argued, were nothing to the point. The Home Office was generally successful in the

---

[74] Of women and girls aged 15–49, UNICEF, *Statistical Profile on Female Genital Mutilation/Cutting: Somalia*, December 2013.
[75] *Country Information and Guidance Somalia: Women fearing gender-based harm and violence* Version 3.0, 2 August 2016.
[76] *Country Information and Guidance Somalia: Women fearing gender-based harm and violence* Version 3.0, 2 August 2016, section 4.1.3.
[77] *Home Office Immigration Statistics – April to June 2015: Asylum*. Publication Date: 27 August 2015. Volume 4, Table as 14, Asylum appeal applications and determinations, by country of nationality and sex.

asylum context[78] until 2010, when the Court of Appeal rejected it in *HH (Somalia) & Ors v Secretary of State for the Home Department*,[79] albeit in *obiter dicta*:[80]

> '[The Home Office] "strong" case depends on the proposition that the only appeal afforded by s 82 is against "the decision in principle to remove the appellant from the United Kingdom". It is only when actual removal directions are set, she submits, that an issue can arise in law about the point or route of return, because it is only then that it is known where the appellant is to be returned to.
>
> …
>
> We do not accept [the] "strong" argument. […] … we consider that, in any case in which it can be shown either directly or by implication what route and method of return is envisaged, the [tribunal] is required by law to consider and determine any challenge to the safety of that route or method. That conclusion is consistent … the requirements of the Qualification and Procedures Directive.'

**10.49** 'Technical obstacles' which can include lack of travel documents or other administrative barriers were not to be considered relevant to risk.[81] Any lingering doubt about the requirement to consider the route to the place of reasonable internal relocation, and not just its existence, was dispelled in *J1 v Secretary of State for the Home Department*.[82] The question for the decision-maker, whether Home Office or tribunal, is 'whether at the time of its decision the appellant could be safely returned'.[83] The Home Office cannot simply undertake to delay return until the route to the proposed area of internal relocation becomes safe. The court must determine if there is a risk to the claimant based on a hypothetical return at the date of hearing,[84] even if technical barriers prevent actual removal at that moment. If overcoming the technical barriers, such as provision of appropriate travel documentation,[85] also obviates the risk, then the hypothetical return is safe enough. If the risk on return cannot be overcome in this way, and the claimant must pass through an area where she will be at real risk of serious harm *en route* to the internal relocation alternative, then she is entitled to international protection.

---

[78] But see *MS (Ivory Coast) v Secretary of State for the Home Department* [2007] EWCA Civ 133 regarding ECHR, Art 8.

[79] *HH (Somalia) & Ors v Secretary of State for the Home Department* [2010] EWCA Civ 426.

[80] *HH (Somalia) & Ors v Secretary of State for the Home Department* [2010] EWCA Civ 426, paras 52 and 58.

[81] *HH (Somalia) & Ors v Secretary of State for the Home Department* [2010] EWCA Civ 426, para 82.

[82] [2013] EWCA Civ 279.

[83] *J1 v Secretary of State for the Home Department* [2013] EWCA Civ 279, para 113.

[84] *J1 v Secretary of State for the Home Department* [2013] EWCA Civ 279, paras 96, 102, 108–109.

[85] For example, see *HM and others (Article 15(c)) Iraq CG* [2012] UKUT 00409 (IAC), where returns to Baghdad Airport without correct documentation would have resulted in detention in conditions breaching the serious harm threshold. However, provision of correct documentation obviated this risk. Overcoming the technical obstacle simultaneously overcame the risk of serious harm.

# Exclusion

**10.50** A refugee may be excluded from the Refugee Convention due to their own crimes, whether committed before recognition of their status or after. UNHCR entreats decision makers to apply the exclusion clauses cautiously:[86]

> 'given the possible serious consequences of exclusion, it is important to apply them with great caution and only after a full assessment of the individual circumstances of the case. The exclusion clauses should, therefore, always be interpreted in a restrictive manner.'

**10.51** Article 1F of the Refugee Convention sets out that where there are 'serious reasons' for considering that the applicant has committed crimes against humanity or war crimes[87] (1F(a)), a 'serious non-political crime outside the country of refuge prior to his admission to that country as a refugee' (1F(b)), or 'an act contrary to the purposes and principles of the United Nations' (1F(c)), the claimant may be excluded from recognition as a refugee.

**10.52** 'Serious reasons' is a standard of proof not found in domestic UK law. In *Al-Sirri v Secretary of State for the Home Department*,[88] the UK Supreme Court acknowledged this and established guidelines for applying it:[89]

> '1. "Serious reasons" is stronger than "reasonable grounds".
> 2. The evidence from which those reasons are derived must be "clear and credible" or "strong".
> 3. "Considering" is stronger than "suspecting". In our view it is also stronger than "believing". It requires the considered judgement of the decision-maker.
> 4. The decision-maker need not be satisfied beyond reasonable doubt or the standard required in criminal law.
> 5. It is unnecessary to import our domestic standards of proof into the question.'

**10.53** More concretely, the judgment goes on:[90]

> 'The reality is that there are unlikely to be sufficiently serious reasons for considering the applicant to be guilty unless the decision-maker can be satisfied on the balance of probabilities that he is.'

**10.54** Article 1F(a) of the Refugee Convention is relatively straightforward, since there are international definitions of war crimes and crimes against

---

[86] UNHCR *Guidelines on International Protection: Application of the Exclusion Clauses: Article 1F of the 1951 Convention relating to the Status of Refugees*, para 2.

[87] Annexes V and VI of the UNHCR *Handbook and Guidelines on Procedures and Criteria for Determining Refugee Status Geneva*, Re-issued 2011 (the 'Handbook') sets out a list of international instruments which define war crimes and crimes against humanity. A clear and updated list is set out in Arts 7 and 8 of the Rome Statute of the International Criminal Court 1998.

[88] [2012] UKSC 54.

[89] [2012] UKSC 54 at para 75.

[90] [2012] UKSC 54 at para 75.

humanity. In *R (JS) (Sri Lanka)*[91] the UK Supreme Court confirmed that the Rome Statute of the International Criminal Court 1998 was the starting point for definition of these crimes. The process by which responsibility for such crimes is determined is set out in the Rome Statute at Articles 25 and 30–33. A defence of duress may apply;[92] a defence that the perpetrator was 'just following orders' never can.[93]

**10.55**   The Home Office guidance[94] on the various exclusion provisions states, 'The exclusions (sic) provisions [of Article 1F] are reflected in EU Directives and the Immigration Rules.' This is not strictly accurate. Article 12(2)(b) of the Qualification Directive modified Article 1F(b) of the Refugee Convention by defining the time of admission to the country of refuge as a refugee as 'the time of issuing a residence permit based on the granting of refugee status'. Under Article 12(2)(b), a serious non-political crime committed in the 'country of refuge' ie the UK, prior to the grant of refugee status, amounts to grounds for exclusion. This is contrary to the declarative nature of refugee status, ie that one is a refugee when the Article 1 criteria are met, which means that refugee status is not subsequently granted but recognised as extant. Further, the UNHCR *Handbook*[95] states clearly that Article 1F(b) was not intended to apply to crimes in the country hosting the asylum claim:

> 'Only a crime committed or presumed to have been committed by an applicant outside the country of refuge prior to his admission to that country as a refugee is a ground for exclusion. The country outside would normally be the country of origin, but it could also be another country, except the country of refuge where the applicant seeks recognition of his refugee status.'

**10.56**   The Qualification Directive adds a clarification to Article 1F(c) that the purposes and principles of the United Nations are 'as set out in the Preamble and Articles 1 and 2 of the Charter of the United Nations'.[96] This is not contrary to the intention of the Refugee Convention, and the UNHCR *Handbook*[97] acknowledges this source of the purposes and principles. The *Handbook* goes on to state that 'that the acts covered by [1F(c)] must also be of a criminal nature'[98] and that the Charter relates to UN Member States and not individuals:

---

[91]   [2010] UKSC 15.
[92]   Rome Statute of the International Criminal Court 1998, Art 31. See also *AB (Art 1F(a) – defence – duress: Iran)* [2016] UKUT 376 (IAC).
[93]   Rome Statute of the International Criminal Court 1998, Art 33.
[94]   See the Home Office guidance Exclusion (Article 1F) and Article 33(2) of the Refugee Convention, Version 6.0, 1 July 2016.
[95]   UNHCR *Handbook*, para 153.
[96]   Qualification Directive, Art 12(2)(c).
[97]   See UNHCR *Handbook*, paras 162–163.
[98]   UNHCR *Handbook*, para 162.

'it could be inferred that an individual, in order to have committed an act contrary to these principles, must have been in a position of power in a member State and instrumental to his State's infringing these principles.'[99]

**10.57** However, in *Al-Sirri v Secretary of State for the Home Department* the UNHCR as an intervener accepted that non-state actors could be guilty of acts contrary to the purposes and principles of the UN. The Supreme Court also found that the necessary 'international dimension'[100] could be expressed in terrorism if it was intended to influence events in other countries or was committed in response to them: 'The test is whether the resulting acts have the requisite serious effect upon international peace, security and peaceful relations between states.'[101]

**10.58** Note that Article 3 of the ECHR has no such limitation. A claimant found to meet the exclusion criteria, but accepted to have a well founded fear of FGM that she cannot avoid would likely be granted 'restricted'[102] leave to remain in the UK, perhaps for six months at a time. This could continue until the Secretary of State reached the view that the risk was no longer operative and sought to remove her, or she became eligible for leave to remain on some other basis.

**10.59** If a recognised refugee commits serious crimes, or a series of lesser crimes, and is considered a threat to public security, the Refugee Convention's protection may be withdrawn as per Article 33(2), though the absolute right not to be subject to inhuman and degrading treatment in Article 3 of the ECHR may prevent actual removal. Article 14(4) of the Qualification Directive faithfully transposes Article 33(2); both require reasonable grounds for regarding the refugee (or claimant) as a danger to the security of the UK, or conviction of a particularly serious crime coupled with constituting a danger to the community. The 'particularly serious crime' in Article 33(2) is interpreted in domestic law by s 72 of the Nationality, Immigration and Asylum Act 2002 (NIAA 2002) as a conviction leading to a two-year prison sentence. In *EN (Serbia) v Secretary of State for the Home Department*,[103] the Court of Appeal found that the requirements of conviction and posing a danger to the community were conjunctive, not alternatives, and that together they raised a rebuttable presumption of revocation of refugee status. The conviction need not be in the UK though the offence must be considered through the lens of UK law. The Home Office guidance[104] states:

---

[99] UNHCR *Handbook*, para 163.
[100] UNHCR *Guidelines on International Protection: Application of the Exclusion Clauses: Article 1F of the 1951 Convention relating to the Status of Refugees*, para 17.
[101] [2012] UKSC 54 at para 40.
[102] See the *Asylum Policy Instruction: Restricted leave*, Version 1.0, 23 January 2015; and *Chahal v United Kingdom* (1996) 23 EHRR 413.
[103] [2009] EWCA Civ 630.
[104] *UNCHR guidance Exclusion (Article 1F) and Article 33(2) of the Refugee Convention*, Version 6.0, 1 July 2016.

'Section 72 also applies where a person who is convicted overseas, is sentenced to a period of imprisonment of at least 2 years and could, if convicted in the UK for a similar offence, have been sentenced to at least 2 years. However, what counts for the purposes of section 72(2) and (3) is not the maximum sentence that could have been imposed, or the time a person actually spends in prison or detention, but the period of imprisonment to which they were sentenced.'

**10.60**   Article 14(5) of the Qualification Directive allows application of Article 14(4) before a recognition of refugee status, so even where the rather stricter criteria of Article 1F of the Refugee Convention cannot be made out, a claim may be pre-emptively precluded from recognition.

**10.61**   This long exegesis leads to the most likely scenarios for exclusion in FGM cases. The first is where the claimant may fall to be excluded from protection as a refugee because of her crimes against humanity, war crimes, terrorism etc. This is straightforward, to the extent that exclusion ever is; she may be excluded from the protection of the Convention and/or the Qualification Directive, but if return to her country exposes her, or her daughter, to the risk of FGM and the other elements apply, then she will be protected from *refoulement* by Article 3 of the ECHR. An as-yet entirely hypothetical scenario arises for cutters who claim to be refugees, or are already recognised as refugees in the UK. Offences relating to the infliction of FGM in the UK carry a penalty of up to 14 years' imprisonment.[105] A 'professional' or prolific cutter might be expected to receive a sentence at the higher end of the range, but in any event more than two years' imprisonment, thus invoking s 72 of the NIAA 2002. But this is speculation, since there has never been a conviction in the UK under this law. Laws prohibiting FGM in countries with high prevalence generally carry much lower penalties, including fines,[106] and in any event are generally equally unenforced. It is unlikely that a tribunal will have the clarity of an FGM-related conviction upon which to decide if a claimant should be excluded under Article 1F(b) of the Refugee Convention, and must find other reasons and evidence for finding that an alleged cutter should be excluded from the Refugee Convention or that s 72 of the NIAA 2002 applies.

**10.62**   There are other possible bases for exclusion from the protection of the Refugee Convention under Articles 1D and 1E. These are far narrower. 1D holds that someone who is 'at present receiving' receiving the assistance of a branch of the UN other than UNHCR cannot benefit from the Convention. This applies exclusively to the United Nations Relief and Works Agency for Palestine Refugees (UNRWA) which operates in Occupied Palestinian Territory (Gaza and the West Bank), Jordan, Lebanon, and Syria. The Court of Justice of

---

[105] Crown Prosecution Service, Female Genital Mutilation Legal Guidance, referencing the 2003 Act, http://www.cps.gov.uk/legal/d_to_g/female_genital_mutilation/#a05.
[106] Eg Eritrea, a country with an 83% prevalence rate (of women and girls aged 15–49, UNICEF, *Statistical Profile on Female Genital Mutilation/Cutting*: Eritrea, July 2014) the penalty upon conviction is a fine of 5,000 to 10,000 Nafka (£262–£524) or a two to three year prison sentence, Thato Motaung, Zero tolerance for female genital mutilation in Eritrea?, 6 February 2015, https://africlaw.com/2015/02/06/zero-tolerance-for-female-genital-mutilation-in-eritrea/.

the European Union (CJEU) has interpreted Article 1D to mean that only voluntary departure from UNWRA protection, unmotivated by risk of harm or other reasons beyond her control, would invoke this exclusion clause.[107] In any event, UNWRA describes FGM as 'uncommon'[108] among Palestinian women and girls.

**10.63**  The final exclusion clause, Article 1E of the Refugee Convention, is of even more limited application. It simply establishes that Refugee Convention protection is not necessary where a claimant has somewhere else to go:

> 'This Convention shall not apply to a person who is recognized by the competent authorities of the country in which he has taken residence as having the rights and obligations which are attached to the possession of the nationality of that country.'

**10.64**  If an asylum claimant already has an unfettered right to reside in a safe country or indeed the UK[109] whether by virtue of citizenship or some other legal status, regardless of whether they would be at risk in their home country, they may be excluded from protection. The burden is on the Secretary of State to prove this.

## Procedural powers: Borders, Citizenship and Immigration Act 2009, s 55: 'best interests'

**10.65**  In an FGM case or indeed any asylum case, there is at least in theory a burden on the tribunal to implement 'the highest standards of fairness'.[110] The claimant should be allowed to bring evidence that supports her claim, and the case should be managed appropriately to facilitate this which may entail adjournment and/or directions to both parties. This is particularly important for expert evidence that may be adduced to counter a Home Office point of refusal about country conditions or medical evidence. This principle applies in any asylum claim, regardless of the vulnerability of the claimant. In practice the argument may be simplified where there is a child involved and the UK has special obligations.

**10.66**  Article 3(1) of the UN Convention on the Rights of the Child states:

> 'In all actions concerning children, whether undertaken by public or private social welfare institutions, courts of law, administrative authorities or legislative bodies, the best interests of the child shall be a primary consideration.'

---

[107]  *Mostafa Abed El Karem El Kott and others* (C-364/11).
[108]  UNRWA Annual Report of the Department of Health, 2006: 'Furthermore, practices harmful to women, such as female genital mutilation, are uncommon among the refugee population.'
[109]  UN High Commissioner for Refugees (UNHCR), *UNHCR Note on the Interpretation of Article 1E of the 1951 Convention relating to the Status of Refugees*, March 2009, para 4, available at: http://www.refworld.org/docid/49c3a3d12.html.
[110]  *SH (Afghanistan) v Secretary of State for the Home Department* [2011] EWCA Civ 1284 at para 8.

**10.67**  Despite ratifying the UN Convention on the Rights of the Child (UNCRC) in 1991, the UK maintained reservations with respect to immigrant children and children in custody until 2008. Notwithstanding the UNCRC's influence on ECHR jurisprudence in the UK through both the HRA 1998 and the ECtHR,[111] it has not been incorporated into UK law. However, 'the spirit, if not the precise language'[112] of Article 3(1) has been given effect in immigration matters by way of s 55 of the Borders, Citizenship and Immigration Act 2009 (BCIA 2009). Section 55 states:

'(1)  The Secretary of State must make arrangements for ensuring that—
    (a)  the functions mentioned in subsection (2) are discharged having regard to the need to safeguard and promote the welfare of children who are in the United Kingdom, and
    (b)  any services provided by another person pursuant to arrangements which are made by the Secretary of State and relate to the discharge of a function mentioned in subsection (2) are provided having regard to that need.
(2)  The functions referred to in subsection (1) are—
    (a)  any function of the Secretary of State in relation to immigration, asylum or nationality;
    (b)  any function conferred by or by virtue of the Immigration Acts on an immigration officer; ...'

**10.68**  On the face of it, the obligation to take into account the 'best interests' of children would seem to have direct application to children at risk of FGM. In practice, however, this is not generally the case. The main reason is that where an application for international protection has been made, consideration of the claim will focus on the risk of serious harm as noted above. If such a risk is found, the UK's obligations of non-*refoulement* and the ensuing grant of status take precedence, and in any event there is no tension between recognition of the need for international protection and a child's best interest if that indicates she should stay in the UK. If it would seem on the facts of the case that, absent the risk of serious harm, the child's best interest would be to return to her home country, the risk of serious harm will carry more weight than any other consideration. A child accepted to be at risk of FGM will not be *refouled* on lesser grounds such as continuation of education in her home country or separation from family members there.

**10.69**  *ZH (Tanzania) v Secretary of State for the Home Department*[113] is a powerful statement by the UK Supreme Court of the primacy of a child's best interests in immigration matters, which in that case resulted in the child's mother being allowed to stay in the UK despite her 'appalling' immigration history. However, the children in that case were British, and the Secretary of State had no power to forcibly remove them from the UK. The relevant immigration decision was directed at their mother, not them, but the

---

[111]  *Neulinger v Switzerland* (41615/07) [2010] ECHR 1053 (6 July 2010).
[112]  *ZH (Tanzania) v Secretary of State for the Home Department* [2011] UKSC 4, Baroness Hale at para 23.
[113]  [2011] UKSC 4.

assumption was that if their mother was removed, they would go with her, thus bringing them within the remit of s 55. It has become axiomatic in these cases that the starting point for 'best interests' is that a child will remain with her parents. As a result, the Court of Appeal now approaches s 55 cases by starting with the parents' or carers' immigration status, and where they have no entitlement to remain, the assumption that the children will remain with them points strongly to their removal.[114]

**10.70**   In addition to the apparent lack of application in FGM cases due to the primacy of international protection law, the Upper Tribunal (IAC) found in *MK (section 55 – Tribunal options)*[115] that while the s 55 duty requires more than 'mere lip-service' by the Secretary of State, the burden of showing a breach rests with the appellant on the balance of probabilities. There is 'no onus'[116] on the Secretary of State to show compliance with the duty. However, it was also found (and later approved by the Court of Appeal) that when either the First-tier Tribunal or Upper Tier find that an adequate assessment of a child's best interests has not been made, they should exercise their case management powers to invite or to compel parties, including the Secretary of State, to provide sufficient evidence to do so. This power should be noted alongside the required standard of fairness in asylum cases that involve a child, whether it is the child who is at risk of FGM or not.

## CONCLUSION

**10.71**   The UK's *Multi-agency statutory guidance on female genital mutilation* dated April 2016 says little about asylum claims except that:[117]

> 'If the girl or woman is from overseas, and fleeing potential FGM, applying to remain in the UK as a refugee can be a complex process requiring professional immigration advice.'

**10.72**   This is true, as far as it goes. In practice, claimants may find it difficult to find a reputable representative. The number of solicitors' firms with a legal aid contract to undertake asylum work, as in many publicly funded areas of law, continues to fall.[118] But a claimant's difficulties are not solved by simply finding a lawyer. Irrespective of the claimant's fear for herself or her daughter, after a claim is refused by the Home Office a representative must make an assessment of the prospects of success. Unless the claim is adjudged to be more likely than not to succeed, Legal Aid Agency (LAA) rules dictate that public funding must be withdrawn and the claimant must face the tribunal without benefit of representation, unless the case has wider public significance or some

---

[114]   *EV (Philippines) & Ors v Secretary of State for the Home Department* [2014] EWCA Civ 874.
[115]   [2015] UKUT 223 (IAC).
[116]   *MK (section 55 – Tribunal options)* [2015] UKUT 223 (IAC).
[117]   Section D.2.8.
[118]   House of Commons Justice Committee, Justice – Eighth Report: Impact of changes to civil legal aid under Part 1 of the Legal Aid, Sentencing and Punishment of Offenders Act 2012, March 2015. See Section 5.

other special factor.[119] Representatives are incentivised to be ruthless in this assessment, on pain of their practice and livelihoods. If a firm's success rate in publicly-funded appeals falls below 40%, their legal aid contract may be withdrawn by the LAA; errors tend to the side of caution.[120]

**10.73** This assessment may be taken out of the representative's hands, regardless of their experience or expertise. As set out above, the Home Office may declare that the case has no prospects of success before an independent immigration judge and certify it as clearly unfounded[121] thus preventing the in-country appeal. For certification to be lifted, the claimant must apply for judicial review. It has been noted that the Home Office may rely more on a country's aspirations than its actions when deciding that the only legitimate view is that an FGM claim cannot succeed. Under scrutiny, many 'clearly unfounded' certifications are withdrawn and the appeal may continue. However, judicial reviews are exempt from the usual practice in English law that a permission refusal on the papers may be renewed orally to develop the arguments. The Civil Procedure Rules and the Upper Tribunal Procedure Rules allow for the certification of applications for judicial review as 'totally without merit' (TWM), which prevents an oral renewal.[122] Unfortunately, the volume of new cases and the Upper Tribunal's case backlog may incentivise TWM certificates as a way of managing the workload,[123] and appeals that should be heard by the tribunal may never reach it.

**10.74** The challenges in the process do not end if a claimant is fortunate enough to reach the tribunal. Like all asylum claims, FGM claims must be examined on their specific facts, notwithstanding the general country situation. Where information is out of date, or there is no country guidance, or the claimant's circumstances are unusual, it is best practice to engage a country expert, who may be able to assist the tribunal. Even where there is background evidence, it may not be clear about the pressures a woman from a particular ethnicity may face to undergo FGM, a country's willingness to protect women, the availability of GBV refuges or services, or the status of female-headed households and their employment prospects. Such evidence is particularly important where there is no FGM country guidance case, which perhaps surprisingly is the situation for many countries with extremely high FGM prevalence, including Burkina Faso (76%),[124] Djibouti (93%),[125] Egypt

---

[119] Civil Legal Aid (Merits Criteria) Regulations 2013, SI 2013/104; Civil Legal Aid (Merits Criteria) (Amendment) Regulations 2016, SI 2016/781.

[120] Legal Aid Agency, *2013 Standard Civil Contract Specification: General Rules*, May 2016. KPI 6 – Quality: Immigration CLR, 2.66 KPI 6A: 'You must achieve a positive outcome in at least the following proportion of cases: 40%.'

[121] As per the Nationality, Immigration and Asylum Act 2002, s 94(2).

[122] See Tribunal Procedure (Upper Tribunal) Procedure Rules 2008, SI 2008/2698 (as amended) at r 30; and Civil Procedure Rules 1998, SI 1998/3132, r 54.12(7).

[123] Robert Thomas, 'Immigration Judicial Reviews: Resources, Caseload, and "System-manageability efficiency"' (2016) 21(3) *Judicial Review*.

[124] Of women and girls aged 15–49, UNICEF, *Statistical Profile on Female Genital Mutilation/Cutting: Burkina Faso*, December 2013.

(87%),[126] Eritrea (83%),[127] Ethiopia (74%),[128] Guinea (97%),[129] Mali (89%),[130] Mauritania (69%)[131] and Sierra Leone (90%).[132]

**10.75** Despite this, the representatives' judgment as to the appropriateness of expert evidence is not determinative. The Legal Aid Agency must also agree. In order to fund an expert report, the LAA must receive at least three bespoke quotes from competing experts.[133] The representative cannot rely upon an advertised fee or course of dealing, no matter how many times an expert has provided reports. If negotiation with the LAA is slow, or the LAA disagrees with the relevance or value for money of an expert (or the representative's assessment of the merits of a case) then the claimant may require an adjournment to ensure her evidence and representation is in place. Adjournments are generally only granted in the tribunal where the likely timeline of the progress of the case is clear, eg an expert has agreed to provide a report by a certain date, which may be contingent upon the LAA's acquiescence to funding that expert's instruction in the case. Notwithstanding the affirmation of the importance of 'fairness' as noted above in *SH (Afghanistan) v Secretary of State for the Home Department*,[134] a refusal of an adjournment for expert evidence is a serious setback.

**10.76** The challenges of FGM asylum claims present real barriers to justice for some claimants. As the statutory guidance implies, professional immigration advice is crucial to understand and navigate the frameworks of international protection law in the UK.

---

[125] Of women and girls aged 15–49, UNICEF, *Statistical Profile on Female Genital Mutilation/Cutting: Djibouti*, December 2013.

[126] Of women and girls aged 15–49, UNICEF, *Statistical Profile on Female Genital Mutilation/Cutting: Egypt*, February 2016.

[127] Of women and girls aged 15–49, UNICEF, *Statistical Profile on Female Genital Mutilation/Cutting: Eritrea*, July 2014.

[128] Of women and girls aged 15–49, UNICEF, *Statistical Profile on Female Genital Mutilation/Cutting: Ethiopia*, December 2013.

[129] Of women and girls aged 15–49, UNICEF, *Statistical Profile on Female Genital Mutilation/Cutting: Guinea*, July 2014.

[130] Of women and girls aged 15–49, UNICEF, *Statistical Profile on Female Genital Mutilation/Cutting: Mali*, December 2013.

[131] Of women and girls aged 15–49, UNICEF, *Statistical Profile on Female Genital Mutilation/Cutting: Mauritania*, December 2013.

[132] Of women and girls aged 15–49, UNICEF, *Statistical Profile on Female Genital Mutilation/Cutting: Sierra Leone*, February 2016.

[133] Legal Aid Agency, Guidance on the Remuneration of Expert Witnesses, April 2015 – 'Generally require at least three alternative quotes. When this is not possible you should provide copies of correspondence attempts and details of steps taken and research conducted in an attempt to obtain alternative quotes.' Legal Aid Agency, CW3C – Immigration and Asylum checklist v1.3 (September 2016); Also 'Where there are no rates set out in the Remuneration Regulations prior authority may be sought and 3 alternative quotes (or an explanation why it has not been possible to obtain 3 quotes) should be provided to the LAA. The quotes will need to include details of both the hourly rate and total number of hours quoted. You must also include a copy of the Court Order and the expert's CV.'

[134] [2011] EWCA Civ 1284.

# CHAPTER 11

# RESOURCES AND USEFUL CONTACTS

## RECOMMENDED READING

Hibo Wardere, *Cut: One Woman's Fight Against FGM in Britain Today* (Simon & Schuster, 7 Apr 2016)

Nawal El Saadawi, *Walking Through Fire: A Life of Nawal El Saadawi* (Zed Books Ltd, London & New York, 15 April 2009)

Kameel Ahmady, *Female Genital Mutilation In Iran (A Research Report)*, 2 June 2015

Guinea: The Office of the United Nations High Commissioner for Human Rights (OHCHR), *Summary of the OHCHR Report on human rights and the practice of female genital mutilation and excision in Guinea*, April 2016

Royal College of Obstetricians and Gynaecologists, *Female Genital Mutilation and its Management*, July 2015

For a detailed survey of the health impacts of FGM see the study by Efua Dorkenoo, *Cutting the Rose: Female Genital Mutilation, The Practice and its Prevention* (Minority Rights Publications, 1994)

## CONTACTS, HELPLINES AND CLINICS

### Helplines

- NSPCC helpline; email fgmhelp@nspcc.org.uk; Telephone: 0800 028 3550
- National Domestic Violence Helpline; http://www. nationaldomesticviolencehelpline.org.uk/; Telephone: 0808 2000 247 (24-hour)

## FGM PROTECTION ORDERS (FGMPOS)

HM Courts Service Application forms for FGMPOs and information in different languages on how FGMPOs can protect people: www.gov.uk/female-genital-mutilation-protection-order

## FGM SUPPORT SERVICES

To find FGM support near you, try the FGM help and advice postcode finder on https://www.gov.uk/female-genital-mutilation-help-advice

## FORCED MARRIAGE

HM Government (2014) *The Right to Choose: Multi-agency statutory guidance for dealing with forced marriage*: www.gov.uk/guidance/forced-marriage

HM Government (2014) *Multi-agency practice guidance: handling cases of forced marriage*: www.gov.uk/guidance/forced-marriage

## FORCED MARRIAGE UNIT

The Government's Forced Marriage Unit can be contacted for advice on forced marriage issues on 020 7008 0151 (Monday–Friday, 9am–5pm; call 020 7008 1500 and ask for the Global Response Centre in emergencies outside of these hours); fgmenquiries@homeoffice.gsi.gov.uk

### Home Office FGM Unit

The Unit:

- provides outreach support to local areas to support them in developing their local response to fighting FGM and to raise awareness of the unit;
- identifies and highlights examples of effective practice across local areas and professional groups;
- promotes available FGM resources;
- works with the police, Border Force, the Crown Prosecution Service and the College of Policing to improve the identification and prosecution of offenders;
- has an overview of all government work to fight FGM and works closely with the voluntary and community sector, survivors and professionals to develop cross-cutting policies and processes.

## OTHER ORGANISATIONS

- 28 Too Many; http://28toomany.org/; email: info@28toomany.org; Telephone: 020 8447 1904
- Africans Unite Against Child Abuse; http://www.afruca.org/
- Agency for Culture and Change Management UK (ACCM UK); email: info@accmuk.com
- BAWSO; http://www.bawso.org.uk/; email info@bawso.org.uk; Telephone: 029 20644 633; 24-hour helpline: 0800 731 8147
- Birmingham Against FGM; email: cypfcomms@birmingham.gov.uk
- Bristol against Violence and Abuse (BAVA); http://www.bava.org.uk/types-of-abuse/female-genital-mutilation/
- Dahlia Project (support group): http://www.manorgardenscentre.org/dahlia-support-fgm-survivors/. Telephone: 020 7281 8970
- Daughters of Eve; http://www.dofeve.org/ (text them on 0798 303 0488)
- Equality Now; http://www.equalitynow.org/; Telephone: 020 7304 6902
- FGM National Clinical Group; http://www.fgmnationalgroup.org/index.htm
- Foundation for Women's Health Research & Development (FORWARD); http://forwarduk.org.uk/; Telephone: 020 8960 4000
- Freedom Charity; https://www.freedomcharity.org.uk//; Telephone: 0845 607 0133 or text 4freedom to 88802
- Iranian and Kurdish Women's Rights Organisation (IKWRO); http://ikwro.org.uk/; Telephone: 020 7920 6460
- Karma Nirvana; http://www.karmanirvana.org.uk/; Telephone: 0800 599 9247
- London Black Women's Health and Family Support (bwhafs); http://www.bwhafs.com/services.php; Telephone: 020 8980 3503
- London Safeguarding Children Board; http://www.londonscb.gov.uk/event/fgm-task-and-finish-group-meeting/
- Manor Gardens Health Advocacy Project (North London); http://www.manorgardenscentre.org/; Telephone: 020 7281 7694
- Ocean Somali Community Action (OSCA); http://www.oceansomali.org.uk/; Telephone: 020 7987 5833
- Southall Black Sisters (SBS); http://www.southallblacksisters.org.uk/; Telephone: 020 8571 0800

## LEGAL INTERVENTIONS

Children and Family Court Advisory and Support Service, information on legal interventions to safeguard children: www.cafcass.gov.uk/grown-ups/professionals/care.aspx

Department for Education (2015) Information sharing: advice for practitioners providing safeguarding services to children, young people, parents and carers: www.gov.uk/government/publications/safeguarding-practitioners-information-sharing-advice

## MANDATORY REPORTING

Home Office (2015) *Mandatory reporting procedural information*: www.gov.uk/government/publications/mandatory-reporting-of-female-genital-mutilation-procedural-information

Department of Health (2015) *Mandatory reporting resources for healthcare professionals*: www.gov.uk/government/publications/fgm-mandatory-reporting-in-healthcare

Home Office (2016) *Fact sheet on mandatory reporting of female genital mutilation*:          www.gov.uk/government/publications/fact-sheet-on-mandatory-reporting-of-female-genital-mutilation

## MATERIALS FOR PUBLIC AWARENESS-RAISING

To order hard copies of materials, email the FGM Unit: FGMenquiries@homeoffice.gsi.gov.uk

To order the Statement Opposing FGM (also know as the 'Health Passport') which sets out the law on FGM and the help and support available and is available in 11 languages, visit the Department of Health orderline website: www.orderline.dh.gov.uk

NSPCC FGM helpline: 0800 028 3550
www.nspcc.org.uk/preventing-abuse/child-abuse-and-neglect/female-genital-mutilation-
email: fgmhelp@nspcc.org.uk

National Domestic Violence Helpline: 0808 2000 247 (24-hour) www.nationaldomesticviolencehelpline.org.uk/

ChildLine: 0800 1111
www.childline.org.uk

## PREVALENCE DATA

UNICEF FGM international data: http://data.unicef.org/child-protection/fgmc.html

A Macfarlane and E Dorkenoo, *Prevalence of Female Genital Mutilation in England and Wales: National and local estimates* (London: City University London and Equality Now, 2015): http://openaccess.city.ac.uk/12382/

HSCIC, NHS England FGM data: www.hscic.gov.uk/searchcatalogue?q=%22female+genital+mutilation%22&area=&si

## RESOURCES FOR HEALTHCARE PROFESSIONALS

Department of Health (2015) *Female Genital Mutilation: Risk and Safeguarding – Guidance for professionals*: https://www.gov.uk/government/uploads/system/uploads/attachment_data/file/525390/FGM_safeguarding_report_A.pdf

Health and Social Care Information Centre, Information on the Female Genital Mutilation Risk Indication System: www.hscic.gov.uk/fgmris

Health and Social Care Information Centre, Information on the Female Genital Mutilation (FGM) Enhanced Dataset Information Standard (SCCI2026): www.hscic.gov.uk/fgm

Department of Health and Health and Social Care Information Centre (2015)

## RESOURCES FOR POLICE

College of Policing (2015) *Authorised Professional Practice: Female Genital Mutilation*: www.app.college.police.uk/app-content/major-investigation-and-public-protection/female-genital-mutilation/?s=female+genital+mutilation#prevention

Crown Prosecution Service, *Provision of Therapy for Child Witnesses Prior to a Criminal Trial*: www.cps.gov.uk/publications/prosecution/therapychild.html

Ministry of Justice (2011) *Achieving Best Evidence in Criminal Proceedings: Guidance on interviewing victims and witnesses, and guidance on using special measures*: www.cps.gov.uk/publications/prosecution/victims.html

## SAFEGUARDING GUIDANCE

HM Government (2015) *Working Together to Safeguard Children*: www.gov.uk/government/publications/working-together-to-safeguard-children–2

Welsh Government (2007) *Safeguarding Children: Working Together under the Children Act 2004*: www.gov.wales/topics/health/publications/socialcare/circular/nafwc1207/?lang=en

Welsh Government (2001) *Framework for the Assessment of Children in Need and their Families*: http://gov.wales/topics/health/publications/socialcare/guidance1/assessing/?lang=en

HM Government (2015) *What to do if you're worried a child is being abused*: www.gov.uk/government/publications/what-to-do-if-youre-worried-a-child-is-being-abused–2

Department of Health (2015) *Female Genital Mutilation: Risk and Safeguarding – Guidance for professionals*: www.gov.uk/government/uploads/system/uploads/attachment_data/file/418564/2903 800_DH_FGM_Accessible_v0.1.pdf

Department for Education (2015) *Keeping Children Safe in Education*: www.gov.uk/government/publications/keeping-children-safe-in-education–2

Department for Education (2015) *Children Missing Education: Statutory guidance for local authorities*: www.gov.uk/government/publications/children-missing-education

All Wales Child Protection Procedures Review Group (2011) *All Wales Protocol: Female Genital Mutilation*: www.wales.nhs.uk/sitesplus/888/page/67421/

## TRAINING AND AWARENESS FOR PROFESSIONALS

Home Office, e-learning module FGM: How to recognise and prevent it: www.fgmelearning.co.uk

E-learning for healthcare, e-learning modules for healthcare professionals in England: www.e-lfh.org.uk/programmes/female-genital-mutilation/

Welsh Government, Live Fear Free: Training on Domestic Abuse, Sexual Violence and Violence against Women: http://livefearfree.gov.wales/guidance-for-professionals/national-training-framework/?lang=en

Home Office (2015), FGM resource pack (including case studies and links to organisations and resources to support local work to tackle FGM): www.gov.uk/government/publications/female-genital-mutilation-resource-pack/female-genital-mutilation-resource-pack%20%20

## COMMISSIONING SERVICES

Imkaan, Accredited Quality Standards for working with black and minority ethnic (BME) women and girls and harmful practices: Forced marriage (FM), Female genital mutilation (FGM) and 'Honour-based' violence (HBV): http://imkaan.org.uk/iaqs

Department of Health (2015) *Commissioning Services to Support Women and Girls with Female Genital Mutilation*: www.gov.uk/government/publications/services-for-women-and-girls-with-fgm

## UNDERSTANDING THE FGM ENHANCED DATASET

www.gov.uk/government/publications/safeguarding-women-and-girls-at-risk-of-fgm

Royal College of Obstetricians and Gynaecologists (2015) *Female Genital Mutilation and its management (Green-top Guideline No. 53)*: www.rcog.org.uk/en/guidelines-research-services/guidelines/gtg53/

Royal College of Nursing (2015) *Female Genital Mutilation*: www.rcn.org.uk/clinical-topics/female-genital-mutilation

General Medical Council, *Guidance on child protection examinations*: www.gmc-uk.org/guidance/ethical_guidance/13430.asp

General Medical Council (2008) *Consent: Patients and Doctors Making Decisions Together*: www.gmc-uk.org/guidance/ethical_guidance/consent_guidance_index.asp

General Medical Council (2009) *Confidentiality*: www.gmc-uk.org/guidance/ethical_guidance/confidentiality.asp

General Medical Council (2013) *Intimate Examinations and Chaperones*: www.gmc-uk.org/guidance/ethical_guidance/21168.asp

## USEFUL CONTACTS

Child Protection Helpline
Telephone: 0808 800 5000 (advice for adults worried about a child)

Childline
Telephone: 0800 1111 (24 hr free helpline for children)
https://www.childline.org.uk/

Daughters of Eve
http://www.dofeve.org/

Equality Now
http://www.equalitynow.org/

FGM National Clinical Group
http://www.fgmnationalgroup.org/

FGM Safeguarding guidance:
https://www.gov.uk/government/publications/safeguarding-
women-and-girls-at-risk-of-fgm
FGM Risk Indication System: www.hscic.gov.uk/fgmris
FGM Enhanced Dataset reports published by HSCIC:
www.hscic.gov.uk/fgm

FGM Risk Indication System: www.hscic.gov.uk/fgmrisFGM Enhanced Dataset
reports published by HSCIC: www.hscic.gov.uk/fgm

Foundation for Womens' Health Research & Development (FORWARD)
Telephone: 020 8960 4000
http://forwarduk.org.uk/

Foreign and Commonwealth Office
Telephone: 020 7008 1500
fgm@fco.gov.uk

London Safeguarding Children Board
59 Southwark Street
London, SE1 0AL
Telephone: 020 7934 9683
http://www.londonscb.gov.uk/event/fgm-task-and-finish-group-meeting/

Metropolitan Police
Child Abuse Investigation Command/Project Azure
Telephone: 020 7161 2888
http://content.met.police.uk/Article/Female-genital-mutiliation/
1400009693144/1400009693144

National Society for the Prevention of Cruelty to Children (NSPCC)
Telephone: 0808 800 5000
https://www.nspcc.org.uk/

# ASYLUM

Information on claiming asylum in the UK: www.gov.uk/claim-asylum

## POLICE

Police forceswww.gov.uk/contact-police

Metropolitan Police Servicehttp://content.met.police.uk/HomeProject Azure Partnership Team: 020 7161 2888

# APPENDIX 1

## APPLICATION FOR A FEMALE GENITAL MUTILATION PROTECTION ORDER

▶ Print form    ▶ Reset form

FGM001

## Application for a
## Female Genital Mutilation (FGM)
## Protection Order

Part 1 of Schedule 2 to the
Female Genital Mutilation Act 2003

| To be completed by the court | |
|---|---|
| Date issued | |
| Case no. | |
| Name of court | |
| Fee charged/ remission ID | |

Please read the accompanying notes as you complete this form

### 1. About you (the applicant)

Are you (tick only one box)

☐ the person who is to be protected by this order (see page 7)

☐ a relevant third party (see page 7)

Full name

**If you do not wish your address to be made known to the respondent** leave this space blank
and if you have not already done so, complete Confidential address form C8. See notes on page 7

Address

Postcode

Phone no. (optional)

Date of birth (if under 18 years)

**For relevant third parties**

Name of organisation (if applicable)

Position held in the organisation

**Your solicitor's details** – if you are representing yourself leave blank

Full name

Name of firm

Address

Reference no.

Phone no.

Fax no.

Postcode

DX no.

Fee account no.

2.  **About the person to be protected**

☐ Mrs    ☐ Miss    ☐ Ms    ☐ Other (please specify)

Full name

**If you do not wish your address to be made known to the respondent** leave this space blank and if you have not already done so, complete Confidential address form C8. See notes on page 7.

Address

Date of birth (if known)

☐ Tick this box if you do not know the date of birth but you believe the person to be protected is under 18 years.

Postcode

3.  **Your reasons for applying on behalf of the person to be protected**

If you are a Relevant Third Party complete this section

State briefly your reasons including what you know of the circumstances of the person to be protected.

## 4. About the respondent(s)

If there are more than two respondents please continue on a separate sheet.

**Respondent 1**

☐ Mr ☐ Mrs ☐ Miss ☐ Ms ☐ Other (please specify) [＿＿＿＿＿]

Full name

[＿＿＿＿＿＿＿＿＿＿＿＿＿＿＿＿＿＿＿＿＿＿＿＿＿＿＿＿＿]

Address

[＿＿＿＿＿＿＿＿＿＿＿＿]   Date of birth (if known) [＿｜＿｜＿｜＿｜＿｜＿]

Postcode [＿｜＿｜＿] [＿｜＿]

**Respondent 2**

☐ Mr ☐ Mrs ☐ Miss ☐ Ms ☐ Other (please specify) [＿＿＿＿＿]

Full name

[＿＿＿＿＿＿＿＿＿＿＿＿＿＿＿＿＿＿＿＿＿＿＿＿＿＿＿＿＿]

Address

[＿＿＿＿＿＿＿＿＿＿＿＿]   Date of birth (if known) [＿｜＿｜＿｜＿｜＿｜＿]

Postcode [＿｜＿｜＿] [＿｜＿]

**5.  The order(s) for which you are applying**

State what you want the order to say (see examples on page 7). Give full details in support of your application below (continue on a separate sheet if necessary) or in a separate statement. Include details of any encouragement or enticement that the respondent has used.

☐   Tick this box if you wish the court to hear your application without notice being given to the respondent. The reasons relied on for an application being heard without notice must be stated in the witness statement (verified by a statement of truth) in support. See notes for guidance on page 7.

**6.  At the court**

If you or the person to be protected requires an interpreter, you must tell the court now so that one can be arranged.

Will you or the person to be protected need an interpreter at court?

☐  No

☐  Yes, please specify the language and dialect

> [ ]

If you or the person to be protected has a disability for which you require special assistance or facilities, please state what is needed. The court staff will then get in touch with you.

> [ ]

Please say whether the court needs to make any special arrangements for you or the person to be protected to attend court (e.g. providing you with a separate waiting room)

> [ ]

**7.  Other information**

> [ ]

**8.  Other proceedings and orders**

If you are aware of any family proceedings or orders in force involving you, the respondent(s) or the person to be protected, then where known, state the type of proceedings.

**9.  Statement of truth**

*[I believe] *[The applicant believes] that the facts stated in this application are true.

*I am duly authorised by the applicant to sign this statement.

Print full name

Name of applicant solicitors firm

Signed                                          Dated

(Applicant) (Applicant's solicitor)

**Proceedings for contempt of court may be brought against a person who makes or causes to be made, a false statement in a document verified by a statement of truth**

*delete as appropriate                    ▶ Print form   ▶ Reset form

**This application is to be served upon the respondents and the person to be protected by the order.**

## Application for a FGM Protection Order

# Notes for guidance

Please read these notes with the leaflet **FGM700 - FGM Protection Orders**

### Section 1 – Applicants

There are three types of applicant. The person to be protected, someone on their behalf and a relevant third party.

If you are the person to be protected and are applying yourself for an order, with or without legal representation, you are also the applicant. Fill in section 1 only, and then go to section 4.

A relevant third party applicant is a person or organisation that is allowed to make an application on behalf of another without the leave of the court. Only the Lord Chancellor can make a person or organisation a relevant third party, for example a local authority.

If you are not a relevant third party and you are not the person who is to be protected by the order you can still make the application, but you need the court's permission. The court can give you the form (FGM006) to apply for permission.

### Address details

If you do not wish your address, or the address of any person named in the application form to be made known to the respondent, leave the space(s) on the form blank and complete Confidential Address Form C8. The court can give you this form.

### Section 2 – Person to be protected

This section only needs to be completed if you are applying on behalf of someone. If you are the person to be protected by the order, leave this section blank.

### Address details

If you do not wish the address of the person to be protected to be made known to the respondent, leave the space blank and complete Confidential Address form C8. The court can give you this form.

### Section 4 – Respondents

A person who you want the court to make an order against is called the respondent. There may be more than one respondent.

If you know of other people who may become involved as a respondent include their details in section 6.

### Section 5 – The Order

A FGM Protection Order provides protection to victims of or potential victims of FGM. Each FGM Protection Order is specific to each case and contains terms that change the behaviour of the respondent and other people.

Examples of what you might want the court to order are:

- that the respondent does not take you or the person to be protected abroad with the purpose of committing or attempting to commit FGM

- that the respondent does not enter into any arrangements in the UK or abroad for FGM to be performed on you or the person to be protected

- that the respondent surrenders their passport or any other travel documents and/or the passport of the person named in the application.

In section 5 or in a separate statement say why you are applying and give full details.

### Urgent orders

An urgent order made by the court before the notice of the application is served on the respondent is called a without notice order. In deciding whether to make a without notice order the court will consider all the circumstances of the case, including:

- any risk of a FGM procedure being carried out on the person to be protected or another person, if the order is not made immediately

- whether it is likely that the applicant will be deterred or prevented from pursuing the application if an order is not made immediately

- whether there is reason to believe that the respondent is aware of the proceedings but is deliberately evading service and the person to be protected or the applicant will be seriously prejudiced by the delay.

If you are applying for a 'without notice' order you must include the reasons why the court should deal with the application without notifying the respondent first. You must provide a witness statement verified by a statement of truth. The court can tell you how to do this.

If the court makes a 'without notice' order, it must give the respondent or other person an opportunity take representations about the order as soon as just and convenient at a full hearing.

**Further details**

Further information on making an application is contained in the leaflet FGM700 Female Genital Mutilation Protection Orders. The leaflet contains information on coming to court, and what happens if a respondent or other person fails to obey a court order. You can download this leaflet and details of your local court from our website http://hmctsformfinder.justice.gov.uk

# APPENDIX 2

# NATIONAL FGM CENTRE: ASSESSMENT OF A CASE

**Developing excellence in response to FGM**

# National FGM Centre:

## Assessment of a case

Funded by

Department for Education

# Copyright Notice

# Contents

This document contains the following:

# Summary

**A risk assessment will be done with a family using the National FGM Centre's risk assessment tool to determine an outcome of potentially high, potentially medium and potentially low. The risk assessment would be done at the beginning of an intervention from the National FGM Centre, and at the end of an intervention to assess whether the risk has been decreased. In between this, intensive work would be done with the family unit as a whole to increase their understanding of FGM and the risks associated with it, and to determine the children's and parents understanding of risky behaviours and how to protect themselves from it.**

The intention of the targeted interventions is to ensure families have a sound understanding of safeguarding as a whole and particularly in terms of FGM. For children, it is to ensure they understand how to identify risk and protect themselves from it, and for parents to be able to identify risk and protect themselves and their daughters from it.

**Time frame needed:** 2 weeks minimum; 4 weeks ideal

**Number of sessions:** 6 minimum; 12 ideal

**Hours per session (estimate):** 2-3 hours

**Hours needed for assessment writing:** 5 hours

**Hours in total of preparation time needed:** 4 hours

**Estimate of total hours of intervention:** 22+ hours on 6 sessions, 33+ hours on 12 sessions

**Tools used for targeted interventions:**

- National FGM Centre risk assessment tool
- National FGM Centre pack for targeted interventions with children
- National FGM Centre pack for targeted interventions with parents
- National FGM Centre outcomes grid
- Resources such as stationary etc.

Funded by
Department for Education

Local Government Association

Believe in children
Barnardo's

# Brief outline of National FGM Centre intervention with children

**All sessions share one common theme: to ensure that children understand their body belongs to them and no one else, and that if they are worried about something, that they can speak to someone they trust.**

### Session 1: 'all about me'

The all about me activity is designed to **open up discussions with children about their lives**, and for a worker to get to know the children and vice versa.

A scrap book is given to the child or children that they keep for the duration of the work undertaken, in which they can express themselves through drawings rather than words in between sessions. Drawings are explored at every session.

Optional – a disposable camera is given to the child or children which they can use to capture moments of their lives and their surroundings as they please, which is said to have therapeutic abilities (Weiser, 1999). Pictures are then printed, explored and stuck in the scrap book.

### Session 2: 'my life, my culture!'

The 'my life, my culture!' activity is designed to allow children to **explore their backgrounds and their cultures** – both good cultural traditions, and bad cultural traditions. Children are to understand that as long as culture does not harm us, that it is good

### Session 3: family trees – an innovative way to approaching genograms

**Outcome:**

- **For children to be able to identify members of their family and network that they deem are protective, and be confident about approaching them should they ever be worried about an issue.**

Although genograms are typically drawn with parents and are a good way of determining who is around a family, giving children a voice and allowing children to draw their own genograms or 'family trees' allows a worker to see from the child's perspective, who they determine to be of significance in their lives. It provides the child with the opportunity to express the relationships they have with family members, or other important people in their lives. It also provides the worker with the opportunity to explore who the child feels is their biggest protector in their tree, as well as highlighting who they do not feel has significance in their lives and who does not.

### Session 4: therapeutically exploring worries and anxieties

Outcomes:

- **For children to understand that speaking about worries they have is healthy**
- **For children to gain an awareness of how to manage worries**

This activity focuses on managing stress and anxiety. Children work through worries they have, and discussions are had about how to manage those worries in the present and in the future. Children make a 'calm down jar' in which they can add glitter, or any small items that slowly float around – proven to be calming and therapeutic. Children then work through who they can speak to if they ever have worries.

### Session 5: healthy relationships

Outcome:

- **For children to be able to identify healthy relationships, unhealthy relationships, and how to protect themselves from the latter.**

This session focuses on what a healthy relationship looks like and what an unhealthy relationship looks like, and how children can protect themselves from unhealthy ones. Children also explore physical, emotional and sexual abuse through quizzes and interactive activities. Sexual abuse is explored through the use of the NSPCC PANTS rule.

### Session 6: 'I have rights!'

Outcome:

- **For children to have an understanding of their rights**

This session was developed to ensure that children are aware of and understand their rights as children, using the United Nations Convention on the Rights of the Child (UNCRC). The National FGM Centre 'rights' tool explores important articles within the UNCRC throughout the session. Interactive activities and quizzes are used during the session

### Session 7: 'body rights'

Outcome :

- **For children to reflect on the basic biology taught to them in school, and apply it to body rights.**

This session is a follow on from 'I have rights!'. Whereas 'I have rights' focuses on children's rights as a whole, 'body rights' take this one step further by exploring body rights through the use of curriculum lead biology. Children will gain an understanding of what the different parts of the body are, what their functions are, and the importance of ensuring that they are not purposely changed or damaged through various activities.

Funded by
Department for Education
Local Government
Believe in children
Barnardo's

3

### Session 8: 'nobody changes my body!'

**Outcomes:**

- **For children to understand what Female Genital Mutilation is physically**
- **For children to understand why people may practice Female Genital Mutilation**
- **For children to understand that Female Genital Mutilation is illegal in the UK.**

This activity aims to introduce the topic of Female Genital Mutilation and how girls can protect themselves in an age-appropriate manor. It can also be used with boys to introduce the topic. The National FGM Centre lesson plan is used for this session. This session also brings together all learning from previous sessions.

### Session 9: 'nice, not nice.'

**Outcome:**

- **For children to demonstrate and apply the learning from past sessions by being able to identify risky, or 'not nice', behaviours, from non-risky, or 'nice' behaviours**

This activity is designed to allow the child to reflect on good and bad scenarios, and explain why they are good or bad.

### Session 10: presentations

Children are encouraged to present the work and learning they have done over the past sessions to the worker, and to give feedback on what they enjoyed, what could have gone better, and learning they will take forward with them. This is done through the use of National FGM Centre activity tools.

# Brief outline of National FGM Centre intervention with parents

**1-2 sessions are needed with parents to ensure they understand what FGM is, the consequences it has, and are able to demonstrate effective safety planning to safeguard their daughters from the practice.**

**Outcomes:**

- For the parents to understand what FGM is
- For the parents to understand FGM is illegal
- For parents to understand the health implications of FGM
- For parents to understand the safeguarding implications of FGM
- For parents to be able to demonstrate safety planning

### Session 1: basic awareness

The National FGM Centres basic awareness booklet on FGM is used to explain the basics of FGM to each parent separately. The session is interactive, and allows the parent to engage with the worker. An assessment of their knowledge is undertaken through various exercises, such as quizzes.

### Session 2: safety planning

Using the work the children have completed, including the family tree, culture exercise, children's rights and body rights, parents are encouraged to demonstrate their knowledge from the previous session, not only through the use of a quiz, but also through their ability to demonstrate their safety planning abilities.

**Outcomes for the family**

- Children are able to safeguard themselves from harm, and feel confident in speaking to someone should any issue arise
- Parents awareness of FGM and its consequences has increased, and they are able to demonstrate that they have understood the harmful consequences it has
- Parents are able to demonstrate effective safety planning

**Outcomes for the local authority**

- A full FGM risk assessment would be done on a family at the beginning of an intervention, and at the closing of an intervention, to determine change
- A list of outcomes, specific to FGM, developed by the National FGM Centre would be used throughout the process Intervention by a specialist FGM worker have taken place that ensure the children are very confident in safeguarding themselves from all forms of harmful behaviours
- Intervention by a specialist FGM worker have taken place with parents around FGM

# The Report

**A full, in-depth report on the outcomes and analysis of the intervention will be provided to the local authority, outlining the intervention and work taken place that can then be used in court cases.**

**Such a report would provide:**

- Background to the direct work (i.e. reason for intervention, and country profile data using the National FGM Centre World map and Knowledge Hub
- Tools used with the children
- Tools used with the parents
- Analysis of the engagement of the family, and particularly parents
- Outline of each session done and analysis on the effectiveness of the work
- Debriefs from an interpreter (if one was used)
- General observations of the family + any observations of care of new-born's
- Conclusion and analysis using the National FGM Centre outcomes grid

# Pricing

**Below are the pricing for either a 6 or 12 week intervention and assessment (including report).**

| | |
|---|---|
| **6 week intervention** | **12 week intervention** |
| **£ 3,158** | **£ 4,696** |

# Contact Details

**For more information on pricing, intervention or the National FGM Centre in general please feel free to contact us:**

**Tel:** 0208 498 7137

**Email**: nationalfgmcentre@barnardos.org.uk

**Website**: http://nationalfgmcentre.org.uk/

**Twitter**: @FGMCentre

Developing excellence
in response to FGM

# APPENDIX 3

---

# FEMALE GENITAL MUTILATION AND ITS MANAGEMENT

Royal College of
Obstetricians &
Gynaecologists

# Female Genital Mutilation and its Management

Green-top Guideline No. 53

July 2015

NICE accredited

www.nice.org.uk/accreditation

# Female Genital Mutilation and its Management

This is the second edition of this guideline, which was previously published under the same title in 2009. Prior to this, an RCOG statement with the same title was published in 2003.

Executive summary of recommendations

*Complications of female genital mutilation (FGM)*

Clinicians should be aware of the short- and long-term complications of FGM.

*The legal and regulatory responsibilities of health professionals*

FGM and UK law

All health professionals must be aware of the Female Genital Mutilation Act 2003 in England, Wales and Northern Ireland and the Prohibition of Female Genital Mutilation (Scotland) Act 2005 in Scotland. Both Acts provide that:

1. FGM is illegal unless it is a surgical operation on a girl or woman irrespective of her age:
   (a) which is necessary for her physical or mental health; or
   (b) she is in any stage of labour, or has just given birth, for purposes connected with the labour or birth.
2. It is illegal to arrange, or assist in arranging, for a UK national or UK resident to be taken overseas for the purpose of FGM.
3. It is an offence for those with parental responsibility to fail to protect a girl from the risk of FGM.
4. If FGM is confirmed in a girl under 18 years of age (either on examination or because the patient or parent says it has been done), reporting to the police is mandatory and this must be within 1 month of confirmation. [*New 2015*]

Female genital cosmetic surgery (FGCS) may be prohibited unless it is necessary for the patient's physical or mental health. All surgeons who undertake FGCS must take appropriate measures to ensure compliance with the FGM Acts. [*New 2015*]

Re-infibulation is illegal; there is no clinical justification for re-infibulation and it should not be undertaken under any circumstances. [*New 2015*]

What are the legal and regulatory responsibilities of health professionals in their evaluation of women with FGM?

When a woman with FGM is identified:

The health professional must explain the UK law on FGM. [*New 2015*]

The health professional must understand the difference between recording (documenting FGM in the medical records for data collection) and reporting (making a referral to police and/or social services) and their responsibilities with regards to these (Appendix I). [*New 2015*]

The health professional must be familiar with the requirements of the Health and Social Care Information Centre (HSCIC) FGM Enhanced Dataset and explain its purpose to the woman. The requirement for her personal data to be submitted without anonymisation to the HSCIC, in order to prevent duplication of data, should be explained. However, she should also be told that all personal data are anonymised at the point of statistical analysis and publication. [*New 2015*]

The health professional should be aware that it is not mandatory to report all pregnant women to social services or the police. An individual risk assessment should be made by a member of the clinical team (midwife or obstetrician) using an FGM safeguarding risk assessment tool (an example of such a tool can be found at https://www.gov.uk/government/publications/safeguarding-women-and-girls-at-risk-of-fgm). If the unborn child, or any related child, is considered at risk then a report should be made. [*New 2015*]

*What are the principles of FGM management in obstetric and gynaecological practice?*

All acute trusts/health boards should have a designated consultant and midwife responsible for the care of women with FGM (Appendix II).

All gynaecologists, obstetricians and midwives should receive mandatory training on FGM and its management, including the technique of de-infibulation. They should complete the programme of FGM e-modules developed by Health Education England. [*New 2015*]

Specialist multidisciplinary FGM services should be led by a consultant obstetrician and/or gynaecologist and be accessible through self-referral. These services should offer: information and advice about FGM; child safeguarding risk assessment; gynaecological assessment; de-infibulation; and access to other services.

Health professionals should ensure that, in consultations with women affected by FGM, the consultation and examination environment is safe and private, their approach is sensitive and nonjudgemental and professional interpreters are used where necessary. Family members should not be used as interpreters.

*How should recent FGM be managed?*

Healthcare professionals should be vigilant and aware of the clinical signs and symptoms of recent FGM, which include pain, haemorrhage, infection and urinary retention. [*New 2015*]

Examination findings should be accurately recorded in the clinical records. Some type 4 FGM, where a small incision or cut is made adjacent to or on the clitoris, can leave few, if any, visible signs when healed. Consideration should be given to photographic documentation of the findings at acute presentation. [*New 2015*]

Legal and regulatory procedures must be followed (Appendix I); all women and girls with acute or recent FGM require police and social services referral. [*New 2015*]

*How should FGM be managed in gynaecological practice?*

What should the referral pathway be for women with FGM?

Women may be referred by their general practitioner (GP) to a hospital gynaecology clinic. The referral should be directed to FGM services, if available, or to the designated consultant obstetrician and/or gynaecologist responsible for the care of women and girls with FGM.

Women should be able to self-refer. [*New 2015*]

All children with FGM or suspected FGM should be seen within child safeguarding services. [*New 2015*]

How should women with FGM be assessed in gynaecological practice?

Women with FGM may present with symptoms directly attributable to their FGM or with co-existing gynaecological morbidity. Gynaecologists should ask all women from communities that traditionally practise FGM whether they have had the procedure. [*New 2015*]

Clinicians should be aware that psychological sequelae and impaired sexual function can occur with all types of FGM.   `C`

Examination should include inspection of the vulva to determine the type of FGM and whether de-infibulation is indicated, as well as to identify any other FGM-related morbidities, e.g. epidermoid inclusion cysts. [*New 2015*]   ✓

All women should be offered referral for psychological assessment and treatment, testing for HIV, hepatitis B and C and sexual health screening. Where appropriate, women should be referred to gynaecological subspecialties, e.g. psychosexual services, urogynaecology, infertility. [*New 2015*]   ✓

Gynaecologists should be aware that narrowing of the vagina due to type 3 FGM can preclude vaginal examination for cervical smears and genital infection screens. De-infibulation may be required prior to gynaecological procedures such as surgical management of miscarriage (SMM) or termination of pregnancy (TOP).   ✓

What is the role of de-infibulation in gynaecological practice?

Women who are likely to benefit from de-infibulation should be counselled and offered the procedure before pregnancy, ideally before first sexual intercourse.   ✓

Women offered de-infibulation should have the option of having the procedure performed under local anaesthetic in the clinic setting in a suitable outpatient procedures room (Appendix III).   ✓

What is the role of clitoral reconstruction?

Clitoral reconstruction should not be performed because current evidence suggests unacceptable complication rates without conclusive evidence of benefit. [*New 2015*]   `D`

*How should FGM be managed in pregnancy?*

What level of care do women with FGM require?

Women with FGM are more likely to have obstetric complications and consultant-led care is generally recommended. However, some women with previous uncomplicated vaginal deliveries may be suitable for midwifery-led care in labour.   ✓

How should women with FGM be identified in pregnancy?

All women, irrespective of country of origin, should be asked for a history of FGM at their booking antenatal visit so that FGM can be identified early in the pregnancy. This should be documented in the maternity record. [*New 2015*]   ✓

Women identified as having FGM should be referred to the designated consultant obstetrician or midwife with responsibility for FGM patients. Local protocols will determine which elements of care should be undertaken by these individuals and which may be undertaken by other appropriately trained midwives or obstetricians (Appendix IV).   ✓

What antenatal documentation is required to demonstrate that legal and regulatory processes have been adhered to?

The midwife or obstetrician should ensure that all relevant information is documented in the clinical records (Appendix I). [*New 2015*]   ✓

How should antenatal care be managed?

Referral for psychological assessment and treatment should be offered.   ✓

The vulva should be inspected to determine the type of FGM and whether de-infibulation is indicated. If the introitus is sufficiently open to permit vaginal examination and if the urethral meatus is visible, then de-infibulation is unlikely to be necessary. ☑

Screening for hepatitis C should be offered in addition to the other routine antenatal screening tests (hepatitis B, HIV and syphilis). [*New 2015*] ☑

De-infibulation may be performed antenatally, in the first stage of labour or at the time of delivery and can usually be performed under local anaesthetic in a delivery suite room. It can also be performed perioperatively after caesarean section (Appendix III). ☑

The midwife or obstetrician should discuss, agree and record a plan of care (see Appendix IV). This may be documented in a preformatted sheet. ☑

Women should be informed that re-infibulation will not be undertaken under any circumstances. [*New 2015*] **D**

How should intrapartum care be managed?

If a woman requires intrapartum de-infibulation, the midwife and obstetrician caring for her should have completed training in de-infibulation or should be supervised appropriately. ☑

If de-infibulation planned for the time of delivery is not undertaken because of recourse to caesarean section, then the option of perioperative de-infibulation (i.e. just after caesarean section) should be considered and discussed with the woman. [*New 2015*] ☑

Labial tears in women with FGM should be managed in the same manner as in women without FGM. Repairs should be performed where clinically indicated, after discussion with the woman and using appropriate materials and techniques. **D**

How should intrapartum care be managed for women identified as having FGM in pregnancy for whom there has been no agreed documented plan of care?

The impact of FGM on labour and delivery should be sensitively discussed and a plan of care agreed. [*New 2015*] ☑

How should postnatal care be managed?

A woman whose planned de-infibulation was not performed because of delivery by caesarean section should have follow-up in a gynaecology outpatient or FGM clinic so that de-infibulation can be offered before a subsequent pregnancy. [*New 2015*] ☑

The discharging midwife should ensure that all legal and regulatory processes have been adhered to prior to discharge (Appendix I). [*New 2015*] ☑

1.  Purpose and scope

The purpose of this guideline is to provide evidence-based guidance on the management of women with female genital mutilation (FGM) and those who are considered to be at risk. It covers the clinical care of women before, during and after pregnancy, including the legal and regulatory responsibilities of health professionals. The focus of this guideline is on practice in the UK. Although much of the content is applicable to all four constituent countries, the regulatory framework in Scotland and Northern Ireland differs to that described here; further information is available elsewhere.[1,2]

For a global perspective on FGM, further information is available from other sources.[3,4]

2.   Introduction and background epidemiology

*2.1   Definition and classification*

Female genital mutilation, also known as 'female genital cutting', 'female genital mutilation/cutting' or 'cutting', refers to 'all procedures involving partial or total removal of the external female genitalia or other injury to the female genital organs for non-medical reasons'.[3,5] The widely accepted classification of FGM developed by the World Health Organization (WHO) in 1995 and updated in 2007 is shown in Table 1. FGM is practised for a variety of complex reasons, usually in the belief that it is beneficial for the girl.[4] It has no health benefits and harms girls and women in many ways. FGM is a human rights violation and a form of child abuse, breaching the United Nations Convention on the Rights of the Child,[4] and is a severe form of violence against women and girls.[6]

**Table 1.**   WHO FGM classification[3]

| | |
|---|---|
| **Type 1:** | Partial or total removal of the clitoris and/or the prepuce (clitoridectomy). |
| **Type 2:** | Partial or total removal of the clitoris and the labia minora, with or without excision of the labia majora (excision). |
| **Type 3:** | Narrowing of the vaginal orifice with creation of a covering seal by cutting and appositioning the labia minora and/or the labia majora, with or without excision of the clitoris (infibulation). |
| **Type 4:** | All other harmful procedures to the female genitalia for non-medical purposes, for example: pricking, piercing, incising, scraping and cauterization. |

*2.2   Global epidemiology*

UNICEF estimates that worldwide over 125 million women and girls have undergone FGM.[4] It is a traditional cultural practice in 29 African countries. FGM prevalence by country is shown in Figure 1. Outside Africa, FGM is also practised in Yemen, Iraqi Kurdistan and parts of Indonesia and Malaysia. Far smaller numbers have been recorded in India, Pakistan, Sri Lanka, the United Arab Emirates, Oman, Peru and Colombia.

The type of FGM varies between countries. FGM type 3 (infibulation) is practised almost exclusively in Africa, with the highest prevalence in northeastern Africa, including Somalia, Sudan, Ethiopia, Eritrea and Djibouti. FGM prevalence also varies within countries, where it may be associated with particular ethnic groups. FGM is almost always carried out on girls between infancy and the age of 15, but the age at which girls are mutilated varies considerably between countries. It is estimated that in over half of countries practising FGM, girls are cut under the age of 5 years. In some communities adult women may undergo re-infibulation following childbirth.

Those performing FGM are usually traditional practitioners with no formal medical training, who practise without anaesthetics using crude instruments such as knives, scissors or razor blades. However, in some countries health professionals undertake a substantial number of FGM procedures. These include Egypt, where doctors undertake the majority of FGM procedures, Sudan and Kenya. Globally, the trend towards medicalisation of FGM is increasing.[4]

As a result of migration, there has been a substantial increase in the number of girls and women with FGM living in North America, Australia, New Zealand and Europe.[4]

*2.3   UK epidemiology*

It has been estimated that 137 000 women and girls in England and Wales, born in countries where FGM is traditionally practised, have undergone FGM, including 10 000 girls aged under 15 years. These provisional interim estimates were derived by combining published data on FGM prevalence in FGM-practising countries with census and birth registration data in England and Wales.[7] There are

**Figure 1.** Prevalence of FGM. Percentage of girls and women aged 15–49 who have undergone FGM, by region/country. Source: UNICEF[4]

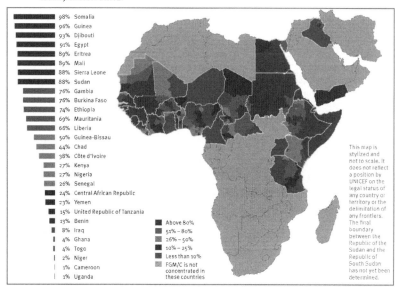

98%  Somalia
96%  Guinea
93%  Djibouti
91%  Egypt
89%  Eritrea
89%  Mali
88%  Sierra Leone
88%  Sudan
76%  Gambia
76%  Burkina Faso
74%  Ethiopia
69%  Mauritania
66%  Liberia
50%  Guinea-Bissau
44%  Chad
38%  Côte d'Ivoire
27%  Kenya
27%  Nigeria
26%  Senegal
24%  Central African Republic
23%  Yemen
15%  United Republic of Tanzania
13%  Benin
8%  Iraq
4%  Ghana
4%  Togo
2%  Niger
1%  Cameroon
1%  Uganda

Above 80%
51% – 80%
26% – 50%
10% – 25%
Less than 10%
FGM/C is not concentrated in these countries

This map is stylized and not to scale. It does not reflect a position by UNICEF on the legal status of any country or territory or delimitation of any frontiers. The final boundary between the Republic of the Sudan and the Republic of South Sudan has not yet been determined.

**FGM/C** female genital mutilation/cutting

no published studies on the prevalence of FGM in Scotland or Northern Ireland. There is anecdotal evidence that girls are taken from the UK to their country of origin to undergo FGM and that FGM also takes place in the UK.[8]

In order to capture data about numbers of women with FGM receiving care from the National Health Service in England, the Department of Health implemented an FGM data set in 2014. In April 2015, an enhanced data set was introduced, requiring all acute trusts, general practices and mental health trusts to record FGM data and return patient-identifiable data to the Health and Social Care Information Centre (HSCIC). Information can be found on the HSCIC website: http://www.hscic.gov.uk/fgm.

## 3.   Identification and assessment of evidence

This guideline was developed in accordance with standard methodology for producing RCOG Green-top Guidelines. MEDLINE, EMBASE and the Cochrane Library were searched. The search was restricted to articles published between 2007 and January 2014 and limited to humans and the English language. A top-up literature search was performed in April 2015. The databases were searched using the relevant Medical Subject Headings (MeSH) terms, including all subheadings, and this was combined with a keyword search. Search terms included 'FGM', 'female genital cutting', 'female genital mutilation', 'circumcision', 'infibulation', 'deinfibulation', 'de-infibulation', 'clitoridectomy' and 'defibulation'. The National Guideline Clearinghouse, National Institute for Health and Care Excellence (NICE) Evidence Search, Trip, Guidelines International Network and the Geneva Foundation for Medical Education and Research website were also searched for relevant guidelines. The websites of the WHO, UNICEF, United Nations Population Fund (UNFPA), the Population Council, the Population Reference Bureau, FORWARD

(Foundation for Women's Health Research and Development), Rainbo and the UK Government were searched for relevant reports. Where possible, recommendations are based on available evidence. Areas lacking evidence are highlighted and annotated as 'good practice points'.

### 4. Complications of FGM

**Clinicians should be aware of the short- and long-term complications of FGM.**

#### 4.1 Short-term complications

A systematic review by Berg[9] found that the most common immediate complications from FGM were haemorrhage (5–62%), urinary retention (8–53%) and genital swelling (2–27%), although there were additional studies reporting infection and fever, and three deaths directly attributed to FGM. The methodological quality of these studies was generally poor.

*Evidence level 2+*

There is concern that some type 4 FGM procedures, where a small cut is made adjacent to the clitoris, may now be performed more frequently.[4] This may leave little in the way of long-term scarring and so contemporaneous recording of all findings is crucial.

#### 4.2 Long-term complications

Reported long-term complications of FGM are listed below. The systematic review by Berg[9] demonstrated an association of FGM with urinary tract infection, dyspareunia and bacterial vaginosis. Cohort studies and case reports have also found associations with other sequelae. Most studies are of poor methodological quality.

#### Genital scarring

Genital scarring after FGM can be unsightly and painful. Keloid scarring has been reported in up to 3% of women. Epidermoid inclusion cysts and sebaceous cysts may need surgical excision.[10] Neuroma of the clitoris causing pain has been described.[11-13]

*Evidence level 4*

#### Urinary tract complications

Lower urinary tract symptoms are more common in women with FGM, particularly those with type 2 or type 3 FGM.[14] Poor urinary flow beneath the infibulation scar may result in symptoms of urinary obstruction, and stasis of urine may lead to recurrent urinary tract infection (relative risk [RR] 3.01, CI 1.42–6.38)[9] and to urinary or vaginal calculi.[15] The recommended treatment is de-infibulation.

*Evidence level 2+*

Damage to the urethra during FGM of any type may result in a urinary stricture or fistulae. These require assessment by a urologist or urogynaecologist.

There is no evidence that FGM directly increases the long-term risk of genital prolapse or incontinence.[16] However, vaginal narrowing may hamper urodynamic investigation.

*Evidence level 3*

#### Dyspareunia, apareunia and impaired sexual function

Dyspareunia may occur as a result of vaginal narrowing and painful scar tissue (RR 1.53, 95% CI 1.20–1.97). Apareunia and vulvovaginal lacerations during sexual intercourse have also been reported.[9]

*Evidence level 2+*

The removal of sexually sensitive tissue such as the clitoris and labia minora may reduce sexual sensation, while scarring over the clitoris may be painful. Numerous reports exist of various sexual consequences of FGM, including a reduction in desire and arousal, reduced frequency of orgasm or anorgasmia, decreased lubrication and poorer sexual satisfaction.[17-19]

Evidence level 2+

### Psychological sequelae

It is accepted that FGM has psychological effects, and flashbacks, anxiety[20] and post-traumatic stress disorder have been reported.[21] FGM has been linked to an increased incidence of domestic violence in Africa[22,23] but there are no European or UK data on this.

Evidence level 3

### Menstrual difficulties

Haematocolpos due to FGM has been reported. Dysmenorrhoea has also been reported among women with FGM, although the underlying mechanisms are unclear.[13]

Evidence level 3

### Genital infection and pelvic inflammatory disease

FGM has been associated with an increased risk of bacterial vaginosis[9] and herpes simplex virus type 2.[24] However, currently there is no conclusive epidemiological evidence to support an increased risk of pelvic inflammatory disease as a consequence of FGM. One case–control study from Sudan showed similar rates of chlamydia, gonorrhoea and syphilis in women with and without FGM.[25]

Evidence level 2+

### Infertility

At present, there are no well-planned studies that confirm whether or not FGM leads to infertility. Potential factors could include lack of sexual intercourse (apareunia, dyspareunia, impaired sexual function) and ascending infections caused by the FGM procedure. One case–control study showed an association between primary infertility and FGM.[26]

Evidence level 2−

### HIV and hepatitis B infection

Many FGM-practising countries are hepatitis B endemic[27] and some have a high prevalence of HIV.[28] Although mechanisms by which FGM may increase the risk of transmission of hepatitis B, hepatitis C and HIV have been proposed (i.e. sharing of non-sterile instruments and cutting in groups), there is currently no conclusive epidemiological evidence to support this.

### Obstetric complications

Research into the obstetric complications of FGM has been hampered by patchy methodology and the fact that in Africa, where FGM is typically practised, maternal and perinatal mortality and morbidity are already high due to other factors. Obstetric complications have been described with all types of FGM. However, the risks are greater with greater tissue damage.

Maternal complications associated with FGM have been described in Africa, North America and Europe. One large prospective study by the WHO investigated both maternal and perinatal outcomes in 28 000 women in six African countries.[29] A meta-analysis by Berg et al.[30] reviewed maternal outcomes and included some studies from Western countries (USA and Europe), although the majority were from Africa. The meta-analysis reported an increased risk of prolonged labour, postpartum haemorrhage and perineal trauma. The WHO study also found an increased risk of caesarean section and demonstrated an increased need for neonatal resuscitation and risk of stillbirth and early neonatal death.

Evidence level 2−

There are no good quality European or UK studies investigating FGM and perinatal outcomes. However, evidence from epidemiological studies of non-European migrants in Europe has shown a higher incidence of stillbirth[31,32] and neonatal death,[31] so women in the UK from FGM-practising countries may be at higher risk.

Evidence level 2–

Although fistulae have been associated with FGM, studies have not demonstrated that a history of FGM increases the risk of subsequent obstetric fistulae due to obstructed labour.[33]

Evidence level 4

Other obstetric consequences that have been described include fear of childbirth, difficulty in intrapartum monitoring (including application of fetal scalp electrodes and fetal blood sampling), difficulty in catheterisation during labour, wound infection and retention of lochia.[29]

Evidence level 2+

5. The legal and regulatory responsibilities of health professionals

*5.1 FGM and UK law*

All health professionals must be aware of the Female Genital Mutilation Act 2003 in England, Wales and Northern Ireland and the Prohibition of Female Genital Mutilation (Scotland) Act 2005 in Scotland. Both Acts provide that:

1. FGM is illegal unless it is a surgical operation on a girl or woman irrespective of her age:
   (a) which is necessary for her physical or mental health; or
   (b) she is in any stage of labour, or has just given birth, for purposes connected with the labour or birth.
2. It is illegal to arrange, or assist in arranging, for a UK national or UK resident to be taken overseas for the purpose of FGM.
3. It is an offence for those with parental responsibility to fail to protect a girl from the risk of FGM.
4. If FGM is confirmed in a girl under 18 years of age (either on examination or because the patient or parent says it has been done), reporting to the police is mandatory and this must be within 1 month of confirmation.

Female genital cosmetic surgery (FGCS) may be prohibited unless it is necessary for the patient's physical or mental health. All surgeons who undertake FGCS must take appropriate measures to ensure compliance with the FGM Acts.

Re-infibulation is illegal; there is no clinical justification for re-infibulation and it should not be undertaken under any circumstances.

Health professionals must have a clear understanding of the law on FGM so that they can explain it to their patients and so that they understand the basis for reporting concerns to the police and/or social care.[34]

Evidence level 4

FGM is illegal in England, Wales and Northern Ireland under the Female Genital Mutilation Act 2003 and in Scotland under the Prohibition of Female Genital Mutilation (Scotland) Act 2005. Both Acts make it an offence for any person:

(a) to excise, infibulate or otherwise mutilate the whole or any part of a person's labia majora, labia minora or clitoris; or
(b) to aid, abet, counsel or procure the performance by another person of any of those acts on that other person's own body, or
(c) to aid, abet, counsel or procure a person to excise, infibulate or otherwise mutilate the whole or any part of her own labia majora, labia minora or clitoris.

Both Acts also make it a criminal offence to carry out FGM abroad, and to aid, abet, counsel or procure the carrying out of FGM abroad, including in countries where the practice is legal. Both Acts permit surgical procedures that may fall within these categories (carried out by an appropriately registered practitioner) if necessary for the physical or mental health of the woman or if performed during labour or immediately postpartum 'for purposes connected with the labour or birth'. It should be noted that the FGM Acts apply to adult women as well as children.

The Serious Crime Act 2015 reinforced existing FGM legislation and introduced mandatory reporting of FGM in girls under 18 years by healthcare workers, teachers and social workers to the police.[35]

All health professionals should be aware of the Department of Health's guidance on FGM risk assessment and safeguarding.[5]

FGCS refers to non-medically indicated cosmetic surgical procedures, which change the structure and appearance of the healthy external genitalia of women (or internally in the case of vaginal tightening). UK guidance on FGCS is available and this includes the recommendation that FGCS should not normally be carried out on those under 18.[36] The legal status of some FGCS procedures has been called into question and it is likely to be illegal unless necessary to safeguard the patient's physical or mental health (the section 1(2)(a) exemption).  

Evidence level 4

Re-infibulation refers to the resuturing (usually after childbirth) of the incised scar tissue in a woman with FGM type 2 or 3. Previously there was uncertainty as to whether re-infibulation was covered by the FGM Acts.[6] However, it is now accepted that re-infibulation is illegal and should not be performed in any circumstances.

### 5.2   What are the legal and regulatory responsibilities of health professionals in their evaluation of women with FGM?

**When a woman with FGM is identified:**

**The health professional must explain the UK law on FGM.**

D

**The health professional must understand the difference between recording (documenting FGM in the medical records for data collection) and reporting (making a referral to police and/or social services) and their responsibilities with regards to these (Appendix I).**

D

**The health professional must be familiar with the requirements of the HSCIC FGM Enhanced Dataset and explain its purpose to the woman. The requirement for her personal data to be submitted without anonymisation to the HSCIC, in order to prevent duplication of data, should be explained. However, she should also be told that all personal data are anonymised at the point of statistical analysis and publication.**

D

**The health professional should be aware that it is not mandatory to report all pregnant women to social services or the police. An individual risk assessment should be made by a member of the clinical team (midwife or obstetrician) using an FGM safeguarding risk assessment tool (an example of such a tool can be found at https://www.gov.uk/government/publications/safeguarding-women-and-girls-at-risk-of-fgm). If the unborn child, or any related child, is considered at risk then a report should be made.**

✓

To assist health professionals in explaining the law on FGM to their patients, women should be referred to information provided in the Health Passport.[38] This document is available in a range of languages.[39]

The legal and regulatory responsibilities of health professionals are summarised in Appendix I.

**Recording (see Appendix I)**

Recording must be in accordance with the requirements of the HSCIC FGM Enhanced Dataset, which was implemented primarily to improve services for those with FGM. It requires all acute trusts, general practices and mental health trusts to record demographic, clinical and family information for all women with FGM and for these data to be submitted, without anonymisation, to the HSCIC. This should be explained to the woman. However, she should also be told that all personal data are anonymised at the point of statistical analysis and publication. According to Department of Health guidance (http://www.nhs.uk/NHSEngland/AboutNHSservices/sexual-health-services/Documents/2903740%20DH%20 FGM%20Leaflet%20Acessible%20-%20English.pdf), women who object to use of their data in this way should go to http://www.hscic.gov.uk/patientconf for more details.

In accordance with the Enhanced Dataset, when a patient with FGM is identified, the fact that they have had FGM must be documented in the medical records regardless of whether FGM is the reason for presentation. A clinical examination may be indicated to determine the type of FGM and clinicians are required to use the WHO FGM classification (Table 1). For this reason genital piercings must be included as type 4 FGM. The woman should be informed that her personal data will be transmitted to the HSCIC for the purpose of FGM prevalence monitoring and that the data will not be anonymised. Some services, such as sexual health services, are likely to be exempt from returning identifiable FGM data on adult women due to their specific legal obligations regarding confidentiality.

**Reporting (see Appendix I)**

Reporting means making a referral to the police or social services and guidance from the Department of Health is available.[5]

The requirement to report depends on whether an adult or a child is affected. FGM is child abuse and any child with confirmed or suspected FGM, or a child considered to be at risk of FGM, must be reported, if necessary without the consent of the parents. Information should also be shared with the general practitioner (GP) and health visitor. This is in accordance with section 47 of the Children Act 1989.

Local Safeguarding Children Boards (LSCBs) have responsibility for developing inter-agency protocols and procedures for safeguarding. If in any doubt, health professionals must contact their named lead for safeguarding who will advise. The urgency of the referral will vary depending on the type of risk.

There is no requirement to report a nonpregnant adult woman aged 18 or over to the police or social services unless a related child is at risk. The patient's right to confidentiality must be respected if they do not wish any action to be taken. No reports to social care or the police should be made in these cases.[5,34]

It is not mandatory to report every pregnant woman identified as having had FGM to social services or the police. An individual risk assessment must be made by a member of the clinical team caring for the woman during her pregnancy. If the unborn child, or any related child, is considered to be at risk of FGM, then a report must be made to children's social care or the police.

Healthcare professionals must record identified FGM in antenatal notes, screening returns and immunisation notes. Notes should also include whether the woman has been de-infibulated and, where appropriate, referred to further specialist care. A list of specialist FGM clinics is available (please note that this list only covers England).[40]

Following birth, relevant information about the mother's FGM should be recorded in the maternity discharge documentation so that GPs and health visitors are aware of the mother's history. The family history of FGM should also be recorded in the baby's personal child health record ('Red Book').[41]

Where appropriate, healthcare professionals should educate women on how FGM is illegal in the UK and how the practice has serious long-term physical, psychological and emotional consequences.[4]

Evidence
level 4

### 6.    What are the principles of FGM management in obstetric and gynaecological practice?

**All acute trusts/health boards should have a designated consultant and midwife responsible for the care of women with FGM (Appendix II).**

**All gynaecologists, obstetricians and midwives should receive mandatory training on FGM and its management, including the technique of de-infibulation. They should complete the programme of FGM e-modules developed by Health Education England.**

**Specialist multidisciplinary FGM services should be led by a consultant obstetrician and/or gynaecologist and be accessible through self-referral. These services should offer: information and advice about FGM; child safeguarding risk assessment; gynaecological assessment; de-infibulation; and access to other services.**

**Health professionals should ensure that, in consultations with women affected by FGM, the consultation and examination environment is safe and private, their approach is sensitive and nonjudgemental and professional interpreters are used where necessary. Family members should not be used as interpreters.**

D

Each trust/health board should have a designated obstetrician and/or gynaecologist responsible for FGM care. These individuals should be aware of local and/or regional specialist multidisciplinary FGM services. They should remain competent and up to date in all aspects of FGM (including child safeguarding protocols).

The programme of FGM e-modules developed by Health Education England is available free to all healthcare professionals (http://www.e-lfh.org.uk/programmes/female-genital-mutilation). Use of a de-infibulation bench-top trainer as an aid to learning may be considered.

Most UK specialist FGM services are in major cities and may be located in a hospital or community clinic (e.g. GP surgery or sexual health clinic). All FGM specialist services should offer information and advice regarding FGM as well as gynaecological assessment and access to de-infibulation. Some may also offer antenatal care. Specialist FGM services should offer access to psychological assessment and treatment, sexual health screening and treatment and gynaecological subspecialties such as urogynaecology, psychosexual services and infertility. They should work collaboratively with other healthcare providers, including GPs and acute trusts, voluntary sector organisations, the police, social services and schools. Currently referral pathways, clinic hours and service provision vary and there is a need to develop national minimum quality assurance standards for establishing and operating these services.[42]

Evidence
level 4

Guidance about the professional approach to take when women with FGM attend for consultation is available.[34] Health professionals should be nonjudgemental, pointing out the illegality and health risks of the practice without appearing to blame the woman. Appropriate language should be used. Although the term 'FGM' may be understood and accepted by some, referring to being 'cut', 'closed' or 'circumcised' may be more acceptable to many women.[34] A list of local/traditional terms for FGM is available in the Department of Health *Female Genital Mutilation Risk and Safeguarding* guidance.[5]

### 7.    How should recent FGM be managed?

**Healthcare professionals should be vigilant and aware of the clinical signs and symptoms of recent FGM, which include pain, haemorrhage, infection and urinary retention.**

D

Examination findings should be accurately recorded in the clinical records. Some type 4 FGM, where a small incision or cut is made adjacent to or on the clitoris, can leave few, if any, visible signs when healed. Consideration should be given to photographic documentation of the findings at acute presentation. ✓

Legal and regulatory procedures must be followed (Appendix I); all women and girls with acute or recent FGM require police and social services referral. D

Healthcare professionals should be aware of the clinical signs and symptoms of FGM and record their examination findings accurately in the clinical records. The legal and regulatory procedures are outlined in Appendix I.

8. How should FGM be managed in gynaecological practice?

*8.1 What should the referral pathway be for women with FGM?*

Women may be referred by their GP to a hospital gynaecology clinic. The referral should be directed to FGM services, if available, or to the designated consultant obstetrician and/or gynaecologist responsible for the care of women and girls with FGM. ✓

Women should be able to self-refer. ✓

All children with FGM or suspected FGM should be seen within child safeguarding services. ✓

All hospitals are expected to identify women with FGM and assess appropriately. In areas of low prevalence there must be clear pathways for referral to FGM services, including self-referral.

*8.2 How should women with FGM be assessed in gynaecological practice?*

Women with FGM may present with symptoms directly attributable to their FGM or with co-existing gynaecological morbidity. Gynaecologists should ask all women from communities that traditionally practise FGM whether they have had the procedure. ✓

Clinicians should be aware that psychological sequelae and impaired sexual function can occur with all types of FGM. C

Examination should include inspection of the vulva to determine the type of FGM and whether de-infibulation is indicated, as well as to identify any other FGM-related morbidities, e.g. epidermoid inclusion cysts. ✓

All women should be offered referral for psychological assessment and treatment, testing for HIV, hepatitis B and C and sexual health screening. Where appropriate, women should be referred to gynaecological subspecialties, e.g. psychosexual services, urogynaecology, infertility. ✓

Gynaecologists should be aware that narrowing of the vagina due to type 3 FGM can preclude vaginal examination for cervical smears and genital infection screens. De-infibulation may be required prior to gynaecological procedures such as surgical management of miscarriage (SMM) or termination of pregnancy (TOP). ✓

The clinical management of women with FGM in gynaecological practice is summarised in Appendix II.

*8.3 What is the role of de-infibulation in gynaecological practice?*

Women who are likely to benefit from de-infibulation should be counselled and offered the procedure before pregnancy, ideally before first sexual intercourse. ✓

**Women offered de-infibulation should have the option of having the procedure performed under local anaesthetic in the clinic setting in a suitable outpatient procedures room (Appendix III).**

De-infibulation is a minor surgical procedure to divide the scar tissue sealing the vaginal introitus in type 3 FGM. The need for de-infibulation can be determined on inspection of the external genitals by an experienced health professional. De-infibulation is sometimes termed a 'reversal' of FGM; however, this is incorrect as it does not replace genital tissue or restore normal genital anatomy and function.

De-infibulation is recommended if the introitus is not sufficiently open to permit normal urinary and menstrual flow, vaginal examination, comfortable sexual intercourse and safe vaginal delivery. It may also be necessary to permit cervical smears, sexual health screens and gynaecological surgery (e.g. SMM, TOP). In practice it will be required for most women with type 3 FGM, as the vaginal introitus will be narrowed.

De-infibulation can usually be performed under local anaesthetic in an appropriately equipped room for minor procedures or in a delivery suite room. Occasionally a spinal or general anaesthetic is required. One recommended method of de-infibulation is shown in Appendix III.

### 8.4   What is the role of clitoral reconstruction?

**Clitoral reconstruction should not be performed because current evidence suggests unacceptable complication rates without conclusive evidence of benefit.**

Several publications, including a large retrospective study,[43] claim that reconstructive clitoral surgery can restore clitoral function. However, surgery cannot replace clitoral tissue removed at FGM and it is also possible that surgical exploration of the clitoral area may result in further damage to the clitoral nerves and vasculature and loss of sensation. It is debatable that these procedures improve clitoral sensation, although improving the genital appearance may have benefits for some women. Existing studies are retrospective with poor follow-up and they lack standardised assessment of sexual function. In the study by Foldès,[43] 2938 women underwent surgery but only 29% attended for follow-up and 4% required hospital readmission because of surgical complications. There is a need for well-designed clinical trials to investigate the safety and effectiveness of this procedure.

Evidence level 3

### 9.   How should FGM be managed in pregnancy?

### 9.1   What level of care do women with FGM require?

**Women with FGM are more likely to have obstetric complications and consultant-led care is generally recommended. However, some women with previous uncomplicated vaginal deliveries may be suitable for midwifery-led care in labour.**

Women with FGM are more likely to have obstetric complications and consultant-led care is generally recommended. However, some women who have previously had one or more uncomplicated pregnancies and have delivered vaginally may be considered low risk, provided that they have no history of post-delivery re-infibulation.

### 9.2   How should women with FGM be identified in pregnancy?

**All women, irrespective of country of origin, should be asked for a history of FGM at their booking antenatal visit so that FGM can be identified early in the pregnancy. This should be documented in the maternity record.**

**Women identified as having FGM should be referred to the designated consultant obstetrician or midwife with responsibility for FGM patients. Local protocols will determine which elements of care should be undertaken by these individuals and which may be undertaken by other appropriately trained midwives or obstetricians (Appendix IV).**

Pregnancy is a time when the majority of women engage with healthcare services. It presents a key opportunity to identify women with FGM, provide information and advice, address healthcare needs and assess the risk to the unborn child and to other female family members. In the UK, it is normal practice to defer vaginal examination of pregnant women until the onset of labour, unless there is a clinical indication. For this reason, early identification of FGM in pregnancy is best achieved by asking all women booking for antenatal care whether they have a history of FGM.[41] It is good practice if possible to obtain such a clinical history from the patient in the absence of a partner or other family member. It might be important to consider that some women may not know if they have been exposed to FGM. | Evidence level 4

The clinical management of pregnant women is summarised in Appendix II.

### 9.3 What antenatal documentation is required to demonstrate that legal and regulatory processes have been adhered to?

**The midwife or obstetrician should ensure that all relevant information is documented in the clinical records (Appendix I).**

The information in the clinical records should include documentation that FGM has been recorded in accordance with the HSCIC Enhanced Dataset, as well as other information as shown in Appendix I.

### 9.4 How should antenatal care be managed?

**Referral for psychological assessment and treatment should be offered.**

**The vulva should be inspected to determine the type of FGM and whether de-infibulation is indicated. If the introitus is sufficiently open to permit vaginal examination and if the urethral meatus is visible, then de-infibulation is unlikely to be necessary.**

**Screening for hepatitis C should be offered in addition to the other routine antenatal screening tests (hepatitis B, HIV and syphilis).**

**De-infibulation may be performed antenatally, in the first stage of labour or at the time of delivery and can usually be performed under local anaesthetic in a delivery suite room. It can also be performed perioperatively after caesarean section (Appendix III).**

**The midwife or obstetrician should discuss, agree and record a plan of care (see Appendix IV). This may be documented in a preformatted sheet.**

**Women should be informed that re-infibulation will not be undertaken under any circumstances.**

For women with type 3 FGM, where adequate vaginal assessment in labour is unlikely to be possible, de-infibulation should be recommended antenatally, usually in the second trimester, typically at around 20 weeks of gestation. Antenatal de-infibulation as an elective procedure ensures that the procedure is performed by an appropriately trained midwife or obstetrician. However, women may prefer de-infibulation during labour, as this is the usual practice in some countries where FGM is prevalent.

There have been no randomised trials conducted on measures that may improve outcomes for pregnant women with a history of FGM.[44] However de-infibulation (when the introitus is narrowed) and selective episiotomy (depending on assessment at the time of delivery) may improve clinical outcomes.

Women should be informed that re-infibulation will not be undertaken under any circumstances.[37] They should also be informed of the health consequences of re-infibulation and the benefits of not re-infibulating. | Evidence level 4

### 9.5   *How should intrapartum care be managed?*

**If a woman requires intrapartum de-infibulation, the midwife and obstetrician caring for her should have completed training in de-infibulation or should be supervised appropriately.**

**If de-infibulation planned for the time of delivery is not undertaken because of recourse to caesarean section, then the option of perioperative de-infibulation (i.e. just after caesarean section) should be considered and discussed with the woman.**

**Labial tears in women with FGM should be managed in the same manner as in women without FGM. Repairs should be performed where clinically indicated, after discussion with the woman and using appropriate materials and techniques.** D

Women with FGM should generally be delivered in units with immediate access to emergency obstetric care and should have intravenous access established in labour and blood taken for full blood count and group and save. However, in certain circumstances women with FGM may be considered low risk and midwifery-led care in labour may be appropriate (see section 9.1).

The technique of de-infibulation at delivery is similar in principle to de-infibulation performed at other times (see Appendix III). However, in contrast to de-infibulation prepregnancy, antenatally or in the first stage of labour, when either a scalpel or scissors may be used, at delivery the incision should be made with scissors (rather than a scalpel) just before crowning of the fetal head. Lidocaine without adrenaline (epinephrine) should be used. Once the procedure has been performed, the need for episiotomy should be assessed; this is commonly required (irrespective of FGM type) due to scarring and reduced skin elasticity of the introitus.

In women for whom intrapartum de-infibulation was planned to permit safe vaginal delivery, emergency caesarean section may result in the woman having an ongoing need for de-infibulation during a subsequent pregnancy. If feasible from the perspective of maternal and fetal wellbeing, the option of perioperative de-infibulation, after safe caesarean delivery of the baby, should be discussed with the woman prior to transfer to theatre. This scenario may be discussed with women antenatally.

Guidance for repair of perineal and genital trauma is available[45] and should be followed for women with FGM, for example, in the case of labial tears. | Evidence level 4

### 9.6   *How should intrapartum care be managed for women identified as having FGM in pregnancy for whom there has been no agreed documented plan of care?*

**The impact of FGM on labour and delivery should be sensitively discussed and a plan of care agreed.**

If vaginal examination is not possible or intrapartum procedures and urinary catheterisation are not feasible, then de-infibulation in the first stage of labour should be recommended. An epidural should be offered to cover the procedure and for subsequent examinations and delivery. If vaginal access is adequate then de-infibulation can be performed at the time of delivery under local anaesthetic (see section 9.5).

### 9.7   *How should postnatal care be managed?*

**A woman whose planned de-infibulation was not performed because of delivery by caesarean section should have follow-up in a gynaecology outpatient or FGM clinic so that de-infibulation can be offered before a subsequent pregnancy.**

**The discharging midwife should ensure that all legal and regulatory processes have been adhered to prior to discharge (Appendix I).**

The designated consultant obstetrician or named specialist midwife may consider a postnatal debrief with the patient and her partner, regardless of whether intrapartum procedures were undertaken or not. This represents a further opportunity to educate the family on FGM. All the appropriate legal and regulatory processes should be documented as shown in Appendix I. The discharging midwife should ensure that the documentation is complete.

10. Recommendations for future research

- The rates of stillbirth and neonatal death in women with FGM.
- Interventional trials to assess the role of de-infibulation in improving pregnancy outcomes and the optimal timing of de-infibulation.
- Clinical trials to investigate the safety and effectiveness of clitoral reconstruction.
- The role of psychological assessment and treatment in the antenatal care of women with FGM.

11. Auditable topics

- The proportion of women asked about FGM at booking (100%).
- The proportion of healthcare professionals who are familiar with the HSCIC FGM Enhanced Dataset (100%).
- The proportion of healthcare workers (gynaecologists, obstetricians and midwives) who have received training on FGM and its management (100%).
- The proportion of pregnant women identified as having FGM who are referred to a designated consultant obstetrician or specialist midwife with responsibility for FGM patients (100%).
- The proportion of women identified as having FGM who are offered screening for hepatitis B, hepatitis C, HIV and syphilis (100%).
- The quality of documentation of FGM in the medical records, including ensuring information is transferred to the community.
- Number of referrals made to social services and/or police.

12. Useful links and support groups

- Department of Health. *Commissioning services to support women and girls with female genital mutilation*. London: DH; 2015 [https://www.gov.uk/government/publications/services-for-women-and-girls-with-fgm].
- Department of Health. *Female Genital Mutilation Risk and Safeguarding. Guidance for professionals*. London: DH; 2015 [https://www.gov.uk/government/publications/safeguarding-women-and-girls-at-risk-of-fgm].
- Patient information leaflets may be ordered from the Department of Health [https://www.orderline.dh.gov.uk/ecom_dh/public/saleproduct.jsf?catalogueCode=2903740].
- FORWARD (Foundation for Women's Health Research and Development) [http://www.forwarduk.org.uk].
- Multi-agency practice guidelines have been produced by the Home Office and the Department for Education to support front-line professionals to prevent FGM [https://www.gov.uk/government/publications/female-genital-mutilation-guidelines].
- NHS Choices. *Female genital mutilation*
  - For patients: [http://www.nhs.uk/Conditions/female-genital-mutilation/Pages/Introduction.aspx].
  - For professionals: [http://www.nhs.uk/nhsengland/aboutnhsservices/sexual-health-services/pages/fgm-for-professionals.aspx].
- Orchid Project (a charity dedicated to ending female genital cutting) [http://orchidproject.org/].

## References

1. Baillot H, Murray N, Connelly E, Howard N; Scottish Refugee Council; London School of Hygiene and Tropical Medicine. *Tackling Female Genital Mutilation in Scotland. A Scottish model of intervention.* Glasgow: Scottish Refugee Council; 2014.
2. [Department of Finance and Personnel, Northern Ireland]. *Multi-agency practice guidelines: female genital mutilation.* [Bangor, Northern Ireland]: [DFP]; [2014] [http://www.dfpni.gov.uk/multi-agency-practice-guidelines-on-female-genital-mutilation.pdf]. Accessed 2015 May 29.
3. World Health Organization. *Eliminating female genital mutilation: an interagency statement.* Geneva: World Health Organization; 2008.
4. United Nations Children's Fund. *Female Genital Mutilation/Cutting: A statistical overview and exploration of the dynamics of change.* New York: UNICEF; 2013.
5. Department of Health. *Female Genital Mutilation Risk and Safeguarding. Guidance for professionals.* London: DH; 2015.
6. Royal College of Midwives, Royal College of Nursing, Royal College of Obstetricians and Gynaecologists, Equality Now, Unite. *Tackling FGM in the UK: Intercollegiate recommendations for identifying, recording and reporting.* London: RCM; 2013.
7. Macfarlane A, Dorkenoo E. *Female Genital Mutilation in England and Wales. Updated statistical estimates of the numbers of affected women living in England and Wales and girls at risk. Interim report on provisional estimates.* London: City University London; 2014.
8. House of Commons Home Affairs Committee. *Female genital mutilation: the case for a national action plan. Second Report of Session 2014–15 Report, together with formal minutes relating to the report.* HC 201 [Incorporating HC 1091, 2013–14]. London: The Stationery Office; 2014.
9. Berg RC, Underland V, Odgaard-Jensen J, Fretheim A, Vist GE. Effects of female genital cutting on physical health outcomes: a systematic review and meta-analysis. *BMJ Open* 2014;4:e006316.
10. Asante A, Omurtag K, Roberts C. Epidermal inclusion cyst of the clitoris 30 years after female genital mutilation. *Fertil Steril* 2010;94:1097.e1–3.
11. Abdulcadir J, Pusztaszeri M, Vilarino R, Dubuisson JB, Vlastos AT. Clitoral neuroma after female genital mutilation/cutting: a rare but possible event. *J Sex Med* 2012;9:1220–5.
12. Fernández-Aguilar S, Noël JC. Neuroma of the clitoris after female genital cutting. *Obstet Gynecol* 2003;101:1053–4.
13. Kaplan A, Forbes M, Bonhoure I, Utzet M, Martin M, Manneh M, et al. Female genital mutilation/cutting in The Gambia: long-term health consequences and complications during delivery and for the newborn. *Int J Womens Health* 2013;5:323–31.
14. Amin MM, Rasheed S, Salem E. Lower urinary tract symptoms following female genital mutilation. *Int J Gynaecol Obstet* 2013;123:21–3.
15. Yusuf L, Negash S. Vaginal calculus following severe form of female genital mutilation: a case report. *Ethiop Med J* 2008;46:185–8.
16. Peterman A, Johnson K. Incontinence and trauma: sexual violence, female genital cutting and proxy measures of gynecological fistula. *Soc Sci Med* 2009;68:971–9.
17. Berg RC, Denison E. Does female genital mutilation/cutting (FGM/C) affect women's sexual functioning? A systematic review of the sexual consequences of FGM/C. *Sex Res Social Policy* 2012;9:41–56.
18. Andersson SH, Rymer J, Joyce DW, Momoh C, Gayle CM. Sexual quality of life in women who have undergone female genital mutilation: a case–control study. *BJOG* 2012;119:1606–11.
19. Alsibiani SA, Rouzi AA. Sexual function in women with female genital mutilation. *Fertil Steril* 2010;93:722–4.
20. Vloeberghs E, van der Kwaak A, Knipscheer J, van den Muijsenbergh M. Coping and chronic psychosocial consequences of female genital mutilation in The Netherlands. *Ethn Health* 2012;17:677–95.
21. Behrendt A, Moritz S. Posttraumatic stress disorder and memory problems after female genital mutilation. *Am J Psychiatry* 2005;162:1000–2.
22. Salihu HM, August EM, Salemi JL, Weldeselasse H, Sarro YS, Alio AP. The association between female genital mutilation and intimate partner violence. *BJOG* 2012;119:1597–605.
23. Peltzer K, Pengpid S. Female genital mutilation and intimate partner violence in the Ivory Coast. *BMC Womens Health* 2014;14:13.
24. Morison L, Scherf C, Ekpo G, Paine K, West B, Coleman R, et al. The long-term reproductive health consequences of female genital cutting in rural Gambia: a community-based survey. *Trop Med Int Health* 2001;6:643–53.
25. Elmusharaf S, Elkhidir I, Hoffmann S, Almroth L. A case-control study on the association between female genital mutilation and sexually transmitted infections in Sudan. *BJOG* 2006;113:469–74.
26. Almroth L, Elmusharaf S, El Hadi N, Obeid A, El Sheikh MA, Elfadil SM, et al. Primary infertility after genital mutilation in girlhood in Sudan: a case-control study. *Lancet* 2005;366:385–91.
27. Hwang EW, Cheung R. Global epidemiology of hepatitis B virus (HBV) infection. *N Am J Med Sci (Boston)* 2011;4:7–13.
28. Duri K, Stray-Pedersen B. HIV/AIDS in Africa: trends, missing links and the way forward. *J Virol Antivir Res* 2013;2(1).
29. WHO study group on female genital mutilation and obstetric outcome, Banks E, Meirik O, Farley T, Akande O, Bathija H, et al. Female genital mutilation and obstetric outcome: WHO collaborative prospective study in six African countries. *Lancet* 2006;367:1835–41.
30. Berg RC, Odgaard-Jensen J, Fretheim A, Underland V, Vist G. An updated systematic review and meta-analysis of the obstetric consequences of female genital mutilation/cutting. *Obstet Gynecol Int* 2014;2014:542859.
31. Gissler M, Alexander S, Macfarlane A, Small R, Stray-Pedersen B, Zeitlin J, et al. Stillbirths and infant deaths among migrants in industrialized countries. *Acta Obstet Gynecol Scand* 2009;88:134–48.
32. Small R, Gagnon A, Gissler M, Zeitlin J, Bennis M, Glazier R, et al. Somali women and their pregnancy outcomes postmigration: data from six receiving countries. *BJOG* 2008;115:1630–40.
33. Browning A, Allsworth JE, Wall LL. The relationship between female genital cutting and obstetric fistulae. *Obstet Gynecol* 2010;115:578–83.
34. HM Government. *Multi-Agency Practice Guidelines: Female Genital Mutilation.* [London]: HM Government; 2014.
35. Ministry of Justice, Home Office. *Serious Crime Act 2015. Factsheet - female genital mutilation.* [London]: Ministry of Justice; 2015 [https://www.gov.uk/government/uploads/system/uploads/attachment_data/file/416325/Fact_sheet_-_FGM_-_Act.pdf]. Accessed 2015 May 29.
36. Royal College of Obstetricians and Gynaecologists. *Ethical considerations in relation to female genital cosmetic surgery (FGCS).* Ethical opinion paper. London: RCOG; 2013.
37. World Health Organization. *Global strategy to stop health-care providers from performing female genital mutilation UNAIDS, UNDP, UNFPA, UNHCR, UNICEF, UNIFEM, WHO, FIGO, ICN, IOM, MWIA, WCPT, WMA.* Geneva: WHO; 2010.
38. HM Government. *A Statement Opposing Female Genital Mutilation.* [London]: HM Government; 2014.
39. Statement opposing female genital mutilation [https://www.gov.uk/government/publications/statement-opposing-female-genital-mutilation]. Accessed 2015 Apr 20.

40. Department of Health. *NHS Specialist Services for Female Genital Mutilation.* [London]: DH; 2014 [http://www.nhs.uk/NHSEngland/AboutNHSservices/sexual-health-services/Documents/List%20of%20FGM%20Clinics%20Mar%2014%20FINAL.pdf]. Accessed 2015 Apr 20.

41. Health and Social Care Information Centre. *Female Genital Mutilation (FGM) Enhanced Dataset. Requirements Specification.* [Leeds]: HSCIC; 2015.

42. FORWARD. *Reviewing Access to FGM Specialist Services in England (2011).* Research Brief No. 2. London: FORWARD; 2011.

43. Foldès P, Cuzin B, Andro A. Reconstructive surgery after female genital mutilation: a prospective cohort study. *Lancet* 2012;380:134–41.

44. Balogun OO, Hirayama F, Wariki WM, Koyanagi A, Mori R. Interventions for improving outcomes for pregnant women who have experienced genital cutting. *Cochrane Database Syst Rev* 2013;(2):CD009872.

45. National Institute for Health and Care Excellence. *Intrapartum care: care of healthy women and their babies during childbirth.* NICE clinical guideline 190. [Manchester]: NICE; 2014.

Appendix I: Legal and regulatory responsibilities of health professionals

1. Data recording (http://www.hscic.gov.uk/fgm)
- Data recording is mandatory for all women identified as having FGM.
- Document FGM diagnosis in medical records (even if FGM is not the reason for presentation).
- If genital examination is performed and type of FGM is identified, record FGM type (WHO classification).*
- Document further details in accordance with the HSCIC FGM Enhanced Dataset.
- Explain to the woman that her personal data will be transmitted to the HSCIC for the purpose of FGM prevalence monitoring and that the data will not be anonymised.

2. Reporting to police and/or social services in the event of risk to a child (https://www.gov.uk/government/publications/safeguarding-women-and-girls-at-risk-of-fgm)
- Children under 18:
  - If FGM is confirmed (on examination or if the patient or parent says it has been done), refer as a matter of urgency to the police and this should be done within 1 month of confirmation.
  - If FGM is suspected (but not confirmed) or the girl is at risk (but has not had FGM), refer to social services or the police. The urgency of the referral depends on the degree of risk.
- Nonpregnant women with FGM: no requirement to report unless a related child is at risk.
- Pregnant women:
  - A member of the clinical team (midwife or obstetrician) must make an individual risk assessment using an FGM safeguarding risk assessment tool and if the unborn child, or any other child in the family, is considered to be at risk of FGM then reporting to social services or the police must occur.
  - Document maternal history of FGM in the personal child health record ('Red Book') prior to postnatal discharge.
  - If delivery of a baby girl, notify the designated child protection midwife, who should inform the GP and health visitor.

*Genital piercings should be classified as type 4 FGM in accordance with the WHO FGM classification.

**Appendix II:** Clinical management of adult women with FGM in obstetric and gynaecological practice

1. All acute trusts/health boards should have a designated consultant and midwife responsible for the care of women with FGM

2. All women in obstetric and gynaecological practice
- Explain law on FGM, documenting the discussion and referring her to information provided in the Health Passport (https://www.gov.uk/government/publications/statement-opposing-female-genital-mutilation).
- Provide interpreter if required (not a family member).
- Offer referral for psychological assessment and treatment.
- Offer specialist referral as appropriate, e.g. sexual health, urology.
- Make a clinical assessment of FGM (symptoms, examination) and need for de-infibulation.
- Record data in accordance with the HSCIC FGM Enhanced Dataset. These include age at FGM, country where FGM was performed, date of entry to UK (if applicable) and past history of de-infibulation and/or re-infibulation.
- If de-infibulation is indicated, offer before pregnancy – it can usually be performed on an outpatient basis.
- Reporting to social services or the police is only required if a related child is considered to be at risk.

3. Additional management in pregnant women
- Refer to designated consultant obstetrician or specialist midwife with responsibility for women with FGM.
- Local protocols will determine which elements of care (child safeguarding risk assessment, data recording, clinical management) should be undertaken by the designated midwife or obstetrician and which may be undertaken by other appropriately trained midwives or obstetricians.
- Discuss and clearly document a plan of care – preformatted pro formas may be used.
- Make an individual risk assessment using an FGM safeguarding risk assessment tool (an example of such a tool can be found at https://www.gov.uk/government/publications/safeguarding-women-and-girls-at-risk-of-fgm). If the unborn child or any related child is considered to be at risk then reporting to social services or the police must occur.
- Offer screening for hepatitis C in addition to routine screening for hepatitis B, HIV and syphilis.
- If de-infibulation is indicated, discuss, agree and document the timing (antenatal or intrapartum). Inform the woman that re-infibulation after delivery will not be performed under any circumstances.
- Manage as high obstetric risk (increased risk of haemorrhage, perineal trauma and caesarean section), except for women who have had previous pregnancies with uncomplicated vaginal deliveries and no history of post-delivery re-infibulation.
- Document maternal history of FGM in the personal child health record ('Red Book') prior to postnatal discharge.
- If delivery of a baby girl, notify the designated child protection midwife, who should inform the GP and health visitor.
- Offer postnatal follow-up if de-infibulation performed intrapartum or if planned de-infibulation did not occur because of delivery by caesarean section.

Appendix III: One recommended method of performing de-infibulation

**1) Type 3 FGM (infibulation)**

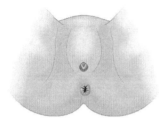

**2) Infiltration of midline scar with local anaesthetic**

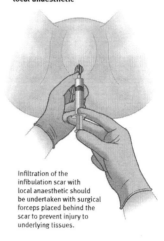

Infiltration of the infibulation scar with local anaesthetic should be undertaken with surgical forceps placed behind the scar to prevent injury to underlying tissues.

**3) Incision of midline scar**

The incision should be made either with scissors or a knife and extended anteriorly until the external urethral meatus is visible.

**4) Suturing of cut edges with absorbable suture**

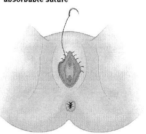

The cut edges may be oversewn with a fine absorbable suture and a paraffin gauze dressing applied.

Appendix IV: Plan of care for women with FGM in pregnancy

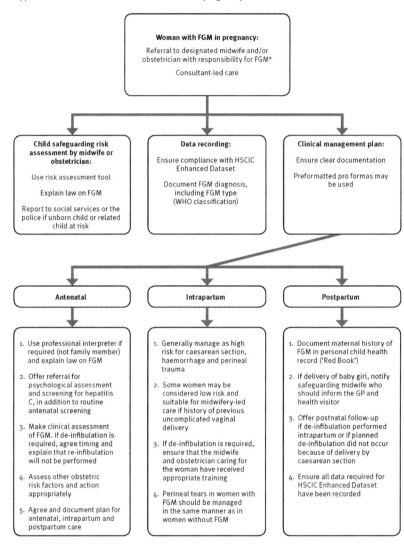

**Woman with FGM in pregnancy:**

Referral to designated midwife and/or obstetrician with responsibility for FGM*

Consultant-led care

**Child safeguarding risk assessment by midwife or obstetrician:**

Use risk assessment tool

Explain law on FGM

Report to social services or the police if unborn child or related child at risk

**Data recording:**

Ensure compliance with HSCIC Enhanced Dataset

Document FGM diagnosis, including FGM type (WHO classification)

**Clinical management plan:**

Ensure clear documentation

Preformatted pro formas may be used

**Antenatal**

1. Use professional interpreter if required (not family member) and explain law on FGM

2. Offer referral for psychological assessment and screening for hepatitis C, in addition to routine antenatal screening

3. Make clinical assessment of FGM. If de-infibulation is required, agree timing and explain that re-infibulation will not be performed

4. Assess other obstetric risk factors and action appropriately

5. Agree and document plan for antenatal, intrapartum and postpartum care

**Intrapartum**

1. Generally manage as high risk for caesarean section, haemorrhage and perineal trauma

2. Some women may be considered low risk and suitable for midwifery-led care if history of previous uncomplicated vaginal delivery

3. If de-infibulation is required, ensure that the midwife and obstetrician caring for the woman have received appropriate training

4. Perineal tears in women with FGM should be managed in the same manner as in women without FGM

**Postpartum**

1. Document maternal history of FGM in personal child health record ('Red Book')

2. If delivery of baby girl, notify safeguarding midwife who should inform the GP and health visitor

3. Offer postnatal follow-up if de-infibulation performed intrapartum or if planned de-infibulation did not occur because of delivery by caesarean section

4. Ensure all data required for HSCIC Enhanced Dataset have been recorded

* Local protocols will determine which elements of care (child safeguarding risk assessment, data recording, clinical management plan) should be undertaken by the designated midwife or obstetrician responsible for women with FGM and which may be undertaken by other appropriately trained midwives or obstetricians

Appendix V: Explanation of guidelines and evidence levels

Clinical guidelines are: 'systematically developed statements which assist clinicians and patients in making decisions about appropriate treatment for specific conditions'. Each guideline is systematically developed using a standardised methodology. Exact details of this process can be found in Clinical Governance Advice No. 1 *Development of RCOG Green-top Guidelines* (available on the RCOG website at http://www.rcog.org.uk/green-top-development). These recommendations are not intended to dictate an exclusive course of management or treatment. They must be evaluated with reference to individual patient needs, resources and limitations unique to the institution and variations in local populations. It is hoped that this process of local ownership will help to incorporate these guidelines into routine practice. Attention is drawn to areas of clinical uncertainty where further research may be indicated.

The evidence used in this guideline was graded using the scheme below and the recommendations formulated in a similar fashion with a standardised grading scheme.

| Classification of evidence levels | Grades of recommendations |
|---|---|
| **1++** High-quality meta-analyses, systematic reviews of randomised controlled trials or randomised controlled trials with a very low risk of bias |  At least one meta-analysis, systematic review or randomised controlled trial rated as 1++, and directly applicable to the target population; or A systematic review of randomised controlled trials or a body of evidence consisting principally of studies rated as 1+, directly applicable to the target population and demonstrating overall consistency of results |
| **1+** Well-conducted meta-analyses, systematic reviews of randomised controlled trials or randomised controlled trials with a low risk of bias | |
| **1−** Meta-analyses, systematic reviews of randomised controlled trials or randomised controlled trials with a high risk of bias |  A body of evidence including studies rated as 2++ directly applicable to the target population, and demonstrating overall consistency of results; or Extrapolated evidence from studies rated as 1++ or 1+ |
| **2++** High-quality systematic reviews of case–control or cohort studies or high-quality case–control or cohort studies with a very low risk of confounding, bias or chance and a high probability that the relationship is causal | |
| **2+** Well-conducted case–control or cohort studies with a low risk of confounding, bias or chance and a moderate probability that the relationship is causal | C A body of evidence including studies rated as 2+ directly applicable to the target population, and demonstrating overall consistency of results; or Extrapolated evidence from studies rated as 2++ |
| **2−** Case–control or cohort studies with a high risk of confounding, bias or chance and a significant risk that the relationship is not causal |  Evidence level 3 or 4; or Extrapolated evidence from studies rated as 2+ |
| **3** Non-analytical studies, e.g. case reports, case series | |
| **4** Expert opinion | |

**Good practice point**

☑ Recommended best practice based on the clinical experience of the guideline development group

This guideline was produced on behalf of the Royal College of Obstetricians and Gynaecologists by:
**Dr NM Low-Beer MRCOG, London and Professor SM Creighton FRCOG, London**

and peer reviewed by:
Dr J Abdulcadir, University Hospitals of Geneva, Geneva, Switzerland; Dr F Abu Amna MRCOG, Preston;
Ms J Albert, London; Dr MM Amin, Kobe University Graduate School of Medicine, Kobe, Japan;
Dr IA Babarinsa MRCOG, Doha, Qatar; Ms O Balogun, National Center for Child Health and Development, Tokyo,
Japan; Dr RC Berg, Norwegian Knowledge Centre for the Health Services, Oslo, Norway; Miss P Buck FRCOG,
Lancashire; Crown Prosecution Service; Department of Health; Professor A Macfarlane, City University London;
Dr R Mori, National Center for Child Health and Development, Tokyo, Japan; RCOG Women's Network;
Professor AA Rouzi, King Abdulaziz University Hospital, Jeddah, Saudi Arabia; Royal College of Midwives;
Dr SMA Saad MRCOG, Paisley; Mr E Vloeberghs, Pharos, Utrecht, The Netherlands; Dr AI. Wright FRCOG, London;
Dr AEA Yagoub MRCOG, Blackpool; and Professor L Yusuf, Addis Ababa University College of Health, Addis Ababa,
Ethiopia.

Committee lead reviewers were: Dr M Gupta MRCOG, London; Dr M Ledingham MRCOG, Glasgow;
Dr AJ Thomson MRCOG, Paisley; and Mr RC Wimalasundera FRCOG, London.

The chairs of the Guidelines Committee were: Dr M Gupta[1] MRCOG, London; Dr P Owen[2] FRCOG, Glasgow;
and Dr AJ Thomson[1] MRCOG, Paisley.
[1] co-chairs from June 2014 [2] until May 2014.

*All RCOG guidance developers are asked to declare any conflicts of interest. A statement summarising any*
*conflicts of interest for this guideline is available from: https://www.rcog.org.uk/en/guidelines-research-services/*
*guidelines/gtg53/.*

The final version is the responsibility of the Guidelines Committee of the RCOG.

The review process will commence in 2018, unless otherwise indicated.

# APPENDIX 4

# FGM SAFEGUARDING PATHWAY

 **Department of Health**

# FGM Safeguarding Pathway

Presentation prompts clinician to suspect/consider FGM e.g. repeated UTI, vaginal infections, urinary incontinence, dyspareunia, dysmenorrhea etc. Also consider difficulty getting pregnant, presenting for travel health advice or patient disclosure (e.g., young girl from community known to practice FGM discloses she will soon undergo 'coming of age' ceremony).

INTRODUCTORY QUESTIONS: Do you, your partner or your parents come from a community where cutting or circumcision is practised? (It may be appropriate to use other terms or phrases)

**No – no further action required**   **Yes**

Do you believe patient has been cut?

**No – but family history**   **Yes**

**Patient is under 18 or vulnerable adult**   **Patient is under 18**   **Patient is over 18**

**If you suspect she may be at risk of FGM:**

Use the safeguarding risk assessment guidance to help decide what action to take:

- If child is at imminent risk of harm, initiate urgent safeguarding response.
- Consider if a child social care referral is needed, following your local processes.

Ring 101 to report basic details of the case to police under **Mandatory Reporting Duty.**

*Police will initiate a multi-agency safeguarding response.*

Does she have any female children or siblings at risk of FGM?

And/or do you consider her to be a vulnerable adult?

Complete safeguarding risk assessment and use guidance to decide whether a social care referral is required.

FOR ALL PATIENTS who have HAD FGM
1. Read code FGM status
2. Complete FGM Enhanced dataset noting all relevant codes.
3. Consider need to refer patient to FGM service to confirm FGM is present, FGM type and/or for deinfibulation.

   a) If long term pain, consider referral to uro-gynae specialist clinic.

   b) If mental health problems, consider referral to counselling/other.

   c) If under 18 refer all for a paediatric appointment and physical examination, following your local processes.

Can you identify other female siblings or relatives at risk of FGM?
- Complete risk assessment if possible OR
- Share information with multi-agency partners to initiate safeguarding response.

Contact details

*Local safeguarding lead:*

*Local FGM lead/clinic:*

*NSPCC FGM Helpline:* 0800 028 3550

Detailed FGM risk and safeguarding guidance for professionals from the Department of Health is available online

FOR ALL PATIENTS:
1. Clearly document all discussion and actions with patient/family in patient's medical record.
2. Explain FGM is illegal in the UK.
3. Discuss the adverse health consequences of FGM.
4. Share safeguarding information with Health Visitor, School Nurse, Practice Nurse.

If a girl appears to have been recently cut or you believe she is at imminent risk, act immediately – this may include phoning 999.

REMEMBER: Mandatory reporting is only one part of safeguarding against FGM and other abuse. *Always ask your local safeguarding lead if in doubt.*

# APPENDIX 5

# SUMMARY OF THE OHCHR REPORT ON HUMAN RIGHTS AND THE PRACTICE OF FEMALE GENITAL MUTILATION AND EXCISION IN GUINEA

April 2016

## 1. INTRODUCTION AND LEGAL BACKGROUND

Female genital mutilation/excision (FGM/E) is strongly anchored in the customs and traditions of 29 countries in Africa and the Middle East,[1] and has been noted elsewhere. WHO estimates that 130-140 million girls and women alive today have suffered some form of FGM/E; more than 30 million girls risk being forced to endure this practice in the coming decade.[2]

Guinea has the second highest prevalence of FGM/E worldwide, after Somalia. Although FGM/E is forbidden by law, it is practised in every region, by all ethnic or religious group and social class, and 97% of Guinean women and girls aged 15-49 have suffered excision.[3] Although FGM/E is decreasing worldwide, a national Demographic and Health Study (EDS) found in 2012 that FGM/E had slightly increased since 2002.[4]

FGM/E involves multiple violations of the human rights of women and girls, and is prohibited in international law, under multiple legally binding conventions to which Guinea is party.

The question is also addressed in the African Charter on Human and Peoples' Rights and the Protocol to the African Charter on Human and People's Rights on the Rights of Women in Africa (Maputo Protocol), which details measures that States must take to eradicate harmful practices with negative impacts on

---

[1]  Benin, Burkina Faso, Cameroon, Central African Republic, Chad, Côte d'Ivoire, Djibouti, Egypt, Eritrea, Ethiopia, Gambia, Ghana, Guinea, Guinea-Bissau, Iraq, Kenya, Liberia, Mali, Mauritania, Niger, Nigeria, Senegal, Sierra Leone, Somalia, Sudan, Togo, Uganda, United Republic of Tanzania, Yemen.

[2]  UNICEF, *Female Genital Mutilation/Cutting: A statistical overview of exploration of the dynamics of change*, July 2013, New York.

[3]  See mapping in UNICEF, *Female Genital Mutilation/Cutting: A statistical overview of exploration of the dynamics of change*, July 2013, New York.

[4]  Guinea's 4th Demographic and Health Study was carried out in October 2012 by the *Institut national de la statistique* (INS).

women's rights. The African Charter on the Rights and Welfare of the Child, ratified by Guinea, requires State Parties to take all appropriate measures to 'eliminate harmful social and cultural practices affecting the welfare, dignity, normal growth and development of the child', particularly 'customs and practices prejudicial to the health or life of the child' and 'those customs and practices discriminatory to the child on the grounds of sex or other status'. In July 2004, African Union Heads of State and Government adopted the Solemn Declaration on Gender Equality in Africa, which expresses deep concern regarding the negative impact of harmful practices on women and invites all Member States of the African Union to take action to completely eradicate such practices.[5]

Guinea's Constitution guarantees respect for the physical and moral integrity of all individuals and for the principles of equality and non-discrimination. The Penal Code prohibits, and provides for life imprisonment for, any mutilation of the genital organs of men (castration) or women (excision).[6] This prohibition is reaffirmed in Guinea's 2008 Children's Code, which makes perpetrators liable to imprisonment of between three months and two years and/or a fine, sanctions which are further strengthened if the victim suffers permanent disability or death. In November 2010, the Guinean Ministry for Social Action, the Advancement of Women and Children's Issues published five decrees which, *inter alia*, prohibited FGM/E in all public and private health centres throughout the country.[7]

## 2. CURRENT SITUATION REGARDING FGM/E IN GUINEA

Guinea's estimated 11 million inhabitants stem from various ethnic groups. In terms of religious belief, Islam dominates in Upper and Middle Guinea and to a lesser extent in Lower Guinea (85% de la population). Christianity (10% of the population) and animism (5%) are more widespread in Forest Region of Guinea (*Guinée forestière*). Most Guinean women have suffered Type 2 FGM/E, in other words the total or partial ablation of the clitoris and labia minora, with or without ablation of the labia majora. According to the 2012 EDS study, 84% of women aged 15–49 have suffered ablation; 8%, infibulation; and 6%, cutting with no removal of flesh. The most extreme form of FGM/E, Type 3 (infibulation), is practised among the Peuhle ethnic group and by the Tomas.[8] Age appears to have no impact on the type of FGM/E practised. The EDS found a 96% prevalence of FGM/E among women aged 15–49 in 2005, and a 97% prevalence in 2012. FGM/E were practised by all ethnic groups without significant disparities, excepting the Guerzé, a mostly Christian and animist group of *Guinée forestière*. While the prevalence of the

---

5    http://www.achpr.org/fr/instruments/declaration-on-gender-equality-in-africa/ (01.07.14).
6    CRC/C/GIN/2, paras 357–358.
7    Ministry of National Solidarity and the Promotion of Women/Ministry of Health and Public Hygiene/Ministry of Security/Ministry of Justice/Ministry of Territorial Administration and Political Affairs.
8    EDS-MICS 2012, pp 328–329.

practice did not shift significantly from 1999 to 2012 among most ethnic groups, among the Guerzé, the EDS noted a significant decline, from 89% in 1999 to 66% in 2012.[9] Studies are underway to determine the reasons for this decrease; relevant stake-holders feel it may be the result of awareness campaigns in *Guinée forestière*.

Although globally FGM/E is more prevalent in rural zones,[10] in Guinea there is no significant difference in prevalence in urban areas (96.8% of women aged 15–49) and rural zones (97%).[11] The prevalence of excision decreases among girls whose mother is more highly educated, and support for FGM/E is greatest among women and girls from poor households (92%) compared to more well-off households (68%).[12] The study also indicates that the practice is being inflicted on girls at a younger age than previously: according to the 2012 EDS study, 69% of women aged 20 to 24 were excised before the age of 10, compared to 61% of women aged 45 to 49. Conversely, among the Guerzé, excision is practised later; 54% of women endure FGM/E after the age of 10.[13]

In Guinea, FGM/E is an initiation rite, not only in the transition from childhood to adolescence and adulthood, but also to prepare the young girl for active life within specific communities.[14] Groups of girls from multiple families[15] are usually excised together, either at home or in camps established for the purpose, with or without ceremonies and festivities. FGM/E usually takes place during school holidays or at harvest time.[16] There is an increasing trend to fewer celebrations and an increase in individual excisions, because of limited financial resources and a desire for greater discretion, due to the potential for legal sanctions. The excision of infants or very young girls is easier to hide from the authorities than the ceremonious excision of large groups.[17] Paradoxically, this more clandestine development of FGM/E may be the result of awareness campaigns in recent years, and the increase in legal sanctions.[18]

---

[9]   EDS-MICS 2012, pp 327–328.
[10]  UNICEF, *Female Genital Mutilation/Cutting: A statistical overview of exploration of the dynamics of change*, July 2013, New York, graph 4.6, p 38.
[11]  EDS-MICS 2012, table 17.2, p 327.
[12]  EDS-MICS 2012, p 331; UNICEF, *Female Genital Mutilation/Cutting: A statistical overview of exploration of the dynamics of change*, July 2013, New York, graph 6.6, p 60.
[13]  EDS-MICS 2012, pp 329–330.
[14]  Plan International, *Tradition and rights – Excision in West Africa*, Regional Office for West Africa, Dakar, July 2006, p 9.
[15]  CRC/C/GIN/2, para 361.
[16]  CRC/C/GIN/2, para Para. 361; General Commissariat for Refugees and Stateless Persons (CGRA/Belgium), French Office for the Protection of Refugees and Stateless Persons (OFPRA/France) and Federal Office for Migration (ODM/Switzerland), *Report on the Mission to the Republic of Guinea*, 29 October to 19 November 2011, Belgium-France-Switzerland Cooperation, March 2012, p 18.
[17]  Plan International, *Tradition and rights – Excision in West Africa*, Regional Office for West Africa, Dakar, July 2006, p 11.
[18]  UNICEF, *Female Genital Mutilation/Cutting: A statistical overview of exploration of the dynamics of change*, July 2013, New York, p 111.

As throughout West Africa, FGM/E is usually practised in Guinea by traditional excision practitioners, often women. The excision is usually carried out without anesthesia or modern hygiene. The wound is treated with traditional concoctions of plants, ash and mud. The cut is made with knives or razor-blades; previously the same knife would be used on all the girls but following awareness campaigns and greater medicalization of FGM/E, some practitioners have abandoned their traditional tools and use a new razor blade for each girl. Excision practitioners do not always disinfect their hands between each intervention.

The 2012 EDS study indicates a trend towards greater medicalization of FGM/E in Guinea.[19] Although 79% of women aged 15–49 were excised by traditional practitioners, the proportion falls to 66% among girls aged 0–14. Health personnel, principally midwives, are increasingly involved, despite the 2010 decree prohibiting the practice of FGM/E in public or private health institutions.[20]

In some areas, health personnel practise a simulated or symbolic excision, usually a pinch or scratch leading to a small release of blood. This technique is said to be practised mainly in small urban health centres where supervision by health services is limited.[21] Its object is to avoid girls suffering from stigma because they are not excised.

Forest, animist, communities, particularly the Guerzé, practise excision in collective procedures, regularly organised, which gather up to 500 girls and women into a single camp and involve costly and spectacular ceremonies. Traditional excision practitioners, known as *Zowo*, identify the place where the camp will be built, often in isolated areas close to a river or water source.[22] Excision takes on religious overtones, with the 'Nyömou' or sacred forest spirit 'giving birth' to initiates during a ceremony. Previously, tradition maintained a calendar for excision, often just before marriage, but today even 2 year-old girls may be excised,[23] and the duration that girls spend in the camps – formerly up to 3 years – has been reduced to a few weeks. Girls who have been excised no longer wear traditional clothing, though they continue to wear a specific uniform and the traditional musical instruments that accompanied the ritual have been replaced by hifi. Excision may cost the parents between 2 and 3

---

[19]   UNICEF, *Female Genital Mutilation/Cutting: A statistical overview of exploration of the dynamics of change*, July 2013, New York, pp 43–44 et graph 5.1; UNICEF Innocenti Research Centre, *Changing a Harmful Social Convention: the practice of excision/female genital mutilation*, 2005, reprinted May 2008, Florence, p 25.

[20]   N° 2464/MSNPFE/MSHP/MS/MJ/MATAP.

[21]   General Commissariat for Refugees and Stateless Persons (CGRA / Belgium), French Office for the Protection of Refugees and Stateless Persons (OFPRA/France) and Federal Office for Migration (ODM/Switzerland), *Report on the Mission to the Republic of Guinea*, 29 October to 19 November 2011, Belgium-France-Switzerland Cooperation, March 2012, p 19, para 3.

[22]   Remarks made by women from the VBG thematic group during the international day against FGM/E, 6 Feb 2014, in NZérékoré.

[23]   Remarks made by women from the VBG thematic group during the international day against FGM/E, 6 Feb 2014, in NZérékoré.

million Guinée francs (roughly 300-400 USD),[24] and often it is the family's ability to pay which determines the age at which a girl is excised. Mother and daughter(s) may be excised on the same day.[25] Following the post-excision healing period, each family must organise in turn a welcome ceremony for the women and girls who have been excised. Excised women and girls are given an additional name, often reflecting their character, social role or physical characteristics.

Broadly speaking, non-excision of girls is considered dishonourable in Guinean society.[26] This is indicated by the use of the term 'washing'; non-excised girls are considered 'dirty', and in every Guinean community, to say that a woman is not excised is a grave insult. Social pressure is such that girls may request excision for fear of being excluded or forced to remain unmarried if they do not suffer the practice. In most countries where FGM/E is practised (19 out of 29), women and girls are largely in favour of abolishing the practice; in Guinea, in 2012, 76% of women and girls wanted the practice to continue – up from 65% in 1999.[27]

Despite its health risks, many women perceive FGM/E as a symbol of female power, an affirmation of self and a liberation from male oppression. The daily lives of many women and girls involves submission, hard labour and deprivation, without the possibility of participating in decision-making. Excision gives women and girls an identity, a certain social and adult status, collective recognition and a sense of belonging to a community.[28] Moreover, the period of initiation ceremonies is free of male authority and daily chores.[29] When they leave the excision camps, girls receive presents, clothes, jewels and food, factors which contribute to encouragement and acclaim for the practice.[30]

According to a 2013 study by UNICEF:

• 32% of women viewed FGM/E as a religious requirement, compared with 25% of men;

• 13% of women felt excision preserved cleanliness and female hygiene, compared with 8% of men;

[24]  World Bank, gross national income per capital is 38.30 USD http://donnees.banquemondiale. org/pays/guinee.

[25]  Plan International, *Tradition and rights – Excision in West Africa*, Regional Office for West Africa, Dakar, July 2006, p 9.

[26]  UNICEF Innocenti Research Centre, *Changing a Harmful Social Convention: the practice of excision / female genital mutilation*, 2005, reprinted May 2008, Florence, p 19.

[27]  EDS-MICS 2012, p. 337; UNICEF, *Female Genital Mutilation/Cutting: A statistical overview of exploration of the dynamics of change*, July 2013, New York, p 87 and diagramme 8.1A, p 90.

[28]  On FGM/E as a factor of social integration in the sub-region cf. Boubacar Traoré Lamine, *FGM/Excision – Attitudes and perceptions in the West African sub-region, problems and prospects*, pp 5–7.

[29]  Plan International, *Tradition and rights – Excision in West Africa*, Regional Office for West Africa, Dakar, July 2006, p 15.

[30]  Plan International, *Tradition and rights – Excision in West Africa*, Regional Office for West Africa, Dakar, July 2006, p 13.

- 10% of women felt there was no advantage to FGM/E, compared with 40% of men;

- 6% of women felt FGM/E aimed to preserve virginity, compared with 12% of men;

- 5% of women felt FGM/E improved marriage prospects, compared with 7% of men;

- 3% of women and 2% of men felt FGM/E enabled men to experience more sexual pleasure.[31]

Any effective intervention strategy must take into account the beliefs that surround this practice. Moreover, to criticise FGM/E and impose its prohibition could be interpreted by communities as Western or neo-colonial interference, and could inspire resistance. FGM/E is accompanied by multiple initiation rites including some which promote positive cultural and traditional values that do not violate human rights. Recognising and encouraging the cultural heritage of Guinean communities must be a central part of all awareness-raising initiatives which aim to abolish FGM/E.

UNICEF found that 68% of Guinean women and 57% of men viewed excision as a religious practice, notably of Islam. This belief is propagated by some religious leaders, despite the 2007 religious edict or fatwa by the al-Azhar Council of Islamic Research which states that FGM/E have no basis in Islam and constitute a sin. There is also a widespread perception that excision is a hygiene issue which enables women to pray properly.[32]

In 2014, the General Secretariat for Religious Affairs, a Government body charged with regulating religious affairs, declared that FGM/E was not an Islamic obligation and organised a number of workshops for imams on the subject. The Roman Catholic Church also prohibited excision in an open letter by the Archbishop of Conakry to all believers in 2012. It will be essential to involve religious authorities in awareness campaigns regarding FGM/E, so that they can dismantle the perception of the religious requirement of FGM/E.[33]

The persistence of FGM/E is also linked to superstition. Medical complications are often attributed to spirits or devils.[34] The excision practitioners may be said to have magical powers. It should be noted that in the first decade of the 21st century, Guinea suffered repeated rebel incursions as a result of armed conflicts in neighbouring countries. These developments heightened a withdrawal into community ties, particularly in *Guinée forestière*, which has suffered

---

[31] UNICEF, *Female Genital Mutilation/Cutting: A statistical overview of exploration of the dynamics of change*, July 2013, New York, tableaux 6.2 et 6.3, pp 67–68.

[32] UNICEF, *Female Genital Mutilation/Cutting: A statistical overview of exploration of the dynamics of change*, July 2013, New York, p 69.

[33] UNICEF, *Female Genital Mutilation/Cutting: A statistical overview of exploration of the dynamics of change*, July 2013, New York, p 72.

[34] Plan International, *Tradition and rights – Excision in West Africa*, Regional Office for West Africa, Dakar, July 2006, p. 16.

inter-ethnic violence. In this context, initiation camps may be viewed as a cultural affirmation and a form of protection against enemy groups.

In numerous West African communities, including Guinea, virginity until marriage and female conjugal fidelity are viewed as of great importance. Ablation of the clitoris as a means of domination of women's sexuality is congruent with cultures of male domination. Excision is viewed as a way to preserve these virtues, limit women's desire, prevent masturbation and preserve morality, chastity and fidelity.[35] Some believe that FGM/E improves sexual intercourse and procreation.

## Impunity

The persistence of FGM/E is in large part due to an absence of vigorous action by judicial authorities to ensure their prevention and eradication. Thousands of young girls are excised across the country every year, during school vacations, with the full knowledge of judicial personnel, including prosecutors and instructing magistrates. Generally speaking, legal texts prohibiting FGM/E are not respected. Excision practitioners are rarely subjected to legal proceedings. No administrative or legal sanction has to date been taken against any medical professional for participation in FGM/E, although according to the EDS 2012 and a recent study by the Ministry for Social Action, the Advancement of Women and Children's Issues, a growing number of excisions take place in health centres, violating the 2000 law on reproductive health.

This is compounded by the fact that the Justice sector in Guinea is poorly funded, and several prefectures with more than 100,000 inhabitants can count on only two magistrates, one legal clerk and fewer than five police officers or gendarmes. When these personnel do seek to address FGM/E issues they are frequently subjected to serious pressures, including threats. On several occasions when alleged perpetrators have been arrested and charged, groups of women have burst into offices and threatened physical violence if they were not immediately released.

This situation may be shifting to some to degree. In July 2014, a court in Mafanco, in Matam commune in Conakry, sentenced an 80-year old excision practitioner to a two year suspended sentence and a fine of 1,000,000 GNF. However, since then, only 16 arrests for FGM/E have been reported, with 8 convictions. In each case these court verdicts have not been commensurate with the harm caused, being limited to suspended sentences and insignificant fines.

---

[35] Plan International, *Tradition and rights – Excision in West Africa*, Regional Office for West Africa, Dakar, July 2006, p 14; UNICEF, *Female Genital Mutilation/Cutting: A statistical overview of exploration of the dynamics of change*, July 2013, New York, p 33; UNICEF Innocenti Research Centre, *Changing a Harmful Social Convention: the practice of excision/female genital mutilation*, 2005, reprinted May 2008, Florence, p 20; Gomis Dominique and Wone Mamadou Moustapha, *Excision in Senegal: meaning, significance and lessons learnt from the national response*, UNICEF, Dakar, August 2008, p 4.

It should be noted that the punitive application of law will not in itself be sufficient to alter widespread practice. Indeed, it could lead to more clandestine practice targeting younger children, for greater discretion,[36] or to cross-border practice, given the free circulation of people in the ECOWAS economic community.

In some countries, State authorities do not actively dissuade the population from practising FGM/E, and may even support their practice, with financial or material contributions to excision ceremonies, in order to cultivate their electoral base. Women's groups in Guinea frequently request and receive such support from local authorities, undermining the legal prohibition of FGM/E. Moreover, some religious leaders, particularly imams, encourage the practice of FGM/E during Friday prayers and on widely influential religious radio broadcasting. Furthermore, the practice of FGM/E may be a significant source of revenue for health personnel, as well as for excision practitioners.

Numerous awareness campaigns by the government and national and international partners have justly emphasised the health risks of FGM/E.[37] This has unfortunately encouraged the increasing medicalization of excision and may have contributed to the perception that in a medical setting, FGM/E is authorised and presents no risk. This interpretation could undermine work to change community mentalities regarding the practice.[38]

## 3. ACTIONS TO COMBAT FGM/E

Over the past 15 years, the Guinean Government has made notable progress setting up norms and institutional frameworks to combat FGM/E. Numerous legislative texts and regulations to prevent and sanction FGM/E have been adopted.[39] In 2011, the Office for protection of Gender, Children and Morals (OPROGEM) was restructured and located in each of the country's 8 regions, as well as a number of police stations. In 2012, the Government drew up a National Strategic Plan for the Abandonment of Female Genital Mutilation, *2012–2016 (NSP)*, with a roadmap for operationalization in 2013. This was followed by extensive training of judicial and security personnel, as well as training and awareness raising for medical and paramedical personnel and in the context of medical schools. An awareness-raising kit has been produced for use in primary school classes. Other training and awareness-raising campaigns have been organised with local authorities, traditional and religious chiefs, traditional communicators (griots) and performers, including poster campaigns, and advertisements on TV and radio.

---

[36]  Plan International, *Tradition and rights – Excision in West Africa*, Regional Office for West Africa, Dakar, July 2006, p 30.

[37]  UNICEF Innocenti Research Centre, *Changing a Harmful Social Convention: the practice of excision/female genital mutilation*, 2005, reprinted May 2008, Florence, pp 25–26.

[38]  Plan International, *Tradition and rights – Excision in West Africa*, Regional Office for West Africa, Dakar, July 2006, p 28.

[39]  See section 2.

The Office of the High Commissioner for Human Rights participates actively in the gender thematic group within the UN Country Team in Guinea, and in the sub-cluster focusing on gender-based violence. These groups provide a framework for reflection and discussion with the national authorities regarding ways to fight discrimination and violence inflicted on women and girls. In partnership with the authorities, medical and teaching professionals, NGOs, human rights defenders and other civil society actors, the Office has organised and participated in numerous awareness-raising activities on FGM/E. The Nzérékoré sub-Office has assisted partner NGOs to form three thematic groups, including one on gender-based violence, enabling better cooperation, and the Office has given technical and financial assistance to partner NGOs particularly in *Guinée forestière* and Upper Guinea.

Other UN entities are also active in the fight against FGM/E in Guinea, including UNFPA, UNICEF and UNDP, which in 2013–14 invested 1,000,000 USD to fight gender-based violence (including FGM/E) through training and awareness-raising within communities, and with judicial, security and health personnel.

National and international NGOs also give significant assistance to the government in drawing up strategies to fight gender-based violence including FGM/E. In 2012, the German aid agency *Deutsche Gesellschaft für Internationale Zusammenarbeit* (GTZ) assisted the Government's strategic plan (PNS). In 2013–14 *Sabou Guinée*, a domestic NGO working on the rights of the child, organised training programs for judicial personnel, members of children's clubs, teachers and members of women's associations.

A number of NGOs have worked with communities on topics such as the maintenance of other initiation rites while abandoning excision. Several communities responded favourably to the idea of abandoning FGM/E on condition that their cultural heritage be preserved.[40]

GTZ organised discussion groups[41] and workshops for non-excised girls and their parents, to strengthen self-esteem and encourage them to become community role-models. Several parents also proposed to organise initiation celebrations without excision.[42] Since 2013, the NGO Humanitaire pour la protection de la femme et de l'enfant (HPFE) has also been working with non-excised girls in *Guinée forestière*. This approach, which seeks to acclaim and celebrate non-excised girls, is also followed in Upper Guinea and some areas of *Guinée forestière* by NGOs participating in the FGM Joint

[40]   Plan International, *Tradition and rights – Excision in West Africa*, Regional Office for West Africa, Dakar, July 2006, pp 31–32.
[41]   UNICEF Innocenti Research Centre, *Changing a Harmful Social Convention: the practice of excision/female genital mutilation*, 2005, reprinted May 2008, Florence, p 34.
[42]   Deutsche Gesellschaft fur Technische Zusammenarbeit (GTZ), *Use of action research for impact monitoring: lessons learnt from the Dialogue of Generations and Training for non-excised girls in Guinea*, Federal Ministry for Economic Cooperation and Development, 2005, Eschborn, pp 9–10.

Programme. The US Embassy has contributed more than 1,500,000 USD to a 12-month national programme to accelerate the abandonment of FGM/E (October 2014–October 2015); its goal is to contribute to protecting 65,000 women in 300 districts and 900 villages, who are at risk of mass excision ceremonies.

## 4. CONCLUSIONS AND RECOMMENDATIONS

The Office of the High Commissioner for Human Rights makes the following recommendations:

To the Government:

Effective measures should be taken to fight FGM/E including when performed in a medical setting:

- Ensure the proper application of the law, with independent and impartial investigation of every suspected case of FGM/E, leading to prosecution for perpetrators and their accomplices;

- Ensure the application of disciplinary measures under the joint order of 2010 for any health personnel violating the law, with a supervisory mechanism to detect the practice of FGM/E by health personnel;

- Prohibit broadcasting by private or public media of messages encouraging FGM/E, in accordance with the Ministerial order of 2010;

- Strengthen training of judicial personnel regarding national laws and regional and international norms on FGM/E, with adequate human and material resources to carry out their work, including, if necessary, protection measures;

- Mobilise all actors involved in FGM/E (regional, prefectoral and local government; justice; police; civil society and NGOs; development partners; women's rights defenders; traditional associations; religious and traditional leaders, etc.) in a concerted programme to fight impunity for these crimes;

- Strengthen training for health personnel, teachers, social workers and other professionals to detect and treat women and girls who have suffered FGM/E, or who are at risk of the practice, with health and psychological support;

- Strengthen the institutional framework and measures to promote the eradication of FGM/E, in support of the Multisectoral National Council for Coordination of FGM Action, including creation of effective regional and prefectoral committees and focal points in all relevant locations;

- Intensify systematic gathering of quantitative and qualitative data on FGM/E, including in health centres, with more qualitative research to better understand the socio-cultural factors which could encourage abandonment of FGM/E; draw up effective strategies to eliminate FGM/E; gather good practices regarding prevention and elimination of FGM/E, particularly in West Africa;

- Strengthen awareness campaigns and dialogue with communities, customary chiefs, religious leaders and traditional communicators (griots), notably via the RENACOT network and other traditional structures, as well as with parents, media, women's organisations and young people, to better involve them in the fight against FGM/E;

- Ensure effective involvement of the General Secretariat of Religious Affairs in setting up actions to promote elimination of FGM/E, and to identify, train and accompany the more influential religious leaders in the promotion of this goal by encouraging them to make public statements regarding the non-religious character of the practice;

- Integrate within the curricula of schools, universities and training centres fundamental training on women's rights, male/female equality, violence against women and girls, reproductive health, maternal health and FGM/E, and their consequences;

To civil society:

- Monitor and document cases of FGM/E, report them to judicial authorities and file formal judicial complaints;

- Continue to develop programmes for awareness, mediation and advocacy with political, administrative, traditional and religious authorities, as well as with urban and rural communities;

- Support non-excised women and girls in their efforts to resist social pressure; mobilise and involve them in awareness exercises;

- Give appropriate health, social and legal support to the victims of excision;

To the international community:

Assist Governmental and civil society actors with financial and technical support in order to further efforts aimed at eradicating FGM/E and to contributing to improving the rights of women in Guinea.

# INDEX

References are to paragraph numbers.